WOMEN AND
THE POLITICS OF PLACE

WOMEN AND
THE POLITICS OF PLACE

Edited by Wendy Harcourt
and Arturo Escobar

Kumarian
Press, Inc.

Women and the Politics of Place
Published in 2005 in the United States of America by Kumarian Press, Inc.,
1294 Blue Hills Avenue, Bloomfield, CT 06002 USA

Production and design by Rosanne Pignone, Pro Production
Copyedited by Nancy Burnett, Golden Cypress Publication Services
Proofread by Beth Richards
Index by Robert Swanson

The text for *Women and the Politics of Place* is set in Times Roman 10.5/14.
Printed in the United States of America on acid-free paper by Thomson-Shore, Inc.
Text printed with vegetable oil-based ink.

   The paper used in this publication meets the minimum requirements of the American National Standard for Information Sciences—Permanence of Paper for printed Library Materials, ANSI Z39.48-1984

Library of Congress Cataloging-in-Publication Data
Women and the politics of place / edited by Wendy Harcourt and
   Arturo Escobar.
      p.   cm.
   Summary: "This book analyzes the mobilization of women's economic and social justice movements by challenging traditional views"—Provided by publisher.
      Includes bibliographical references and index.
      ISBN 1-56549-207-2 (pbk. : alk. paper) — ISBN 1-56549-208-0
         (hardcover : alk. paper)
   1. Women in politics. 2. Women in development. 3. Body, Human—Social aspects. 4. Place (Philosophy). 5. Marginality, Social. 6. Social movements. 7. Women—Social conditions. I. Harcourt, Wendy, 1950–   II. Escobar, Arturo, 1952–
HQ1236.W58518 2005
305.42'09172'4—dc22

                                                              2005018016

14 13 12 11 10 09 08 07 06 05   10 9 8 7 6 5 4 3 2 1

Contents

v

Part Two Women, Place, and
Struggles Related to the Environment

Part Three The Diverse Economy:
Women, Place, and Alternative Economies

Part Four Displacements: Women on the Move

List of Tables and Figures

Tables

Figure

Acronyms

AGM	alternative globalization movement
AMC	Asian Migrant Centre
AWID	Association for Women's Rights in Development
BSF	Bologna Social Forum
CVO	professional civil society organization
DAWN	Development Alternatives for Women in a New Era
ENDA	Environment Development Alternatives
EU	European Union
G8	Group of 8
GDP	gross domestic product
GJSM	Global Justice and Solidarity Movement
GNP	gross national product
IMF	International Monetary Fund
IUCN	International Union for the Conservation of Nature
JBG	*Junta del Buen Gobierno*
KKJS	Koel Karo Jan Sanghathan
MDGs	Millennium Development Goals
NAFTA	North American Free Trade Agreement
NGO	nongovernmental organization
Nufo	North-Karelian Youth Forum
PCN	*Proceso de Comunidades Negras*
PPA	participatory poverty assessment
SID	Society for International Development
TAMWA	Tanzania Media Women's Association

UMWA	Uganda Media Women's Association
UN	United Nations
UNCED	United Nations Conference on Environment and Development
WAF	Women's Action Forum
WEDO	Women's Environment and Development Organization
WICEJ	Women's International Coalition for Economic Justice
WPP	Women and Politics of Place
WSF	World Social Forum
WTO	World Trade Organization

Preface

n today's world, places are no longer isolated, nor are they pure, static, or just traditional. Places are clearly made and affected by their encounters with global processes."

The book *Women and the Politics of Place* is the outcome of a seven-year-long exploration of the relationship among women, globalization, and place-based politics. The process of exploration had several aims. The first was to document how women in place are living their lives at different levels of resistance and creativity in the face of what are often perceived as overwhelming and largely abstract global forces. The second was to bring together some of the exciting people known to the editors who were undertaking activist research on place and women's political mobilization. The process gave the space for women and men of different cultures, intellectual and activist backgrounds, and ages who are interested in place-based politics to work together on some of the underlying theoretical issues that link place, women, body politics, environment, community, activism, justice, and alternative globalization. In this, the book built on an earlier collective research project, 'women on the 'Net,' to which some of the authors belonged.[1] The third was to create a group process that was mutually supportive and challenging, yet found new ways of working that were neither purely academic nor activist-oriented. Instinctively the group strove to find its own unique balance reflecting the personalities and political concerns of everyone involved, as well as the possibilities offered by cyber networking and meeting places afforded by transnational and national networking.

Several key events marked the book's pathway. The first was a debate among the book's editors, Wendy Harcourt and Arturo Escobar, around 'global' organizing, and how to bring together feminist and ecological politics and theory in a discussion on women and globalization that cut through binary local/global divides. The result was an issue of *Development* vol. 41 no. 2, entitled "Globalism and the Politics of Place," published in June 1998. On the strength of the interest generated around that journal issue a Rockefeller Foundation grant was awarded to the Society for International Development for further research and also a meeting in 2001 where many of the authors first met. The meeting, held at the Foundation's Research and Study Center in Bellagio, Italy, set the framework for *Development* vol. 45 no. 1, "Place, Politics and Justice: Women Negotiating Globalization." This second *Development* issue was published in March 2002 in both English and Spanish and was launched at the University of Oregon in Eugene, Oregon in April 2002. The four-day Eugene meeting held on the boundaries of the university and community attracted a diverse range of academics and activists from the community. The meeting was unusual for both academic and community meetings. It was marked by learned discussions and heated debate stimulated by reports, performances, and analysis from community activist groups, young women filming, a running commentary on the wall of the meeting room, dancing and singing, and shared personal maps and stories. The deep sense of connectedness among the group indicated that this was the beginning—not the end—of the process. A leaflet and CD were produced for wider dissemination, and members of the project were invited to various venues, including international meetings in Australia, Germany, India, the United States, Italy, and Tanzania. We also found in Kumarian Press a supportive and enthusiastic publisher.

The response of women's groups, research communities, and activists made it clear that the project was answering an important need. Equally important was the friendship that grew with the frank discussions, e-mailing, and occasional meetings among the group members. In addition the personal difficulties faced at different times by nearly all the authors, from brushes with death to the loss and critical illness of loved ones, to major changes in life situations, were shared and recovery quietly supported. The richness of the book reflects the honesty of this process and how each of us grappled with difficult issues at personal, political, and theoretical levels.

The group continues to be positive and committed to many creative outcomes, learning from the pain as well as happiness such intimate and long-term engagement for political change brings. We are very grateful to the commitment of all of those involved in the book, from its inception to its completion. We particularly acknowledge the contributions and support of: Lourdes Arizpe, Fonu Bain-Vete, Kitt Bohn-Willeberg, Guy Bentham, Susan Garfield, Jim Lance, Sandi Morgen, Lila Rabinovich, Evelyn Schielke, Lynn Stephen, Nadra Sultan, Lynn Szwaja, and Nahda Younis Sh'ada. We hope that the book will be of use to all of those who join us in our collective, place-based activities for gender, economic, and social justice.

Wendy Harcourt, Arturo Escobar, Laura Mª Agustín, Sonia Alvarez, Lamis al-Shejni, Fatma Alloo, Marisa Belausteguigoitia, Randa Farah, Katherine Gibson, Julie Graham, Libia Grueso, Liisa Horelli, Smitu Kothari, Khawar Mumtaz, Michal Osterweil, Dianne Rocheleau, Yvonne Underhill-Sem, and *Gerda Wekerle.*

Note

1. One result of that collaboration was the edited collection, *Women@Internet: Creating cultures in cyberspace* (Harcourt 1999).

Introduction
Practices of Difference:
Introducing *Women*
and the Politics of Place

Arturo Escobar and Wendy Harcourt

This book is born out of different attempts by a small group of theorists and activists to make sense of women's mobilizing transnationally around place. The core of the book comes from stories of women's actions in different parts of the world. Building on the experiences of women's mobilizations around sexual and reproductive rights, land and community, contested economic terrains, rural and urban environments, and global capital, we develop a framework that highlights the interrelations among place, gender, politics, and justice. We call this framework 'Women and the Politics of Place' (WPP).

We see this book as contributing to the analysis of political movements (the women's movement and economic and social justice movements, including those evolving around the World Social Forum processes). Here our book contributes to a dual rearticulation of politics. On the one hand, our book is a challenge to the traditional left to be aware of how the place-based practices of women involve an interrelated set of transformations around body, environment, and the economy that could provide alternative ways forward in their mobilizations, as explained by the WPP framework. For example, when opposing economic restructuring it is important to take into account factors affecting body, environment, and home that are made invisible by conventional political ideologies. On the other hand, women's groups involved in sexual, health, and reproductive rights issues could also use the language

1

and perspective provided by WPP to reinterpret their struggles as enmeshed in broader environmental and economic processes.

In putting this book together, the question of why women and why
place emerged in multiple ways. As the project unfolded, we started by
theorizing place to mean what women define as their environment and
what determines their livelihoods, being, and identity; that is, body,
home, local environs, and community—the arenas that women are motivated to defend, define, and own politically.[1] In putting together the
present book, we decided on a 'women and the politics of place' conception that brings together into one framework discourses and struggles about: the body, usually the focus of the women's rights movement;
the environment, the interest of ecology movements; and diverse economies, usually the concern of global social and economic justice movements. In other words, our conceptual framework aims to analyze the
interrelations created in women's struggles among body, environment,
and economies in all of their diversities (diverse embodiments, diverse
ecologies, diverse economies). In doing so we aim to demystify theory
that ignores women's experiences of their lived bodies, the local economy, and the environment in order to relocate their politics of place as
key to our understanding of globalization. We deliberately are focusing
on women rather than speaking of feminist analysis or gender relations.
We see the political importance of looking at women mobilizing in
place, beginning with how women themselves experience it. We do this
in order to not blur their specific experiences with the men with whom
they are often working. Too often the differences for women and men
become smoothed away in progressive analytical frameworks. Knowledge about women continues to be hardest to come by, and although
many of us work in feminist theory, we try in this book not to assume
that readers share that knowledge, but instead bring it in when it helps
explain the story we are telling.

The question, 'Why women?' is meant to underline that we are not
talking about all women. Generally speaking, we are focused on the experiences of subaltern women, although we also write about other women
who are mobilizing on behalf of subaltern women. By 'subaltern' we
adopt the Gramscian framework (and the meaning later used by Raymond
Williams and Stuart Hall, among others) to mean those groups that, in a
given hegemonic formation, occupy subordinate positions vis-à-vis the

dominant groups in relation to questions of work, exploitation, racism, ethnicity, and other forms of cultural subordination. So, for instance, in the patriarchal capitalist formations of today's neoliberal societies, groups such as poor urban women of color, migrant domestic workers, indigenous peoples, many ethnic minorities, poor rural communities, and so on would fit this category.

However, we are not interested in just any subaltern activities; we are interested in those in which the defense of place becomes a politics of place—that is, when subaltern women become engaged in collective political struggles around place, linking subaltern voices with collective action against inequality. Furthermore, among these latter we chose to focus on transformative politics of place as opposed to reactionary defenses of the status quo by subaltern groups. This transformative politics may involve resistance, but it also involves reappropriation, reconstruction, reinvention, even relocalization of places and place-based practices; and the creation of new possibilities of being-in-place and being-in-networks with other human and nonhuman living beings. Our choice of which women and which places has emerged from the group's own interests and concerns; there is no attempt to cover a representative sense of place or women (see the Preface for an account of the project's history). This book does reflect a very broad range of interests, places, and women, illustrating the international setting of the group and the feminist (or, some might argue, the Social Forum) spirit of working collectively and horizontally across disciplines, ages, genders, race, and place.

Each of the chapters that follow enables us to look through different lenses at women's place-based struggles in different parts of the world. From narratives emerging from Papua New Guinea, Eastern Africa, Pakistan, the Dominican Republic, the Colombian Pacific, Canada, India, South East Asia, the United States, Finland, Mexico, Europe, Palestine, and the Middle East, we discover the intelligent, courageous, and decided efforts by women's groups to engage in what we call 'politics of place.' The experiences narrated by these chapters show how women in their various struggles around place are defending it, transforming it, redefining it, recreating it in nontraditional locations, even leaving it—and in so doing are creating a new form of politics. Our book tries to show how these responses challenge dominant social, cultural, and economic trends at regional, national, and global levels.

Challenging Mainstream Academic
Frameworks and Development Regimes

In developing this analytical framework, this book aims to contribute to several debates. The first is to expose how the patriarchal and totalizing character of most established academic frameworks (for instance, about globalization, empire, and geographies of place and space) disempower women, place, and their politics. Patriarchy varies from place to place depending on the power plays, but it is always present and, in using the term, we are underlining the constantly unequal relations of power between men and women as well as among women and among men. In focusing on the stories of women in place-based movements, we aim to show how women engage creatively with globalization in multiple ways, and with particular reference to body politics as core to women's experience of place and politics. In this we are also engaging with feminist theory and practice within the academe and the women's movement.

Secondly we are challenging the current focus of the development regime on women, particularly concerning social problems and issues such as violence against women, reproductive rights, human rights, health, entrepreneurship, market citizenship, and so on. We believe these recent trends in the development apparatus are better understood as a biopolitical response to the consequences of neoliberal globalization. In other words, when confronted with increasing poverty, social dislocation, income disparity, displacement, and violence, the development apparatus responds with carefully targeted interventions at the level of the body, health, and reproduction. Some researchers refer to this biopolitical response as the management of the social. This book aims to make visible their disempowering effects on women and place.

By bringing to the fore women's place-based struggles, we challenge the policy makers, scholars, and NGOs who look at globalization through what we may call 'globalocentric' frameworks. The agents of transformation, in these dominant narratives, are markets, corporations, big governments of the North, the global economy, financial capital, and new technologies. These are indeed real forces transforming the world. In these globalocentric perspectives there is little that people in localities can do. Places, communities, and regions have to adapt or perish, so to speak, and strategies of local and regional development must be devised with the aim of integrating into the global economy according to this or that comparative advantage. Given worldwide circumstances of unequal power, this often means that in order to find their 'competitive niche' places and communities have to overexploit themselves, oftentimes affecting women.

What our book aims to do is show how this form of exploitation is not always accepted; indeed there are veritable struggles over the character and purpose of the use of a place between the planners, policy makers, and those who live and work there. The stories of women in public parks in Toronto creating community gardens; the young women and men forming local networks for alternative economic and cultural projects in the marginalized North Karelia region of Finland; and the cultural struggles by black people for the defense of the Pacific rainforest region in Colombia all show the vibrancy of a different politics of place that is dismissed or made invisible or unimportant in conventional frameworks.

We also argue that the innovative strategies of women around their health, livelihood, home, and rights in the face of global capital are hardly more visible in the globalization literature on the left. Even if these analyses pay some attention to grassroots mobilizations and social movements against globalization, they are equally globalocentric. In leftist narratives what counts most is empire, capital, and modernity, and if one could only confront these big monsters with an equally ambitious project; in other words, only a global type of politics (even if often seen in terms of the articulation of many struggles) could make a dent in the structure of the enemy. Such analyses damage and devalue place-based politics and make invisible women's struggles around body politics in particular. As J. K. Gibson-Graham suggest in Chapter 9, this devaluation arises from the same kind of global- and capitalocentrism that pervades mainstream views. What this means is that most analyses of capitalism render capitalism into an all-embracing entity with the power to absorb, control, co-opt, and shape every form of life, denigrating any place-based resistance and confining it to a set of futile, reformist, or naïve responses. But is this so? Chapters in this book reveal that there are indeed many other dynamics going on, which we call place-based but not place-bound. Or we should say, along with Michal

Osterweil (see Chapter 11), there is indeed a place-based form of glob-alism 'out there,' and this is not a contradiction in terms. On the con-trary, it represents a vibrant and innovative form of politics, one in which women often lead.

Outlining the Framework: Difference and Diversity

This book then tries to chart an emerging set of political practices within a framework of women and the politics of place. Simultaneously, based on these cases, it aims to develop a critical language with which to mount responses to modernity and global capitalism that highlight the creativity, knowledge, and experience of women's groups engaged in place-based politics. This language allows us to talk about women's forms of place-based politics without reducing them to any overarching global logic, but seeing them in their own right and in terms of the translocal effects they may generate through networking and shifts of scale. And, while we recognize the importance of creating a new lan-guage, we are also mindful of the fact that a language is not enough. We are interested in the cultivation of collective political subjects—again, based on practices that already exist, even if aiming at new ones as well—capable of advancing struggles around what we see as three key dimen-sions of place: the body, the environment, and the economy. We refer to these goals as reembodying the body, reembedding the environment, and relocating the economy—or, in the language we hope to develop, diverse embodiments, diverse environments, and diverse economies.

Why so much insistence on diversity? Diversity, first of all, is inher-ent to places. Despite much touted cultural homogenization, places con-tinue to be irreducible to each other or to any single global logic. The fact of having a body and living in place—embodiment and emplace-ment—are fundamental human features. Places are deeply historical and specific; no matter how transnationalized and shaped by larger forces, there is an important sense in which one always lives locally, in place. This also applies to body, environment, and economy. Today, rather than speaking about a seemingly homogenous 'global village,' we rather need to talk, with feminist geographer Doreen Massey (1997), about a 'global sense of place' that recognizes both global influences and local determinations, and hence the fundamental diversity of places. We would emphasize that our valorization of diversity goes hand in hand with a critique of inequality; indeed diversity entails new ways of making connections to rework inequality.

Our question then becomes: is it possible to see anew the multiple different forms that body, environment, and economy take on today, particularly those that might pose interesting challenges to neoliberal globalization? Adopting a more theoretical mode, and extending a notion from Gibson-Graham's analysis of the economy (also see Escobar, 1999), we speak of 'practices of difference' in relation to bodies, environment, and the economy. In other words, place-based struggles reveal that people do inhabit their bodies, relate to their environments, and act like economic subjects through practices that are often quite different from the mainstream and that cannot be reduced to them. This ethnographic observation suggests the possibility of building a in which we conceptualize what diverse embodiments, environments, and economies might look like, as opposed to the current dominant views that emphasize a monocultural landscape of these three aspects of place. Let us explain the main elements of the framework.

Development, the Body Politic, and the Politics of Place

It is clear that bodies are constituted through power; this is particularly clear with 'marked' bodies, such as those of women marked as reproductive and productive bodies that are exposed and vulnerable through various domains of violence and exploitation. This happens as much in 'out-of-the-way' places in remote corners of the world as in the most industrialized societies; perhaps what is striking is, in all these cases, women are often marginalized because of their bodies. In places such as small villages of the eastern Pacific (e.g., Papua New Guinea) women— e.g., young pregnant women—are placed at the margins of community through their lived bodily experience. Yet, as Yvonne Underhill-Sem makes clear in Chapter 1, even in these cases women are able to find room to maneuver through the constellations of power that mark their bodies—whether at the level of home, health facility, work, church, or village—in ways that enact both a diverse embodiment and a politics of place. By resisting traditional and new forms of power, and through 'active positioning,' young bodies, maternal bodies, and working bodies reveal the ways in which bodies define places and vice versa. This may happen in an altogether different way when women choose to leave home; the new places will be marked by the tacking back and forth between body and place, clearly so in the case of sex workers, as in the situations involving Latin American sex workers in Europe discussed by Laura Agustín in Chapter 14. In Underhill-Sem's descriptive expression, bodies are both "materially pinchable and fluid and discursively constituted," and here we find a principle for thinking about diverse embodiments and the relation between body and a politics of place. Through resistance and active positioning, women rearticulate bodies and places; as they reinhabit their bodies and struggle with and over places, they engage in a transformative feminist politics of place.

That women's body politics is more visible, and hence subject to social control, is well exemplified by the case of development. It could almost be said that every engagement of women with the apparatus of development is an opportunity for their bodies to be seized at the service of a patriarchal, economistic, and managerial 'body politic,' as Wendy Harcourt calls it in Chapter 2. Several decades of strategies for women in/and development attest to this fact. What she means by body politic and biopolitics of development is an entire panoply of institutional (e.g., UN-, NGO-, and state-based) interventions focused on women as working bodies, maternal bodies, sexualized bodies, sick bodies, and even bodies that are subjects of violence and rights. In the 1990s and beyond, this amounted to a veritable and powerful regime for the production of individual and social female bodies; even more, this has happened not only despite tremendous international and feminist concern with the fate of third world women, but largely because of such concern and proliferations of strategies. From this careful examination of women-centered development strategies we learn that feminist experts and NGOs might be better off working with, and for, an emergent subaltern politics of place—women acting in solidarity in place and across place—than relying on the developmentalist management regimes of the female body.

Somewhat similar conclusions are reached by Lamis A. M. al-Shejni for the case of Arab women organizations (see Chapter 15). Here, she poses the question of level of action in a complex discussion around history, identity, and political positioning that differ according to national, regional, or international context. It is important, she warns, to realize that women's politics take very different forms at different levels. What Arab women might be able to do at the level of the Arab region might contradict what they do at the national or more broadly international levels. Often engagement in 'development' allows women to do or not do different things at different levels.

Without wanting to essentialize, it is not a coincidence that the struggles of women activists for gender justice are often centered on and mediated by bodily and emotional resistance and pain. The decolonization of the mind and the decolonization of the body from patriarchal structures go hand in hand. A radical politics of the body and of place suggest that the personal journeys of women are deeply imbued with their political practice; the desire to give voice to women's pain often leads activists to engage in a politics of place. This vision comes out strongly from both Fatma Alloo's narrative of body, self, and politics through which she links her native Zanzibar with Tanzania, Africa, and the world on the basis of media projects with and for women (see Chapter 3); and it is also present in Khawar Mumtaz's account of the founding and workings of Shirkat Gah, a women's rights organization in Pakistan (see Chapter 4). In the practices of this NGO one may find a source of alternatives to the developmentalist body politic. Focused on everyday body politics—the issues and needs of women in terms of health, employment, reproduction, rights, and livelihoods—Shirkat Gah's strategy confronts local patriarchal practices, builds on women's own skills and capacities, and links struggles for women's autonomy with defenses of place, becoming a transformative politics of place—that is, one that embraces at the same time, and at many levels, women's empowerment for bodily integrity, knowledge, and autonomy and their changing sense of self, place, and community. While highlighting the vitality of place-based politics, both chapters also make clear the important role of transnational networks—of movements, but at times engaging with mainstream institutions—for a more effective politics of place in poorer countries of the world.

Politics of Place and Environmental Destruction and Diversity

Smitu Kothari speaks about the agony caused by the disruption of communities—their environments, economies, and knowledge systems—that is in turn caused by development (see Chapter 8). The devaluation of people's place-based knowledge systems and experiences finds one of its most clear consequences in the destruction of habitats; notwith-standing, places continue to be a primary space for maintaining the diversity of human and natural life. This double condition—places and environments as targets of destruction and sites of diversity—is the basis of many place-based environmental struggles. Even urban environments, as Gerda Wekerle shows in her discussion of struggles over public spaces in Toronto (see Chapter 6), are not immune to this double dynamic. For many poor rural communities, the loss of connection to place implies the loss of meaning, subsistence, and security. There is no question that in many cases the vulnerability of place and environment increases with development-driven integration into the global economy. The cultural and economic impact of the loss of commons and territory is as profound in the case of many tribal communities in India as it is in black river communities in the Colombian Pacific with whom Libia Grueso and Leyla Arroyo work (see Chapter 7). For some displaced communities, the need is for remaking place—even in urban sites, as is true for many Dalits in India—but even in these cases the assertion of autonomy and self-rule in place becomes an important goal.

Very often women play a central role in struggles over livelihood and environment, as demonstrated through the experiences of women in India, Colombia, the Dominican Republic, or Canada related in this book (also see Rocheleau, et al., 1996; Martínez Alier, 2002). This is because livelihood is central to family, community, and economy; hence struggles to defend and democratize livelihood have to do with all of these domains in which women have a particular stake. What happens in the spaces of home, work (economy), and place is often enmeshed with what happens to landscapes and ecosystems. As Rocheleau argues, by looking at landscapes and ecosystems through women's eyes one could learn to see them differently—in particular, to see how living beings are integrated with each other through intricate webs of relations (women, men, natural beings, artifacts, even spiritual beings). By following women through each space and level—farm, field, community, organization, and so on—one can learn to appreciate how landscapes are embedded in social relations and vice versa. Landscapes appear as gendered terrains that are always under construction through ecological and social relational webs, not as inert backgrounds for human action.

The result is a multiplicity of diverse ecologies that are struggled over, particularly when livelihood, culture, and bodily integrity and health are at stake, as in the case of the social movement of black communities of the Colombian Pacific. Against the developmentalist attempt at rendering the rainforest into a modernized, plantation-type ecology, this movement emphasizes that the territory is a culturally specific habitat, thus rendering its actions into a politics of place. Rather than women-in-development programs focused on income generation, for instance, women activists highlight the intimate relation between cultural and ethnic rights, on the one hand, and the environment or territory, on the other. Culture, identity, and the defense of the environment thus emerge as the organizing principles of both everyday life and political strategy; the result, as activists see it, is a set of place-based anti-globalization strategies. Something quite similar can be said to occur in the struggles over space and place in Toronto. Even in this thoroughly urban and seemingly modernized environment, there are ongoing relocalization strategies led by women and immigrant minorities, such as the struggles over certain public spaces for community gardens and alternative food systems to ensure nutrition and food security. Often obscured in hegemonic, masculinist narratives of the 'neoliberal city,' this women's politics of place is becoming increasingly visible as a valid and effective form of contesting cities. 'Domesticating' public spaces such as public parks is, again, one form of building diverse environments and economies and of reembedding the environment in a different set of social relations.

Diverse Economies and the Politics of Place

An important part of the WPP framework is to be able to see the many forms of economy that exist in spite of or side by side with capitalist economies. This is an exercise of revisioning beyond the dominant economic thinking through which most of us have been trained to see. As J. K. Gibson-Graham point out, recognizing that there are diverse economies 'out there' is the beginning of imagining a noncapitalist politics of place. As they suggest, what we usually refer to as the 'economy' (in terms of markets, wages, and capitalist enterprises) is only one aspect of the economic activity in which people engage. By looking at places through the framework of the diverse economy, we are able to see that there are indeed other 'really existing forms of economy'; these might be related to communities, cooperatives, migrant organizations, subsistence activities, local exchanges, self-employment, and so on, and in many of these women are central. One of the key principles here is to ask: what do local women do with the wealth ('surplus') that is generated locally? The answer is that oftentimes this surplus is recirculated into the community in ways that cannot be described as capitalist at all. On the contrary, what one sees is women engaged in building ethical spaces of interdependent economic activity that are a far cry from competitive and individualistic capitalist practices.

Within a WPP framework, we need to learn to see these diverse economic activities and nurture them; this means cultivating new ways of being subjects of the economy, actually desiring these different subjectivities and acting on such desire individually and collectively. In this way we will be able to see the power of place to bring about more economic diversity. This does not happen by itself; and oftentimes it requires cultivating interests and capacities, as in the case of the Asian cases discussed by Gibson-Graham or the Finnish women and young people's networks of social cohesion described by Liisa Horelli in Chapter 10. The result is that, rather than just a node in an inescapable capitalist system, place-based efforts emerge as sites and seeds of economic diversity. This exercise of revisioning allows us to speak of a globally emergent movement of place-based economic construction— a crucial dimension of our WPP framework.

Women on the Move: Being-in-Place and Being-in-Networks

Dianne Rocheleau has coined the felicitous phrase, 'rooted networks' to signal that what is at play with most human groups today are systems of multiple and movable roots. Perhaps no other situation makes this condition as real as that of refugees. In analyzing the Palestinian case, Randa Farah shows vividly how even in refugee camps people recreate a sense of place through processes in which women are central (see Chapter 13). Women's contribution in this regard is far from being restricted to the domestic arena or to a role as preservers of culture, as dominant Orientalist and male views would have it. Their place-making practices are integral to the cultural and political struggles against displacement or occupation; resisting gender oppression as much as colonial occupation, Palestinian women weave personal and collective struggles—from home to camp and beyond—into a collective historical process of place making.

A similar weaving of gender and anticolonialist elements is found at play in the struggles of Zapatista women in Chiapas. Here, as Marisa Belausteguigoitia indicates in Chapter 12, women's struggles necessarily articulate actions that transform patriarchal understandings of place in terms of tradition with actions that challenge dominant representation of the nation and make indigenous women's lived experiences and self-expression invisible. What emerges are conceptions of autonomy that enable women to defend their multiple identities: as indigenous, Mexican, and women. To do so, they have to engage in a politics that transforms images of women, patriarchal body politics, and eurocentric conceptions of the nation. The result, in the last instance, is a hopeful renaming and remaking of places that hybridize tradition and modernity in creative ways and that serve as antidote against imperializing trade agreements imposed by the United States. Laura Agustín pushes even harder against a comfortable concept of place by looking at cosmopolitan spaces inhabited by women on the move through many places—such as migrant sex workers in Europe—in their search for work, security, money, pleasure, and satisfying livelihoods. She challenges the romanticizing tendency to link women with cozy ideas of home or stable notions of place in our fast-moving, violent, globalized world, where for many women living transnational lives, place can be somewhere they want or need to move away from: ". . . for millions of people all over the world, the birth and childhood place is not a feasible or desirable one in which to undertake more adult, ambitious, or unconventional projects, and moving to another place is a positive solution." Diverse embodiments, environments, and economies look very different from the perspective of the women described by Agustín.

WPP is therefore also a framework for thinking about the politics of place 'beyond place.' Most movements of today, from the Zapatistas to the Italian alternative globalization movements, can be described as enacting a new form of 'place-based globalism,' as Osterweil calls it. There are two aspects to this formulation: on the one hand, most of today's movements can be described as place-based yet transnationalized struggles (Harcourt and Escobar, 2002); on the other hand, they are engaged in a new kind of politics that often emphasizes the local, the cultural, the present, and the possibilities of other ways of being. For these movements, not only the content but also the process and the very form of politics are of consequence. In some ways at least, this combination of features suggests a certain feminist understanding of being, doing, politics, and globality. The sense of globality one sees emerging out of many of the so-called global movements is one that does not search for universal validity or an all-embracing global reality, no matter how alternative; but one that seeks to preserve heterogeneity and diversity, even as, and precisely through, new kinds of alliances and networking that we refer to as self-organizing, decentralized, and nonhierarchical 'meshworking.' In short, these movements want to be practicing, already, the kinds of worlds they would like to bring into being. This kind of prefigurative politics is also an important element in WPP.

The concept of meshwork is meant to suggest that place-based groups often do not work in isolation. Rather, they engage in dynamic vertical and horizontal networking, connecting among themselves and with others in places far and near, across cultural, political, racial, and ethnic divides. The concept of network is central to processes of globalization. Using global networks, such as the Internet and the networks set up by transnational NGOs, enables place-based movements to exchange information, support, solidarity, and experiences. Through 'networking' they participate integrally in the reshaping of global processes. Most resistance networks operate partially through, or at least by engaging with, dominant networks. The newer movements, however, could be said to engage in meshworks. These nonhierarchical and self-organizing networks often grow in unplanned directions. They involve two parallel dynamics: strategies of localization and of interweaving. While they engage with dominant networks, they tend to retain a characteristic plurality. This does not mean that meshworks are necessarily 'morally superior' to dominant hierarchical networks, but they do tend to enact an oppositional politics.

We find a great degree of resonance between our framework and this new set of movement practices; this includes the exciting political spaces being created by the World Social Forum process.[2] Embedded in our framework is also a constructive perspective for thinking about the planet itself in terms of multiple senses of communities and activism which, without overlooking differences, aims at redrawing borders and building novel forms of connection (Anzaldúa and Keatin, 2002).

A WPP Framework

The table below is an attempt to summarize our Women and the Politics of Place framework in the spirit of J. K. Gibson-Graham's model for diverse economies. The model highlights the three domains (body, environment, economy); it suggests that what feeds the model ('intellectual and political activity') are observations and analysis of embodied, ecological, and economic difference experienced in women's place-based mobilizations, as shown in the few examples in the table. Collective discussions (in the forms of informal conversations, listservs, and workshops) around how to build on these experiences using the framework could be particularly exciting in moving to collective action. From the concept of 'difference,' we might move on to envision (e.g., through discussion and model building) actually existing or imaginable diverse embodiments, environments, and economies. The aim is to reconnect politically and practically—through reembodying, reembedding and relocalizing—women's experience of place, body, environment, and economy. The political side of the process will have to do with how individual women and groups are able to rally around this project and organize for it, through movements, networks, and meshworks within a strategy of place-based globalism. The model is meant to be indicative of the kinds of ideas and practices that women and the politics of place entail; the columns are not meant to be stages of the process, since the various thoughts and actions will necessarily overlap and mutually feed into each other. We include this table as a contribution to the analytical toolkit we have tried to develop in this Introduction and will continue to explore in the various chapters. We hope that, by offering the WPP framework for discussion, this book will contribute to the proliferating forms of politics that are challenging the dominant patriarchal and globalocentric narratives of neoliberal globalization today.

Table 1.1 Framework of Women and the Politics of Place

Domain Concept	Difference	Diversity	Project
Body	Embodied Difference (different experiences of the lived and gendered reproductive and productive body)	Diverse Embodiments (unsettling stereotyped ways of experiencing the female body through recognizing specificities and interrelation of places, environments, and economies)	Reembodying the body (specific projects that establish connections between body and place; e.g., organizing against sexual harassment and exploitation in the workplace, self-help healthy/ crisis survival women groups)
Environment	Ecological Difference (women engaged in diverse ecological urban/rural practices, anti-development, etc.)	Diverse Environments (imagining diverse ways to engage with landscape and place; place and culturally rooted conservation and sustainability)	Reembedding the Environment (e.g., specific projects for integrating environment with culture and economy by women working in community-based conservation, antimining, urban gardens, safe water, local forest movements, etc.)
Economy	Economic Difference (different economic practices, alternative livelihoods, caring economies)	Diverse Economies (imagining other economies, including nonmarket transactions, noncapitalist enterprises)	Relocalizing the Economy (women building community economies, including place-based global networks, for e.g., local trading, local currency groups)
Intellectual and Political Activity	Identify discourses & practices of difference (collective debates about what 'we' do differently at the three levels; activist research on different practices; workshops and reflection on processes leading from place-based organizing)	Model building to facilitate vision making (e.g., J. K. Gibson-Graham, Horelli)	Formulation of visions and strategies by women for place-based globalism (e.g., women organizing in peace and environmental movements, feminist dialogues in global justice movements, women's human rights and alternative development networks, etc.)

Notes

1. See the special issue of *Development,* "Place, politics and justice: women negotiating global justice," vol. 45 (1) March 2002. For the sake of brevity we have not included an exhaustive bibliography on place; many of the main works that have influenced our thinking can be found in many of the chapters. See also Escobar (1999, 2001); Harcourt (1999).

2. See *Development,* "The Movement of Movements," vol. 48 (2) June 2005, guest edited by Nicola Bullard, for detailed discussions on the World Social Forum process by those actors shaping them.

Part One

Women, Place, and Body Politics

1

Bodies in Places, Places in Bodies

Yvonne Underhill-Sem

Introduction

A heavily pregnant young woman, hands calloused from long hours of physical work, sporting bruises on the left side of her face, and speaking from lips dotted with inflamed, pus-infected sores, arrived at my house in the midmorning heat to ask for some casual domestic work. She had walked under the public gaze of the local villagers directly to my house, because she was desperate for money to buy things before the impending birth of her first child. Before I, the only nonlocal village resident, could finish saying that, 'in her state,' I could not give her any work, she interrupted, asking whether she could at least have some food. The diverse embodiments that she visually presented spoke of the diverse places that marked her: places of sexual activity, poverty, violence, and indifference. She had been sent from a distant village by her immediate family to help an older male relative who was living alone in a village closer to town. Once there, she was exposed to the unwelcome and often violent sexual activity of the young village boys. These boys were unfazed by the religiously inspired and village-based notions of harmonious, cooperative, kin-based community systems that had brought this young woman to their village. She had also toiled for long hours in her uncle's garden, and had managed the arduous domestic tasks of food preparation and laundry. Fortunately, potable water was piped to all houses. Her older male relative's inability to provide a physically or

20

emotionally nourishing and secure environment resulted in the marking of this young woman's body in such a dramatic, yet sadly not unusual, way.

In this chapter I examine the makings of the diverse embodiments of women in 'out-of-the-way' places. In a scenario such as the one I described above, being in an out-of-the-way place refers in an absolute way to a small village on the edge of a main town in a small country in the eastern Pacific. However, an out-of-the-way place can also have a relative guise because of the array of its constituent parts. This kind of out-of-the-way place could be anywhere in the developing world. It can be a place where semisubsistence livelihoods prevail, where kinship-based contributions are still willingly made, where cultural and social morals are being transformed, and where women too often wear the violent marks of frustration, constraint, anger, poor health, or indifference. It is also a place from which a variety of women's political movements emerge.

All bodies, even those in virtual spaces, are inscribed by many and varied ways and words that their owners, in turn, propagate. Young, pregnant, unsupported women are almost always placed on the margins of communities, because their embodiment provides the visually disturbing evidence of a community unable to care for all its members. Here I look specifically at the complex and often contradictory ways in which the relative subject positioning of women in out-of-the-way places is produced. In the instance I described above, the subject position of my visitor shifted constantly, from being a respectful junior family member, to a sexually interested young woman, daughter, and niece, to a desperate mother-to-be asking a neighbor for food. A few months after I met this young woman, despite attempts to find her, I saw her again when she stepped from behind a screen in the local market. She had become an attractive, delighted, healthy new mother proudly showing me the toothless, chubby, milky smile of her new baby. The ability of this young woman to maneuver through diverse places that were clearly able to mark her body, but not her spirit, points to the importance of understanding the body, and especially the maternal body, as the basis for a politics of place.

My own reading of bodies comes from my relative subject position as a woman of Polynesian heritage, whose bodily appearance is entangled in such diverse places as rural Papua New Guinea, urban New

Zealand, the Cook Islands, and continental Europe. Enmeshed in these places as a daughter, sister, mother, wife, colleague, lecturer, and friend, I am further entangled in the politics of place through my involvement with Development Alternatives for Women in a New Era (DAWN), a global research and advocacy network of women from the economic South. I began thinking about bodies as sites of resistance as I politically navigated the sexual terrains of adolescence, young adulthood, and motherhood. I mostly navigated on my own, but I was increasingly drawn into the more violent turbulence facing friends, family, and my students. Feminist scholarship offered me intellectual guidance and sustenance in my desire to understand and make some differences to women's lives. But my own geographic mobility meant that it was easier politically to express these desires through teaching critical analysis than becoming involved in grassroots activism. Joining DAWN allowed me to understand and support both grassroots and global political activism supported by feminist critical analysis in Asia, Africa, Latin America, and the Caribbean. Understanding the diversity of my own relative subject position over time and space highlights the importance of recognizing that bodies are simultaneously constituted by places and discourses.

My political involvement in DAWN coincided with my growing intellectual engagement with feminist poststructuralist analysis of the body, drawn from research into maternities in Papua New Guinea. DAWN's unrelenting efforts to ensure that the body marked by gender, race, and class remains in view of national and global economic and social policymakers, as well as the male-led civil society organizations, provided the framing for my own understanding of the ever-present maternal body. The fertile tensions between a global recognition of the need to place "reproductive health within a comprehensive human development framework" (Correa, 1994: 64) and my own identification of local constellations of power arrangements in an out-of-the-way place in Papua New Guinea also contribute to subverting masculinist and modernist ways of thinking about bodies. Maternal bodies in this chapter invite particular scrutiny; they are subjected to specific disciplinary regimes (Foucault, 1977), because, as Longhurst (2001: 6) cogently argues, "the pregnant body, it is thought, threatens to expel matter from inside—to seep and leak." Furthermore, the pregnant body confuses

simple subject identities because of the location of at least three different identities in one body.

Out-of-the-way Places

Out-of-the-way places are potent places from which to work and are
ubiquitous in every sense. Any place has an infinite number of sites or
locations, depending on what they are positioned against. When focusing on this position, one must start by understanding why some places
are considered out-of-the-way at certain times, while others are not.
Many responses will likely focus on the relatively small size of the
place and its geographic distance from large population centers. As a
Pacific Islander, I am keenly aware of this argument and the need to
constantly challenge it,[1] because all places, however defined,[2] are
entangled in personal and collective identities. As I have argued previously (Underhill-Sem, 2003), the concept of 'out-of-the-way places'
(Tsing, 1993) usefully suggests an understanding of marginality that
challenges taken-for-granted understandings of center-defined periph-
eries.[3] Instead it invokes the need for a progressive sense of place in
which place is not taken as a preexisting object set in stone but is constituted through the relations of objects and events (Massey, 1994). This
allows for the full layering effects of time and space to work themselves
into making 'places' what they are: historically contingent and globally
located sites of identity.

This argument also applies—to an extent—to the place of the body,
which means, as Rich (1986: 212) notes, "being, though, not with continent or a country or a house, but with the geography closest-in—the
body." Although ever-present in our daily lives, over the last decade
there has been a growing interest in producing academic and popular
knowledge on the body and corporality. Some argue that feminism has
drawn attention to the body as a site of political contestation. Others
refer to the challenges of postmodernism when identifying the contradictions in academic discourse, while for others it is the recognition of
the diversity of bodies in different cultures that highlights the cultural
construction of bodies (Longhurst, 2001). The possibilities of an
embodied approach for transformative development center on the ways

in which it disrupts many taken-for-granted concepts, highlights shifting multiple and contradictory subject positions, and provides insights into the complex constellations of power relations that constitute the worlds we live in. More challenging is the view of the maternal body as a site used to disrupt taken-for-granted understandings. As Jolly (1998: 2) notes in relation to the focus on the maternal body, "we are insistent on how these seemingly natural processes of swelling, bearing, and suck- ling, the flows of blood, semen and milk are constituted and fixed not just by the force of cultural conception but by coagulations of power." So, just as we reinvest place with more thinking, so too must we rein- vest bodies with more thinking.

Diverse Readings of Diverse Embodiments

Bodies are important for how they define places. We are all familiar with ever-present tourist images taken in out-of-the-way places, seduc- ing us to be consumers of 'others' far away. However, it is not only the surface of the body, the inscribed body that is represented in tourist images and takes our attention; it is also the continuum of sensation and energy emanating from the body and providing the means by which social relations occur. Bodies are not just inert and passive matter; they are a source of subjectivity and knowledge. Cultural accounts of bodily processes and experience are best understood in relation to the materi- ality of bodies, because both the cultural and the biological are fields of transformation (Keane and Rosengarten, 2002).

Focusing simultaneously on 'places' and 'bodies' brings together the critical theoretical projects concerning the body, especially its sex- uality, and the economy, especially the political economy (Callard, 1998). Both of these projects have advanced progressive new analyses over the last decade, but convergence has been slow. However, since the body has been identified as the primary site for the exercise of power (inspired by Foucault) and as new geopolitical posturing has increas- ingly identified the intertwined nature of control over resources with global systems of trade and governance, the "fine meshes of the web of power" (Rabinow, 1984: 58) become more important to understand. These 'webs of power' are critical in continuing to define the ways in which women's bodies are constituted, in a myriad of different places. This is not a retreat into relativist positioning; instead it provides a critical feminist lens through which to see and understand how women's agency from a fleshy, postmaterialist position has a transformative, not just destabilizing, effect (Hartsock, 1990).

What are the transformative effects of the fleshiness of maternal bodies? Maternal bodies will continue to be contested terrain, as women remain caught "at the center of the contest between emancipatory promises of 'modernity' and the authenticating claims of 'tradition'" (Jolly, 1997: 135). On the one hand, central government policy to support maternal health through the provision of modern contraceptives, even abortion, runs counter to religious teachings that urge the submission of wives. What is needed is a theoretical position that allows bodies and places to be both grounded and materially 'pinchable,' and also to be fluid and discursively constituted. This theoretical position would make it possible to move between statistical analysis and ethnography in order to produce "convincing representations of the reproduction of inequality" (Haraway, 1997: 22).

Placing Papua New Guinea

Papua New Guinea, in the tropical western Pacific, is an independent country of some four million people bordering the significantly more populous country of Indonesia. Significantly, more than three hundred different languages are spoken among its semisubsistence-based citizenry. Some language groups are as small as a few hundred people, while others extend to several thousand. Just as languages in Papua New Guinea are distinctive and largely place-based, so too are personal identities, in spite of the prevalence of nationalist discourse emerging from the institutions of postcolonial states and the selective expansion of personal mobility. Although globally fashioned cultures, economies, and societies have deeply penetrated many places in Papua New Guinea over many years, though never unproblematically,[4] the politics of place persists.

Alongside the prevalence of diverse languages, the politics of place in Papua New Guinea is worn clearly on people's bodies. Most distinctive are facial and body tattoos and piercing, but it is also possible to read the calloused hands of gardeners, the roughness of impetigo or 'white spot' skin disease, and the bulging stomach of pregnancy. For women in particular, their bodily politics is always more visible and, thus, often more subject to social control. The answers to questions about the circumstances surrounding each tattoo, piercing, callus, skin rash, or pregnancy reveals a diverse constellation of powers that can be read a number of ways. For example, facial tattoos are accepted traditional practice, but some are forced markings. Many urban food gardeners value the skills that come from successfully growing crops on inhospitable dry slopes, while for others the economic necessity of producing food for the purpose of earning cash outweighs the worthiness of the gardening skill involved. And, while the impending birth of a child may be a blessed joy for some mothers, for others it is just as likely to be an unwanted pregnancy resulting from forced sex or lack of contraceptives.

Constituting the Body: Sorcery, Christianity, and Health Care

In Wanigela, Oro Province, Papua New Guinea, gender inequality is clearly evident nationwide. In many places gender inequality is interspersed with other constellations of power. In this case, they include sorcery, Christianity, and the provisions of modern health care. Women move through these constellations of power not only as a way to resist but also in a progressive way that allows them to deal with gender inequalities.

Sorcery, Christianity, and Western medical care are closely connected in Wanigela.[5] Sorcery, in its many forms, was a prevalent organizing force in pre-Christian times and has taken on different forms as it has interacted with Christian influences. Although sorcery is not as widely discussed in Wanigela as in other parts of Papua New Guinea,[6] there is constant reference to the possibilities of being the target of sorcery, and many contemporary practices developed from the fear of being targeted. For example, after the birth of a new child, great care is taken to ensure that the birthing waste is disposed of so it cannot be used in sorcery against the family or wider clan. In addition, mother and child are confined to the house for a number of days. The paradox of vulnerability is clear in this situation: On the one hand, the vulnerability of the mother and child is emphasized by their seclusion and protection.

On the other hand, the potential power of birthing waste is considered to be dangerously strong in the hands of sorcerers, thereby emphasizing the vulnerability of the family or clan. (Even more than one hundred years' influence of Christian missionaries has done little to change these practices.) However, the tension over community versus individual rights is more complex than a simple oppositional issue.

Christianity also has a pervasive place in the life of people in Wanigela. When Christian missionaries introduced education and Western medical care at the end of the 19th century (Barker, 1987, 1990), their influence over both the material and discursive bodies began. In the early 1950s, significant changes to women's bodies occurred because of their involvement with Christianity. Selected young girls were invited to participate in the Anglican Mission's education task of caring for boys: washing and ironing clothes and cooking for the boys who were at the Mission school. Instead of working with their families on daily subsistence gardening activities, the young women spent their days at the mission station, which, being located close to the airstrip, church, and school, was the hub of community activity. Many of these young girls went on to marry the educated boys. Some of them even wore the white wedding dresses that are so closely identified with Christian weddings.

Along with sorcery and Christianity, Western medical care in Wanigela and many other parts of Papua New Guinea has long been credited for its effectiveness in preventing childhood diseases and infections. Health clinics were often well attended, but medical pluralism prevailed. In addition to the use of modern medicine there was a simultaneous use of traditional healing practices, as well as some recourse to sorcery and the use of prayer for divine intervention (Frankel and Lewis, 1989). Within the last century, successive generations of people in the Wanigela area have grown up within the mutually constitutive knowledge bases of 'tradition,' or 'custom,' and Anglican Christianity. As Clifford (2001: 478) writes, "across the Pacific, people have been attaching themselves and their societies to part of Christianity while rejecting, or thoroughly transforming other elements." Identifying the relative influences of 'custom' and Christianity has been complex, especially as the mission stations expanded to include primary schools and health centers.[7]

Women in Wanigela routinely negotiate the practices and language of sorcery, Christianity, and Western medicine. Care is taken to ensure that intimate bodily fluids remain intimate, name taboos are respected, food is available for church events, pharmacy pills and creams are used sparingly and equitably, and so on. This maneuvering does not seem, however, as constrained and regulated; in dealing with these ever-present constellations of power, they more often appear as humorous and generous spirits. Laughter, respectful teasing, and witty retorts permeate the different groups of women as they meet and greet each other in their houses, at the marketplace and church, and on the roads and pathways that interlace the village. In this way women's bodies are simultaneously constituted by the places they move within and through, as well as by the discourses about these places.

The Mothers Union in the Pacific: Thinking Maternally

One of the major ways in which women come together in Wanigela is to attend Mothers Union meetings or events two to three times a week. This is a critical place for women to meet as a group, and although there is a prescribed role for the Mothers Union in the workings of the Anglican Church, this is one of the most public places for women to meet as women.[8] Scheyvens (2003) has argued that it is easy to dismiss innovative feminist development initiatives that focus on women's church groups, especially if the activities center on spiritual growth, sewing, and crafts. Being part of global ideological groups hardly appears to be part of a transformative feminist struggle. However, Christianity has always had localized meanings, because meanings are constantly in tension over colonial, religious, and local agents of change. It is within these place-based meanings that some women have been able to contest global influences.

Sister Helen Roberts, a dedicated missionary who lived in Wanigela from 1947 to her death in 1989, had more influence upon many of the older women than just teaching them sewing, washing, and cooking. As a trained nurse, she became highly skilled at providing basic health care with limited resources.[9] In the 1960s and 1970s, the combination of better medical care and regular immunization for babies and children meant women were healthier and able to have babies more regularly. There was a cohort of women born in the late 1920s who gave birth to seven, eight, nine, ten, eleven, and twelve children. These women were birthing mothers at the time Sister Helen Roberts began working as a medical officer. All of these women had close contact with Sister Helen Roberts, either through working for her, having her assistance during difficult births, being married by her, or, after having seven or eight children at two-year intervals, receiving her encouragement to take the Pill.

The frequent pregnancies of many of her patients must have been of great concern for Sister Roberts, and so she introduced the Pill. Acceptance of the Pill attests to the influence Sister Helen Roberts had upon many of these women and their husbands. She recognized that the married body was also the sexual body that required some help from modern contraceptives, because these mothers hinted that it was hard for them to refuse sex with their husbands. It is no surprise that European women such as Sister Helen Roberts, steeped as they were in their own political, cultural, and moral sensitivities, thought Wanigela women, the main carers of families, needed some extra training to look better after their families (see Jolly and MacIntyre, 1989). To do this they had to train Wanigela women to look after themselves, which included providing clear moral directives about promiscuity and submission. Despite very little knowledge of contraceptives, women in this cohort and their husbands were convinced that taking the Pill was preferable to using traditional methods of birth control. Many even denied any knowledge of traditional methods. Sister Helen Roberts must have been pleased that so many of her patients took her advice of meeting their husbands' needs in the submissive way she believed the Bible guided her to teach them. Many of these women spoke of how they could not say 'no' to their husbands. This contrasts with the idea of 'staying,' or not being sexually active, which older women and an increasing number of younger women referred to when asked about traditional family planning. Yet many of these women also turned to traditional methods of contraception.

The women of Wanigela struggled against their own sense of their ability to cope with their domestic responsibilities, the Church's teachings about the value of wifely submission, and discussions with sisters, mothers, and cousins about how to remain healthy. For many women, the return to traditional forms of contraception was a subtle form of transgressing the hegemony of Christian teaching and Western medical knowledge. Although this may not seem to be a remarkable struggle, on a daily basis it adds up to careful maneuvering within the webs of power that are embedded in the place of Wanigela.

Conclusion

In Wanigela, women were not articulating—from a politics of survival—their needs before, during, and after pregnancy as was the woman I described in the Introduction of this essay. Instead, their politics of place emerges in the way they actively position themselves in relation to how their maternal bodies are regulated; that is, through modern contraception, sorcery, and Christianity. Because women negotiate the ambiguities within their everyday lives, the focus of analysis could expand from including only active resistance to include "active positioning" (Cooper, 1997: 199). This would allow for a politics of place that nourishes just and sustainable alternatives, while engaging with the realities of survival. The impetus to ensure gender equality at the global level is still pressing, especially given the craziness of the twenty-first century, when confusion about human security and violence coheres on women's bodies. But the possibilities for alternative and progressive articulations of bodies in places and places in bodies can be found in out-of-the-way places, which means everywhere. Pregnant bodies will continue to destabilize taken-for-granted notions of undifferentiated asexual bodies.

Notes

1. See papers in *Contemporary Pacific 2001*, 13(1), especially Diaz and Kauani, 2001.

2. See Gegeo (2001) for the range of meanings attributed to 'place' among the Kwao'o speakers of the Solomon Islands in the western Pacific.

3. The binary logic of the concept of 'center-periphery' and the world systems theories from which it emerged most clearly has been under critical scrutiny for some time. See, for instance, Escobar, 1995: 96.

4. This began when missionaries and colonists arrived, and continues to the present day with greater involvement of foreign investors in the economy. Tragically, in July 2001, four young people died in violent confrontations with police after public demonstrations against the government's uncritical acceptance of a World Bank–supported policy of privatization, a key component of its economic strategy.

5. I have come to know Wanigela over the last fifteen years, first as a relative by marriage and then as the site of my doctoral dissertation. It is still one of the places I call home.

6. Even as recently as 2001, some women in Papua New Guinea were violently attacked, often fatally, on suspicion of being witches. See also Dinnen and Ley (2000).

7. These were financially supported by the national government before it embarked on World Bank–prescribed structural adjustment policies in the early 1990s.

8. A new evangelical church also exists in Wanigela, and its women members have a similar 'mothers group.' I know much less about the workings of this group; however, I assume it serves functions that are similar to those of the Mothers Union, as its recruits are from the mainstream Anglican Church.

9. Sister Roberts was fortunate to have had better access to health care supplies than what was accessible during the economic situation of the 1990s, in which the philosophy of 'user pays' applied. However, this should not detract from her considerable tenacity in getting resources for the Collingwood Bay area. For more on the theme of 'Women, Christians, Citizens,' see Douglas (2003).

2

The Body Politic in Global Development Discourse: A Women and the Politics of Place Perspective

WENDY HARCOURT

Introduction: The Body Politic

In this chapter I trace the engagement of global women's movements with 'the body politic' of development discourse on women, the environment, population, and development during the 1990s. I write as a participant working in the women's movement as a feminist researcher employed by an established, international, development nongovernmental organization (NGO). I have worked on body politics both in my writing and as an activist in Australia and the United Kingdom, and in the last decade I have worked internationally as an activist researcher in collaboration with European and southern women's organizations engaged in development policy.[1]

In this chapter I use the term *body politics* in two ways. The first refers to the term as it was developed in the second wave of feminism, beginning with Simone de Beauvoir's foundational *The Second Sex*. This feminist tradition has taken the female body as an entry point for political engagement, both linguistically (see Chapter 9) and politically over a range of issues, such as fighting for abortion rights, Reclaim the Night marches, protesting rape as a weapon in war, protesting against beauty pageants, and so on. These struggles challenge the sense of the female body as 'the other.' Following this tradition, I explore the cultural, social, economic, and political positionings of the physical female

32

body as body politics overlaps with other political battles, particularly in rights, social justice, and environmental movements.

The second use of the term *body politics* is found in development discourse as it constructs and produces individual and collective women's bodies through discourses on 'women in development,' 'gender and development,' and women's empowerment.

Building on the Foucauldian concept of biopolitics (Foucault, 1976; Harcourt, 1986; Charckiewicz, 2004), this chapter explores the historical entanglement of the global women's movement with development through the discourses that constructed and managed the individual and social female body.

A Women and the Politics of Place Perspective on Body Politics

The Women and the Politics of Place (WPP) project helps to conceptualize body politics in several ways. First, it looks at the body not as a static entity locked into culturally defined biological rhythms but as a fluid site of power and political contestation. WPP defines the body as 'the place closest-in' (see Chapter 1), where specific cultural, social, and economic realities are played out with the following result: women in different geographic locations organize to resist constricting, often violent, rules and codes of conduct over and on their bodily existence. Second, WPP opens up the question of how these women are connecting across geographic space and time through various networks or meshworks (see the Introduction to the book) within the apparatus of the global women's movement, environmental movement, and alternative globalization movement. And third, WPP challenges the assumption that a Western knowledge base (feminist, ecological, or alternative) is the given starting point for today's transformative politics. Instead, it seeks out diverse starting points in different 'out-of-the-way' places, 'missed' places, and 'hidden' places that are inhabited by women and that are often the charged places of subaltern resistance to globalization, capitalism, modernization, and development regimes.

The following narrative is divided into three parts. The first was a moment of contestation of development discourses that occurred in the 1970s–1980s as women's movements emerged in diverse parts of the world. This was a moment when feminists working on issues such as trade, population, environment, peace, resource management, and primary health came together and enabled a new set of radical feminist voices to enter the development debate (particularly after the 1985 Nairobi Third World Conference on Women). The second moment was a sustained engagement of these radical voices with development discourse during the late 1980s and early 1990s, resulting in an increase in professionalizing of development, a proliferation of NGOs focusing on women's issues, and a 'politics of truth' that ended up subverting the more radical agenda. This moment reconstructed women's concerns about being perceived as objects of management through powerful discourses around 'gender mainstreaming,' gender and development, and so on. The third moment, which began in the late 1990s and continues to the present day, is marked by disengagement, or at least significant problematizing by the women's movement of the development discourse and apparatus and a decided shift toward interest in other sites of power and knowledge production. Once it became clear that the UN summits and conferences were co-opting rather than changing, the focus turned to global protests against neoliberal globalization, with movements such as the Zapatistas and, since 2000, the World Social Forum process.

The First Moment:
Contesting the Body Politic of Development

My initial entry point into the global debates about women, environment, population, and development was at two of the first women's alternative meetings to the global institutional processes, contributing to the newly emerging 'sustainable development' paradigm. I attended the World Women's Congress for a Healthy Planet held in Miami, Florida, in late 1991 and the series of meetings hosted in the Planeta Femea, or the Women's Tent, at the Global Forum, the nongovernmental forum of the United Nations Conference on Environment and Development (UNCED, the so-called Earth Summit), held in Rio de Janeiro, Brazil, in mid 1992.[2] These meetings were historic moments that allowed global women's movements to consolidate their collective agendas and interact with the official global development discourse characterized by the series of UN conferences in the 1990s.[3]

When I use the phrase 'global women's movements,' I am referring to the thousands of women who have entered into international, agenda-setting arenas from their own regional, local, and place-based perspectives; and who, however self-defined, engage in a translation of their constituency's specific needs into international agendas, thus enabling action at home. They call upon international conventions, institutions, and policy to take into account: women's needs, the complexities of diverse gender differences, and the radical changes required for gender justice to be reached.

Both the Miami and Rio de Janeiro women's events were driven by a strong resistance to the mainstream global development agenda that viewed economic growth as fuel for development and treated 'women,' 'environment,' and 'population' as technical subjects within that overarching goal. The events were characterized by a sense of celebration of women's creativity, alternatives to the mainstream, and cultural diversity. The participants created a vibrant set of messages addressed to the UN establishment about women acting from positions of power, knowledge, and planetary values. The assumption was that, if 'heard' by those in power, these messages could defeat the gender-biased, monocultural, militaristic, and economistic discourse that focused on market, Western science, and elitists' technical solutions to poverty, injustice, and environmental degradation (WEDO, 1992; APDC, September 1992).

It is important to examine not only the ideas that emerged but also the practices through which the emerging discourses came into being. Although the goal was to produce texts with which to infiltrate and change the official UN process, women designed their actions in ways that were decidedly different from UN official practice. The opening ceremony of the Miami meeting was led by the indigenous women of the land where the Miami Hyatt Conference Centre had been built, with a song of welcome to the audience of a thousand or more women from around the world. Leading women from each region of the world gave moving testimonies of the damage development had wreaked upon the land, culture, peoples' bodies, and the balance of nature. The women judges (judges by profession from Australia, Sweden, Guyana, India, and Kenya) then reported their findings, followed by a series of caucus statements by women from each world region, including women of color, indigenous women, and women from the global South. The reports were put together by a team of women each evening and circulated among participants to ensure consensus. They were read at the final ceremony and assembled into one document for the press, world governments, the UNCED Earth Summit Session, and women's and other social movements. The document represented "a compilation of the work, ideas and values of 1,500 women" and a "challenge to women and men to work together to create a safe and sustainable future"(WEDO, 1992: 16).

Planeta Femea, the Women's Tent, organized by the same group as the Miami meeting, was symbolically the largest central tent among the hundreds that were set up for the NGO Global Forum in Rio de Janeiro. It hosted heated debates among representatives of women's networks on economic, political, and social policy issues, leading to successful input into the women's chapter of Agenda 21 (the official outcome of the UNCED governmental meeting). Speeches and panel discussions were interspersed with an international marketplace of open discussion and the trade of crafts and books; and interludes during which local Brazilian women staged demonstrations against mining companies or Nestlé and in favor of breast-feeding. At Planeta Femea, many women's networks and organizations met about different concerns. In the Global Forum they intermingled with ecologists, representatives of the peace movement, trade unions, youth organizations, development NGOs, and local community groups, in what was to become one of the first in a series of events that ran counter to a series of UN meetings held in the 1990s (UNDPI, 1992; WIDE, 1992).

The statements made and discussions held in the Planeta Femea and Global Forum meetings deliberately 'broke out of the boxes' set by the mainstream agenda. The women's far-ranging agenda brought together, in a holistic and critical account of development, all the 'women's issues': sexuality and health, reproductive health and rights, fair pay and access to work outside the home, violence against women, legal rights to land and political decision making, the fight against big corporations that destroy community and nature, the struggle for peace, the need to listen to basic needs of the economic poor, North-South inequalities, and gender blindness of economics and development policy. The concept of environment and development was pushed far beyond the sustainable development paradigm introduced by the official Earth Summit, as women's experiences and shared knowledge combined with politically sophisticated strategies of how to tackle mainstream ideas and policy. The focus was on militarism, debt, trade, and inequality, and expressed a consciousness of the North-South split, particularly around population issues. Even though women expressed celebration and solidarity, it did not lead to a naïve essentialism of all women being able to speak as one. Instead it was about coming together and finding some basis for strategic common ground, along with a shared sense of optimism about the ability of the women's movement to take on the establishment.[4]

In the next six or so years, the practices that emerged to put these ideas into motion in the official arena were complex. Several alliances were formed in order to achieve this goal, some of which received funding to start organizations with offices in the power hot spots (largely Washington, DC or New York). The Women's Environment and Development Organization (WEDO), made up of key women from the environmental, reproductive rights, and economic justice movements, emerged to play a strong role in motivating women to engage with the UN process, with Bella Abzug's team centered in New York (WEDO, 1994; www.wedo.org). An alliance among European, Southern, and American networks that eventually evolved into Women's International Coalition for Economic Justice (WICEJ; www.WICEJ.org) was formed and coordinated from New York (on a voluntary basis), and fed into multiple processes related to the United Nations. Charlotte Bunch at Rutgers brought a strong global focus to women's human rights (Center for Women's Global Leadership; www.cwgl.rutgers.edu). And many other groups, such as Development Alternatives for Women in a New Era (DAWN; www.dawn.org.fj) and Women in Development Europe (www.wide.org)[5] were visibly strengthened through the networking that took place in Miami and Rio de Janeiro, which was evident in their work that spun off into other global and regional events.

The Second Moment: Engagement and Entanglement with the Development Discourse

In this period the global women's movement became a part of the apparatus that created the truth, theory, and values around women, environment, population, and development in the social institutions and practices; and managed and defined women as an object of development discourse.

I am not suggesting that there was a deliberate attempt by UN or government officials to take over the women's agenda; rather, by choosing to become part of the different institutional arrangements, women became embedded in the discourse. Even while protesting the disempowering impacts of development intervention, producing 'counter-knowledge,' and proposing other practices, women were tied into an array of procedures, analyses, reflections, calculations, and tactics that continued the oppression of women through micro strategies that captured the female body as an individual and social subject of development discourse, or what Foucault labeled 'biopower.'

In the 1990s, the aim of the women's movement in engaging with the UN heads of state and intergovernmental meetings was to empower women, change the gender bias and inequities in development policy, and achieve gender justice. These claims were about 'mainstreaming' gender in development, making women's work and lives visible in development policy, and arguing that women were key in putting sustainable development 'into practice'; for example, claiming 'women's rights as human rights' in the Vienna World Conference on Human Rights held in 1994; placing women, reproductive rights, and health at 'center stage' in the population and development conference held in Cairo in 1994; working with social movements to bring gender concerns into 'human-centered development,' 'fair trade,' and 'decent work' at the World Summit on Social Development held in Copenhagen in 1995; adding the previously unspoken issues of sexual choice and violence against women to the more acceptable peace and women's political representation at the Fourth World Conference on Women held in Beijing in 1995; and underlining women's key role in food security in the World Food Summit held in Rome in 1996. These represented paradigmatic shifts, as women and gender were absorbed into the debates. Consequently, women were invited to take up higher positions within the bureaucracy, forms of gender expertise were established, documents were rewritten, and many manuals on how to mainstream gender were presented, as the push continued to have a 'gender perspective' in all areas of development, including trade negotiations in the newly formed World Trade Organization and the Financing for Development Conferences.

By the mid 1990s, in a myriad of places, women 'experts' and the language of gender and women's rights had entered the public sphere of development discourse (Petechesky, 2002). In such discursive practices, the discourse about women and global development—whether it focused on rights, population and social development, food security, empowerment, the environment, or trade negotiations—grew into a small industry of proliferating NGOs, gender experts, and women's networks closely attached to the UN processes. These were the women who could negotiate the maze of corridors in the basement of the United Nations; they understood who was who in the agencies and, at times, worked for those agencies. These were the women who defined the women, or gender, position. Their writings, speeches, and reports charted and interpreted the move from women in development to gender and development; from population to reproductive health; from sustainable development to sustainable livelihoods; and from economic growth to economic justice. They were the ones who lobbied for women's voices to be heard, who could advise on how to mainstream gender, and were among those trusted within government and among the bureaucracy to recommend which participants were funded for the regional and global meetings; they were the experts who could take the message back home.

The micro practices of these talented and committed women helped build the new biopolitical focus on the female body as women negotiated their way through the UN scene. It was this work that established the crucial nature of issues such as violence against women, sexual choice, reproductive rights and health, maternal mortality, access to natural resources, gender justice, gender and trade, and the care economy in global development. By the end of the 1990s, women were no longer 'the poorest of the poor'; they were seen as victims, not subjects, of their own lives. The global process also gave political purpose to the many women concerned about injustice locally; it was a way to move often intractable problems on the national level to the global arena; the UN conferences gave credibility to women's issues that were usually safely ignored on the local front. And, at the same time, the proliferation of UN meetings and the political need to 'engender' the debate provided jobs, careers, and visibility, such as those that male colleagues had been receiving for years, to the women engaged in the struggle.

Yet, with all these efforts, was there a social transformation? Did environmental degradation stop? Did violence against women decrease? Did we move closer to the end of gender injustice? Were women freer to choose, and were women's rights now human rights?

Even without looking up the latest figures, we know that the answer to these questions is a partial yes, but remains mostly no. The ample literature and debates among women's NGOs and women's organizations project a strong sense of frustration. The problem is women entered a dominant set of biopolitical practices that only reinforced many of the oppressive techniques they were challenging in the first place. I do not want to say that women were unaware of the dangers of becoming part of the system, nor were they unaware that the time spent on these big meetings was detracting from other actions. It was a strategic choice, but one that misjudged the way in which power and knowledge work through negotiations, through the very process of dialogue that would allow women to voice concerns, and then turn it into an elaborate process of committees, agreements, loans, and projects within such a straightjacket of terms that the concerns, however genuine, were lost.

Even if we turn to another, perhaps less overtly political strategy of undertaking new knowledge and research, we see similar problems. A strategic choice to back up the engagement with the UN policy machinery was intended to allow women to classify and gather new knowledge and research in order to enter and challenge the global development discourses on technical and scientific grounds. Beyond the question of whether these research processes actually benefited women, the process inevitably had to distort the validity of those 'grassroots' experiences or risk being further marginalized and ignored. There arose a whole industry, composed of both the Women's Bureau within the United Nations and NGOs and researchers outside it, that began to collect 'case studies' that would measure the level of poverty, compare the types of distress, rate the success of 'coping strategies,' find new indicators to measure and show success or failure, and compare and rate one nation's poverty or gender gap against another. There was a concerted search for methodologies to combine feminist thinking with development approaches. 'Women in development,' or 'gender in development,' was described, translated into documents, and researched via qualitative and quantitative measurements to show development policy makers in government, the United Nations, Bretton Woods, and International Financial Institutions (IFIs)—those with the money and decision-making power to determine that gender concerns were valid and scientific, worthy of special policy and funding. While the documents that emerged from the meetings in Vienna, Copenhagen, Cairo, Beijing, Rome, and New York stated that women's situations could be restored to well being, the images that were codified in the documents showed women scrounging in rubbish heaps, women walking in decimated forests with a jar of water on their heads and a baby on their backs, young girls leaning over factory assembly lines or crouched in the sweatshop making Nike shoes, a dying pregnant woman, the scarred face of a victim of acid throwing, the pained eyes of a girl who had undergone female genital mutilation, the pleading expression of the sex worker dying of HIV/AIDS, the huddle of ragged women, and skeletal babies in refugee camps.

Through this kind of codification, the discourse simplified the vastly different experiences of women around the world who came from so many cultures and backgrounds. Through the UN official texts, background reports, statistics, and evidence, these experiences became the generic gendered female body; the poor woman with a specific set of needs and rights. She came in various guises. She was no longer a victim needing aid; instead she was a working subject with productive potential. It was assumed that poor women wanted to get out of the home and were willing and useful agents for development. A whole range of assumptions (often captured in glossy texts with catchy headings) was made about this productive female body: Educate poor women and you educate the next generation. Train poor women for jobs, and your investment is guaranteed. Give poor women credit and the whole family benefits. Teach poor women about sprayed nets to prevent malaria and you save a whole community. Replace the men in a factory with poor women and you have a docile and effective workforce for less pay and less trouble. Sterilize a poor woman and you control unwanted children and prevent the population explosion. These were the messages that reinterpreted the women's movements' arguments for autonomy, rights, and gender equality. The complex links among health, reproductive life cycles, the caring economy, the market economy, the environment, and, by the end of the 1990s, what was increasingly known as globalization, were repackaged into the technical expertise and understandable development concerns. They were put through the UN machine of debate and policy making and emerged as the issues government could agree upon, but did not very often follow up.

This process, despite all the attempts to link social, economic, and gender justice, smoothed away the links in the processes and types of language that were understood by the global development discourse. In the biopolitics of the management of gender and women's rights, the female body and gender issues remained the 'soft' issues of development. So when it came to why there were no real reforms to take these concerns into account, or even why there was less and less money to train women, provide health services, and counter violence against women, the answer could always be that there were other, more pressing concerns to deal with. These included war, failed states, internal conflict, economic crisis, restructuring, liberalizing markets, security, and trade agreements, all of which did not seem, in the end, to have much to do with women's demands, figures, and case studies that were still mostly considered adjuncts to the 'hard' development issues.

For all the women's attempts to bring the multiple needs and concerns of women into the development discourse, it was translated in the body politic as an essentially passive, 'productive, reproductive, and sexualized female body' that was managed and understood through various mechanisms; essentially as new workers with specific health and education needs, as well as the need for special protection from conflict, violence, or unfair work practices, and even sexual exploitation and domestic injustice.

These 'paradigm' shifts were certainly an improvement upon what was accepted in earlier development decades; there was a more holistic understanding of women's lives and a recognition that data on the complexity of their lives was missing; and they needed to be given new space in development projects. As *productive bodies,* women were redefined as the new workforce that needed management and care. The feminization of labor heralded them as the semiskilled factory worker, the home worker, and the informal worker whose industriousness was welcomed. In the more liberal discourse, women's rights to better pay, health, and safety, as well as access to better jobs and other labor markets, were also underlined. 'Third world women' were depicted as enduring double and triple work loads and slaving in the home, fields, or urban slums as the newly recruited global workforce; and, in both urban and rural areas, as the main carers of the environment and culture.

As *maternal bodies,* women needed support to control and space time between children and in the prevention of death during the birthing process. As HIV/AIDS hit the scene in full by the late 1990s, these hard-working maternal bodies became prone not only to high levels of morbidity and mortality but to an epidemic illness that attacked them because of both biological and social reasons. As the discourse became more nuanced, the productive maternal body was overlaid by the *sexualized body,* as case studies began to point to violence against women as a major deterrent against the ability of women to enjoy 'the full benefits of development.' The battered and raped body and the disfigured or sexually exploited woman or girl became another set of icons in development.

The gender and development discourse that emerged from the UN conferences and gender and development programs, and the research that surrounded them, essentially continued to create a colonized poor and marginalized woman who needed to be managed and educated; whose capacity for work and local decision making needed building; and who needed to be controlled reproductively and sexually through a series of development interventions designed for 'women's empowerment.'

From the perspective of place, the specificities of these female bodies are hard to discern. Even if the claim was for regional and cultural difference, the demands of a global discourse smoothed away the differences of place. It was, of course, possible in the gender-aware global development discourse to speak of broadly different concerns and characteristics of women in South Asia, sub-Saharan Africa, the Arab region, Central and Latin America, East Asia and the Pacific, East Europe, and so on. Compared among regions, the average woman could expect different experiences within periods of her life cycle that development policy could predict, monitor, and try to change with more education and better health, more solid investments, and more advantageous markets and trade regimes. Interestingly, women who lived in North America, Europe, and Australasia—with the exception of migrants or indigenous women who became self-defined as 'fourth world' women and were largely outside these debates—were lumped together as the 'developed woman' representing the wealth and values of the West and who more or less had the money, the access, the rights, and the status toward which these other groups of women needed to strive.

These—what I call 'biopolitical prescriptions'—were the unsatisfactory result of the different practices and types of knowledge that the global discourse of gender and development on 'the body politic' produced.

Perhaps the most ironic result of the UN agreements, so belabored and negotiated during thousands of consultations and engagements of members of women's groups in what became known as 'civil society,' is the Millennium Development Goals (MDGs) that emerged out of the Millennium Declaration in 2000 (Harcourt, 2004). The MDGs consist of eight measurable and defined goals with forty-eight indicators attached and a host of UN mechanisms to ensure them: national reports, global campaigns, research projects, UN-wide monitoring, and statistical assessments.

Implementing the MDGs could be viewed as just another UN process to add to the others, but the goals are now determining all aspects of the UN international development agenda. They are complemented by a steady stream of high-level commissions headed by former presidents with former heads of UN agencies or other high-placed officials and academics advising the secretary general on less measurable issues such as peace, migration, and civil society.[6] Cheaper and more efficient than unwieldy heads-of-state affairs, the commission reports come up with recommendations that, not surprisingly, fit well with the MDG process. In fact consultations with civil society are done mainly through e-discussions that 'everyone' is invited to join—sometimes in languages other than English. Knowledge of UN bureaucracy is definitely helpful in these e-discussions, and, even if time and access to a computer does preclude many would-be participants, there are many thousands who can join the discussion.[7]

The Third Moment:
Reorienting Women and the Politics of Place

Not surprisingly, among the women's movements that once buzzed around the UN conferences, there is extreme skepticism of the MDGs (WICEJ, 2004; Harcourt, 2004). While there has been a retreat of the women's movement from the UN arena, new energy has been found in what we call in this book 'place-based struggles,' particularly around the specificity of the lived body in a particular place—while maintaining global connections—and the need to understand the global 'in place.'

Going back to biopower as a way to understand this tiredness and shift of energy, a reverse locus of biopower seems to have emerged, a new kind of 'counterpolitics' that is indeed part of biopolitics. To the extent that women's movements were part of creating the dominant power knowledge, they were also creating within it the nodes of resistance. In the skills learned and knowledge gathered in those micro practices they are also able to resist. The modern functioning of biopower is permeated by a fluid disorder, where power resides not only in the dominant hegemonic structures but also in the engagement and resistance to them.

In quite different processes than those that take place in the halls of the United Nations and in capitols around the world, we can see women's place-based politics or subaltern organizing in the process of building alternatives. For many women who never tried to enter the global development arena, subaltern organizing allows them to continue the struggle against the flows and shifts of different interventions that are snaring democracy and culture in different forms of globalization, degradation, and attack on the community and the commons. These are the women working in economic and social justice movements who are countering the aftermath of structural adjustment and privatization and who are moving into the political spaces opened up by local, political, and economic changes.

The reverse locus of power can be found in the place-based women's movement groups who are using development intervention to counter the management of the female body in numerous ways. Examples of these groups include self-help groups of women working together to rebuild society after conflict or displacement, such as the Women in Black groups in Croatia and Serbia, who are setting up self-help clinics to deal with violence against women in post-war trauma situations and ongoing high levels of domestic violence; the women's groups working for the recognition of women's health rights for migrants dealing with complex issues such as female genital mutilation; and the women's health groups in Bangladesh that are pointing out the need to meet basic health requirements, not just provide family planning clinics. There are many examples of such groups, ranging from Amanitare in Africa to Women on the Waves in central and eastern Europe (Harcourt, 2003). The local fourth world women groups hold on to the diversity of place-based cultural experiences in the face of sometimes overwhelming cultural, economic, and political hegemonies.

The task is not to close down UN or government programs and processes that aim to support women's health, education, reproductive, and productive rights; nor is it to stop research that measures the gender gaps and biases in science and development or charts poverty from a gender perspective. Neither is it wise to retreat into place-based local politics that ignores larger social movements', including women's movements', macro concerns. The point is not to choose one or the other position but to learn from these histories and understand the multiple strategies that are needed to bring into being new schemas of politicization. In modern society we are faced with complex forms of gender oppression that produce, fix, and co-opt gender relations through various techniques. The important issue is for women to act to transform these oppressions, be aware that modern power is fluid and disordered, and understand that consequently their strategies have to be on many levels. The task is to be thoroughly aware of the many ways patriarchal and imperial capitalist, hegemonic power can be expressed and therefore, in a Foucauldian reading of power, resisted.

The framework provided by women and the politics of place suggests that, in the first decade of this century, women's movements are much more readily finding a space in the alternative globalization movement, acting in solidarity in place and across place (WICEJ, 2004). The United Nations is no longer perceived as a site—at least not as a privileged site—of transformative political processes that can push forward a feminist activist agenda. It remains to be seen, however, whether novel events such as the World Social Forum provide effective arenas, or if a new women's place-based politics is yet to evolve.

Notes

1. I am currently chairperson of Women in Development Europe (www.wide-network.org) and program advisor at the Society for International Development (see www.sidint.org).

2. World Women's Congress for a Healthy Planet was held November 8–12, 1991, in Miami, Florida, and was attended by fifteen hundred women from eighty-three countries. Planeta Femea was the Women's Tent organized by the local Brazilian committee with WEDO and DAWN. The documents fed directly into the 1992 Global Forum of the 'Earth Summit.' They also fed into the women's Chapter 24 of the Earth Summit's final declaration, under the section, 'Strengthening the Role of Major Groups' in the Agenda 21 'Program of Action for Sustainable Development'—the final text of agreements that was negotiated by governments at the United Nations Conference on Environment and Development (UNCED) held June 3–14 in Rio de Janeiro, Brazil.

3. The United Nations organized a series of heads of states conferences and summits throughout the 1990s. See the United Nations Web site (www.un.org).

4. See the two paragraphs of the Women's Declaration from the 1992 Global Forum, endorsing the Women's Action Agenda 21 (WEDO, 1992).

5. See "Window on the World" in *Development* 45.1, 46.2.

6. See *Development* 48.1 for a review of the main reports: "Fair Globalization," "Zedillo Report," and "Cardoso Report."

7. For example, the Millennium Project set up a listserv through Action Aid and Panos South Asia to monitor civil society responses to their conclusions on Goal 3 of the MDGs Women's Empowerment.

3

Transforming Passion, Politics, and Pain

In dialogue with Fatma Alloo[1]

WH: When we first spoke about your contribution to the book we spoke about your personal experiences of empowerment. I remember the first title you suggested for this chapter was 'Who Says Women Don't Have Power?' Our discussion turned to how African women have and use sexual power, but don't always understand it as part of their own power. You told me how, in your experience in Zanzibar, sexual power is traditionally taken as a given and is respected, but that respect is being challenged and downgraded with globalization, the onset of tourism, and a selling of bodies, both men and women's, and cultures. Today sexuality is sold through a complex set of cultural and economic processes of exchange. These processes both build on and exploit African women's traditional power of sexuality and desire.

I was very interested in how your own story refutes the traditional way of perceiving African women's exploitation. You have challenged traditional views, fought against violence against women and agitated around other hot topics of 'body politics.' You told me how you built on your own power as a woman, your own sexuality and attraction, that was at first 'used' and, then as you took hold of it, transformed into resistance to the men around you and, in a creative way, to change the structures that were imposed on you.

I am interested in how, within the framework of women and the politics of place, you first became engaged in politics, turning to media

48

and social movement organizing as the way to transform your own life and the exploitation of other women around you.

FA: I have just been asked by the Tanzania Media Women's Association (TAMWA) to document the history of TAMWA. In writing the history I want to explore how the politics of Tanzania, how the place where we live and work, is determined by our history and sets our goals for the future.

Thinking about how to write this history set me in a reflective mood. I started to ask myself, what was the driving force that led me, a traditional Zanzibari woman, to found a national media association in Tanzania? What drove me to form an organization, to portray women's issues in the media as viable and in so doing mobilize women to demand their rights? Why did I become engaged politically in this way? It was a difficult and ambitious project, particularly in 1987 with the beginnings of economic liberalization and the end of a single party socialist economy presided over by Mwalimu Julius Nyerere, one of the great leaders of Tanzania and Africa.

My honest answer to your and my questions is that gender justice was my driving force. The bodily and emotional pain of what it takes to be a woman was the vehicle.

My home is the small island of Zanzibar in the warm Indian Ocean on the east coast of Africa—a dhow (traditional sailing boat) nation. My childhood was happy and peaceful, even if my biological father abandoned my mother and me when I was born and my mother was married off again by her father (as was the tradition) to a man who lived in Mombassa. She left me in the hands of her sister and her mother's family. I grew up with the love of a large extended family, under the protection of my grandfather. My aunt became my mother, my pillar and protector. From her I learned the spirit of struggle and survival.

I grew up in the sixties when the politics of the Cold War were buffeting the island. As I ran in the streets, played marbles and games, I knew little of the 'revolution' brewing in the island of Zanzibar with its half a million people. As President Kennedy sent directives to the Ambassador to stop the revolution in Zanzibar with instructions to prevent another Cuba in the Indian Ocean (Wilson, 1989), instead of Cold War politics I was imagining the flutes on the island as they dance in Lake Victoria. As a young schoolgirl I took the metaphor literally.

WH: This is an intriguing image. What do you mean here?

FA: What I mean is that, as a young girl, I was free and happy and beginning to awaken sexually. Thus dreaming of boys and imagining singing and playing madly in love evoked by the movies from India was part and parcel of my growing up. The movie house was next door to our home, and I used to sneak in and watch the films with astonishment. Little did I realize then the impact it would have in my emotional feeling and awakening as a woman. Thus the flutes and the dance I am referring to evoke in me the happiness of those early childhood days. The expression I think was used by Dr. Livingstone, who said when one pipes in Zanzibar they dance at the shores of Lake Victoria. He meant the influence of trade from Zanzibar was felt on the shores of the lake region. But my image then was of happiness and people dancing on the shores of Lake Victoria!

The story of pain began when I was forced to become a woman overnight, though I was only in my teens. There was turmoil on the island. My parents saw no way out, but to marry their daughters off to 'protect' them from this ordeal. I was married to a noted intellectual of the island, and then followed him as a wife on his travels to British and US universities, eventually settling in Dar-es-Salaam.

I was in this manner exposed to the world and an intellectual environment that helped me to make sense of myself, initially, intellectually. Later on, my 'place' took richer shapes in terms of being a woman, and a Zanzibari and an African in a world that was changing as fast as I was myself. I was deeply influenced by Sembene Ousmane's *God's Bits of Wood* (1970) and Walter Rodney's *How Europe Underdeveloped Africa* (1972). My decolonization process had begun.

Those years at University of Dar-es-Salaam were termed 'revolutionary.' Dar was a center of liberation movement and the University was its pulse. Being surrounded by intellectual revolutionaries then, like Walter Rodney, Clive Thomas, and Kwasi Batchway from Ghana, and many others, triggered in me an appetite for knowledge. I had always told my mother I wanted to study. As I kneaded *chapattis* in the kitchen and as my belly grew with child, I could not help listening to the debates that the revolutionary men were carrying on in my living room. The talk ignited a fire within me, which would eventually break the fetters of conventionalism within my way of living and consume my marriage in its path. This passion led me to thirst for writing, and journalism became my career then.

WH: Can you expand a little more here about your learning experience as a woman and as an African intellectual? I don't know if it is relevant to say here how you perceived yourself as you served those African male intellectuals? Did you feel your own needs, as a woman, were invisible? It would be interesting to know how your lack of voice and your 'houseboundness' and frequent pregnancies led to a rebellion and to your interest in writing and journalism and also to women's movement organizing, as well as eventually to you leaving your marriage and pursuing love outside of it.

FA: Discovering myself as a woman with choices went hand in hand with discovering my own place and its politics, both nationally and also globally. I started to comprehend the global economic forces that rob our continent of its resources and, in the process, labels us poor and colonizes our minds to feel disempowered. Critiques of concepts such as 'underdeveloped' were debated hotly among the intellectuals at the Dar university campus in those days.

As the debates raged so did my being. This unleashed within me a momentum that set me on a political path as an African woman, as a writer, and as a believer in what is right and just. Somewhat naïvely, I set out on this path unaware of all the obstacles that were in the way. My belief in change was deeply linked to liberation theories. I fell head over heals in love with those theories and, in the process, the man (not my husband) who propagated them so eloquently. I wanted to fully live in it, and I did.

Looking back, I realize now that I had failed to see that I, and indeed women, was not part of this leading thinker's political agenda of justice. I was a beautiful, desirable woman who was for conquest, but I was not to be catered to in his busy and starry political agenda. Nor were my own political concerns that centered around women's rights. I had little to guide me then as I found myself on the margins of his life, rejected and not part of the political project he was so vehemently pursuing. Once he had conquered me, the challenge was a done deal. I could now be discarded at his whim. The power of patriarchy was on his side. He won then, and I was broken.

WH: It seems that you, like many women, found that your love for a man led to courageous personal changes, but then, eventually, to a sidelining that sours the love and trust and hope. It reminds me of how often women within social movements end up serving men not working alongside them. These are some of the unspoken power struggles that happen all the time in politics, 'the woman behind the man' syndrome. It is very brave of you to speak out about it.

FA: It was a deeply painful process to realize that this love was not to protect or support me in my own political and personal struggles. It became clear to me that I had to forge my own path if I was to survive. I returned to Dar-es-Salaam. I turned to my writing, to my understanding of women's needs and rights, and found within me a strength and passion that enable me to organize and work with women back in Tanzania and also globally. Thus was born the Tanzania Media Women's Association.

A collective of us had experienced the pangs of birth of womanhood, which manifested itself as TAMWA in 1987. TAMWA was founded together with my colleagues, who had undertaken their own journeys as women and, like me, found their political voice in the media. The seeds of TAMWA, however, had been sizzling since 1980, but the process only surfaced in 1987 as we began to find ourselves.

The will to make a difference for women was our driving force in TAMWA. We wanted to write stories that would carve the way for better conditions of work, better legislation, an end to violence against women, rights to land, rights to inheritance, and, above all, justice, be it for women or for men.

It was an important personal and political experience. I could turn the pain of what I learned as a woman into creating an organization that would voice other women's pain, and together we could bring about change in our country, in our continent, and in our world. In the process I also healed and flourished.

I now engaged my passion for a just world. It empowered me and created a political vision within the association that inspired other women, and we moved mountains to make it happen.

We argued that together we must build, organize. It was the decade of UN conferences, the 1990s. We launched a campaign on violence against women as part also of a global women's movement. Our slogan, *'Women's Rights are Human Rights'* linked up with a global voice in the Vienna UN Conference. In Beijing important strides were taken, and TAMWA played a lead role in media outreach with other women's movements, and even then we took on information technology (IT) as a tool of empowerment.

WH: Do you think your feminist politics, emanating as it does from Zanzibar—your home originally and now once again in your work with NGOs and the Zanzibar Film Festival—has a different 'place-based' politics to mainland Tanzania? Was the fact that TAMWA was created in Dar in Tanzania because of expediency only? What difference did it make for you to be a Zanzibari to begin the network in Dar—and what did it mean when you started a similar women's media agency in Uganda to be a Tanzanian? How does the actual place and history define the political actions you took as a journalist/feminist/intellectual?

FA: TAMWA was a response to the injustice taking place in terms of being a woman. I needed to scream out into the world and have my voice heard. I found my pain was shared by many of the Tanzanian women, but no one had dared to articulate it with the power of the pen. Since at that time I lived in Dar-es-Salaam, my world then was Dar-es-Salaam and the injustices going on in Tanzania. In Tanzania there was a restlessness among women who were feeling the need to move with what was happening around them. TAMWA aimed to capture that restlessness into tangible actions. It was this response to those needs that made it so relevant and unleashed a force in 1987, just when liberalization opened up new organizational channels. At the time I was not aware of all that was happening politically and economically in Tanzania, but I can now see it in retrospect. I see that I was in the right place to be part of a social change in the country where justice was the driving force.

In Uganda, war unleashed a strong concern by many about the human rights abuses, and, as in Dar, I happened to be there at the right moment, driven by my conviction that injustice must be ousted. Given my convictions it was inevitable that I had to be involved. In Uganda I could play a rallying role that the media women who were so embroiled with problems of war could not. So it made it possible for me to create an organization for them that expressed their sentiments.

I was not in Zanzibar in those years, but I suppose if I had been I would probably have become involved in using the media for women and social justice also (as indeed I do today). So I think that wherever one is placed, injustice evokes a strong reaction, be it social or within the family. How the response is manifested depends on the social structure of that particular political and social place.

WH: Does it make sense, then, to ask if you define yourself as a Zanzibari or a Tanzanian or an East African 'African feminist intellectual'? Could TAMWA have been achieved in other parts of Africa—in Addis or Dakar or Harare? What made it possible to emerge as it did then in Tanzania? What were Tanzanian women's specific needs to which you were responding? How is Uganda Media Women's Association (UMWA) different from TAMWA—how do the histories and local politics shape the need for a women's media, and for different forms of political expression?

FA: I define myself as a Tanzanian, but also as a citizen of the globe, too. I speak out against the Empire and on the war on Iraq as much as gender inequality at home. I believe that it is the principles of justice-oriented society that drive me to be who I am and how I speak.

There are media women's associations in various countries of Africa, and TAMWA has been a catalyst. They take a different form according to the needs of women in that country. In Uganda, after the war ended, UMWA was dormant for about ten years, but then the women there realized that the injustices that they were fighting were particular to a war situation, but also they grew to realize it was also patriarchy. It became very active again after ten years of lull. And now they even have their own radio station, MamaFM.

In Kenya the birth of a women's media organization took much more of liberal business organization. It demanded equal opportunity at that level, and it has yet to take on laypeople's sentiments to emerge as a powerful channel for public expression.

WH: Could you also mention how TAMWA interacted with other women's movements—not only media groups—and describe some of their battles against violence, how they connected to other African women's groups, and the process of Beijing and the important role media women played there?

FA: In this exhaustive, if successful process, I also learned that it was not only men who were not to be trusted politically or personally. I began to understand deeply how the social and political relations are founded in patriarchal hierarchy and gender biases. These injustices infiltrate all relations and identities. I learned that women can cause as much pain as men. The mind needs to decolonize from patriarchal values. This cuts across gender, just like violence against women cuts across class and race lines. More importantly I began to feel ghettoized. I needed to grow. I needed to take the space to do so.

The urge to return to my childhood island gripped me more and more. I had left my island as a girl. I wanted to return there as a woman and contribute in my small way as I took my space. I stated to myself, "Zanzibar, here I come, this time to consciously embrace you."

Today, in 2004, I have linked up with many in this political, and intensely personal, journey in a search for solidarity among like-minded people all over the world. In my travels as a media and development activist, I found in national, African, and global arenas that there are many women and men fighting for their rights in the face of the economic and social injustices fueled by neoliberal policies.

When September 11, 2001 took place, we in Africa felt many a September 11 had happened to us on the continent. Yet the world had not squeaked. Who could forget the Rwanda genocide to name but one. But now as we witness the invasion of Iraq, we begin to understand also that our spaces are threatened in the real sense of the word. This time it is not only as women, but also as peoples. It is this force that is being unleashed now. The slogan this time is there is a better world. The Africa World Social Forum is gaining strength and, as Africa organizes the women's movement, is fully part and parcel of it.

WH: In the last two years we have often spoken about how September 11, 2001 did not mean as much to people in Africa as it did to those in Europe and certainly to those in the United States. Africans live every day with violence, insecurities, and attacks from outside. Though I would add that Africa, like all peoples, is suffering the fallout in the 'war on terrorism,' the Iraq war, and the continued domination of US fears and power in all of our 'places.' Can you say a little more about the people-led political processes operating under the broad umbrella of the 'alternative globalization movement'? How has TAMWA, for example, responded? What are the new dimensions for women, for Africa? Could you elaborate a little more on how women's movements are working in the Africa Social Forum, and how the different issues of women's health, rights, access to land, and local struggles are being taken up in the message of sovereignty? What is new and exciting for women's politics in the Social Forum process? Perhaps you could conclude by saying how your journey continues in this Forum process, and how you have found a space there to speak and be heard and allow your political concerns as a woman to be at the heart of peoples' struggles for sovereignty.

FA: I see the World Social Forum as a new global force with which I have become engaged. I see this movement as a reflection of the restlessness we are all experiencing around the globe (Alloo, et al., 2003). In January 2004, I attended the World Social Forum, which took place in Mumbai. This multiple celebration of a peoples' world unleashed a force that has rippled across our continent.

Africa is organizing now as part of this movement of movements. It is time for peoples to organize for change that is guided by us and will benefit us. It is time to challenge the old colonized hierarchies, the failed nation states, and recognize the sham of development cooperation. The era of faith in leaders that are 'elected' has passed. Civil society organizations, and within those groups, many women's organizations, are taking the helm in their hands.

Millions of people in five continents went to the streets on February 15, 2004 to say no to war on Iraq. Even so, war happened. The façade of a sham democracy was exposed. The sovereignty of all peoples is at stake and we have to mobilize effectively for change.

Africa is organizing with civil society taking ownership of processes of change at national, regional, and Pan-African levels. In December 2004 the continent's civil society movements are meeting in Lusaka in an African Social Forum, with the message that sovereignty is ours to determine. The continent needs to claim back its own path, build on its undoubted wealth, and end the leaders' dance of the Empire.

Media has an important role to play in ensuring this change. The information technologies ensure that we can receive the news directly. Now the people do not have to wait or receive thirdhand reports as events take place elsewhere. We witnessed the Twin Towers, we are witnessing Najaf, we are also witnessing Darfur and Rwanda, and we even witness how Kofi Anan declares the war in Iraq as illegal from the UN perspective. We know now how important oil and natural resources are to the world—just some of the riches with which Africa abounds! As women we carry the largest burden of chaos when wars break out. Rape is used as a tool of suppression in wars. Rape as a weapon of war is an acknowledged fact now. As such, women on the continent are aware that, without our engagement directly, situations will not change. Numerous organizations have mushroomed on the continent, trying to engage at national, district, regional, Pan-African, and international levels to see to it that the world becomes a better place. It is an uphill struggle.

WH: When you speak about your work in the Africa Social Forum and work in global movements, how do you see a transformative politics of place working among your 'place-based' work in Tanzania and in the wider setting of African women's politics and global women's politics? What are some of the mechanisms that have emerged from your own concerns in Tanzania (around the body, environment, community, and women entering the public arena)? How does your work in Tanzania and, even closer to home, in Zanzibar contribute to and transform (and vice versa) the different transnational movements (both women and the anti-globalization movement)?

FA: Transformative politics comes from forces that unleash a particular way of organizing. In the movements, the African women's movement in the West had a marked effect in terms of being a catalyst into our own thinking. However the form it took on the continent is our own. The women's movement in Africa reflects our own being as women. It is a movement that says, as women, we are the procreators, mothers, productive. We have to have our rights that recognize all our roles, our needs, and grant us full human dignity.

Places determine politics. The World Social Forum at Mumbai deeply affected our part of the world and brought African women into the heart of the movement of movements. Before, we were locked in, into an NGO culture of organizing, and definitely Mumbai was an eye-opener in terms of ways of organizing.

Last year I attended the Peace March in Perugia, Italy, where social movements came together to listen to how the South builds its movements. I learned a lot about how to mobilize at that forum. Obviously specific place-based histories and cultures we cannot replicate, but visiting other places and seeing ways of mobilizing can stimulate new ways of thinking and actions for social justice back home.

Another international movement event I attended was the Durban Conference on Racism (September 2002), where significant strides were taken on the issues of slavery and reparation. It was a cutting-edge conference because it happened in South Africa, with its history of institutionalized racism in the form of apartheid. I would like to point out that the African Human Rights Charter was the first document on the issue. Now, why do we need an African Human Rights Charter and not anywhere else in the world? Africa rightly should be seen as the cradle of humanity. In Tanzania we have the Oldpai Gorge, where the first human being lived. This continent produced the pyramid. It should be a place of historical knowledge and power, and yet it has squandered many of its productive human resources and is derided as the Dark Continent, even when it gave light to the first human species and earliest civilizations.

So places do matter. Sovereignty needs to be an important factor in today's globalized world founded on a respect for place-based diversity, cultures, and histories. We must all play our roles and say to ourselves, and to our compatriots, *aluta continua*.

Note

1. This dialogue took place 'face to face' and by e-mail during March 2005.

4

The Politics of
Place and Women's Rights in Pakistan

IN DIALOGUE WITH KHAWAR MUMTAZ[1]

WH: You have been working now for many years in Pakistan, in Shirkat Gah (Women's Resource Centre). How do you see the changes that Shirkat Gah (SG) has gone through as it has evolved? To what extent does SG respond to the international rights agenda, and to what extent do you think SG is responding to its own place-based politics for women? What type of 'politics' is SG engaged in—how would you see it as relating to the Women and the Politics of Place (WPP) framework.

KM: Shirkat Gah Women's Resource Centre, formed almost two and a half decades ago, is committed to the empowerment of women. It defines empowerment as 'self-confidence, self-awareness, and self-reliance; freedom to decide and act for oneself, re education, marriage, mobility, and economic activity; and the ability to create new options and choices.' While SG considers Pakistani women as a whole as its overall constituency, in terms of advocacy and changing policies, its development initiatives address women with none or little access to resources and information in urban and rural areas.

SG works both with policy makers and women where they are located, in communities, families, and institutions. Its activities are defined by a women's human rights framework, and the organization is distinct from many other organizations, in that it looks at issues from the perspective of women's everyday lives.

SG has certainly evolved, from a small group of dedicated volunteers to an organization that employs almost one hundred people. It

59

works out of three offices across the country, reaches out to thousands of women, and actively engages with policy makers. After ten years of working out of private homes, SG realized in 1986–87 that, for a meaningful impact on women's lives, it needed to institutionalize with a more formal set up, program, and staff. That is when offices were set up, first in Karachi, followed by Lahore, and later in Peshawar.

Conceptually, Shirkat Gah has always believed in women's agency, and that belief has been the driver of all its strategies and activities from the day it was established. At the time (1975–76), this was a radical departure from the women's organizations in the country, which were basically service and charity oriented, seeing women only as helpless victims. All of SG's endeavors have therefore been directed toward strategic interests of women, and not necessarily practical, service delivery ones. Thus it works with women's groups and organizations within their communities, providing information critical to their lives. They work with women in terms of existing laws and their interface with customary practices, procedures for accessing the judicial process, the extent of rights available under the law, tools for conflict resolution and mediation. Another area is women's reproductive rights, their rights to quality services, access to family planning, and knowledge about their bodies. Similarly, it builds women's skills to speak out, manage their organizations, develop projects, advocate, mobilize, and take collective action. All of these activities fall into the framework of place-based politics. Seeking empowerment at the individual and collective levels, after all, is politics of the most fundamental kind.

As an organization that catalyzed women's organizations in 1981 to form a national women's rights platform Women's Action Forum; (WAF)[2] and challenge the military dictatorship of General Zia-ul-Haq, SG politics has been of upholding human and women's rights as established by international covenants and promoting democratic norms and inclusive democracy. It participated in the UN conferences of the 1990s (through inputs in national reports, preconference mobilization) and linked the local to the international and vice versa. SG networks with regional and international organizations and networks, is the Asia coordination point for the international solidarity network, Women Living Under Muslim Laws,[3] and is a member of Society for International Development (SID), Development Alternatives for Women in a New Era (DAWN), the Association for Women's Rights in Development (AWID), International Union for the Conservation of Nature (IUCN) and regional networks.

WH: What have been some of the place-based concerns of Shirkat Gah?

KM: SG's concerns about women span the whole spectrum, from body politics, the household, the community, and the national to the regional and international. It has been one of the organizations in the forefront of defending women's rights in Pakistan, as well as providing solidarity to individual women in specific instances. Issues that it has campaigned for range from discriminatory legislation (that has had devastating effects on poor women in particular) to the customary practice of killing women in the name of honor; to the right to contraceptives, choice, and protection in marriage, political participation, and representation; to access to natural resources. Solidarity actions have included specific succor in the form of arranging shelter for homeless women, legal assistance to victims of family and domestic violence, for obtaining divorce, custody of children, and maintenance from husbands. In addition, SG has facilitated the building of women's skills and capacities to enable their economic autonomy and confidence. Above all, SG has successfully promoted networking between women of varying backgrounds, classes, and experiences from different regions and locations of Pakistan toward the creation of mutual understanding of the broader parameters of their lives and solidarity. Linking them internationally with women in the Muslim world and to the global women's movement has been undertaken simultaneously wherever possible.

WH: Can you give some examples of your mode of political work in SG?

KM: One of SG's central tasks is to enhance the capacity of women's community-based organizations to deal with women's issues and challenges as they arise in their communities. For instance, women's organizations are approached for advice by families and individuals for drawing up marriage contracts to include clauses for the delegated right of divorce and ensure payment of dowry money (these clauses are usually crossed out by the family and the registrar of marriages). This is a major breakthrough signifying community-level acceptance of the woman's right of divorce, as well as her right to receive the dowry that is routinely denied to her. SG's outreach partner community-based organizations are often asked to mediate in local and family-based conflicts.

An example of SG's mode of work is the facilitation of one of its rural CBO partners in setting up a plant nursery. Running a plant nursery is not an activity normally associated with women in Pakistan. It was established in 1999 at the end of an action research project on women, environment, and health, following extensive discussions among the organization's members. It was started with seed funds from an international donor that enabled its layout and the training of women in basic gardening skills; and training by SG in bookkeeping and accounting, maintenance of records, and management of bank account. Five years later the nursery is flourishing. Its earnings are enough to cover salaries and costs of inputs, leaving a surplus for the organization. The marketing is also completely managed by the organization after initial help from SG. The organization's members have time and again demonstrated their enthusiasm and potential. Even in the opposition from within the village and in some instances from male members of their families, they have continued with resolve and commitment. In the last local government elections they participated fully, and three of the members were returned as local councillors.

A third example is of a group of housebound women in a poor neighborhood of Karachi, where SG facilitated, through skill training and loans, the production of handloom cloth. The cloth was marketed by SG, eliminating the middleman. Over the years women's contribution to their household incomes has increased, leading to the easing of economic pressure, enhanced respect and regard within the families, and growth in self-respect and confidence. At the same time, not only have they had the opportunity to meet other women production workers and learn about the market, raw materials, and management of their own output, but they have also gained awareness of their reproductive and legal rights. Most remarkably, the women, who in the past did not have permission to step out of their homes, are able to purchase raw material from the wholesale market and travel to other cities to participate in special sales or exhibitions. All this activity by the women is now acceptable in families who previously strictly enforced segregation. The impact on women's lives has been dramatic.

Perhaps the most important enabling impact on women in communities where SG has worked is that of women's mobility, within their villages and localities and outside. They seem to have overcome fear and hesitation, are confident, attend meetings and seminars, join in demonstrations, and engage in economic activity.

WH: The WPP framework is particularly interested in 'body politics,' as well as economic and environmental struggles; indeed we are arguing that in all three areas women are resisting and creating new forms of politics. Can you give us any insights based on SG's work?

KM: Shirkat Gah's work illustrates the complex connections among the various levels that place operates in global times. Place for these women includes body, home, community, and the larger physical places, such as the nearest town, city, the metropolitan cities that many can now access, and the world at large that they are connected to through their networks and 'meshworks' (see the Introduction to this book). A political defense of place by women focuses not just on the defense of a community's land or environment or traditional culture in the face of global change, but also on a struggle for women's freedom—often from traditional culture itself—and right to bodily integrity, autonomy, knowledge, and identity that is a mix of modern and traditional discourses. The politics of women's groups defending their place, their body, or their right to rest is not simply at the local level; it is intermeshed with national and international networks. The political work performed by these networks is geared toward pushing for women's economic, social, and political rights.

Women's 'politics of place' is a description of how different women's groups are engaging in complex, multilevel strategies of politics of place: changing their sense of self, their place in the community, their cultural identity, and opening up new types of public political spaces to negotiate gender, economic, and social justice as part of local and global process. As the examples suggest, 'place-based politics' is not purely forms of resistance to modernization or modern capital, or just the defense of traditional culture and land. It is multiple political activities carried out by women, where women's groups are redefining political action to take into account their gender concerns, based on their own needs and in response to various forms of globalization as it is experienced at the level of their daily lives. This process of place-based politics links localities horizontally to other political activities by women's groups that maybe located geographically in other places, building networks that are creating new configurations of culture, power, and identity that are not determined solely by the global, but also by place-based practices. There is, then, a network component to all politics of place, meaning that place is neither simply local nor its politics placebound, even if it continues to be fundamental to people's daily lives.

WH: In a recent study you did on social exclusion, you took a close look at how women are surviving in marginal and excluded areas. Can you explain a little more about the study—how it has understood women's situation in relation to increasing poverty and inequalities?

KM: The study carried out in 2000–2001 was a participatory poverty assessment (PPA) commissioned by the government to bring insights of the poor into the development of Pakistan's poverty reduction strategy.[4] The exercise, spanning all the provinces and administrative regions and covering fifty-one districts, involved teams of men and women going to the poorest village/locality in the districts and staying twelve days each in the poorest and better-off sections of the village/locality. The teams facilitated analysis by the poor of poverty as they experience and perceive it, its causes, and their views on how best to get out of it. Men, women, and children, by ages and other caste and kinship groupings, were engaged in the study, the first of its kind and scale in Pakistan.

Women's exclusion was highlighted across the PPA sites. While confirming the vulnerability of poor households to 'a wide range of adverse shocks . . . trends . . . and seasonal cycles,' it revealed that 'women are much worse off' and that social exclusion as manifested in the political, economic, social, and cultural experience is as much a consequence of poverty as one of its causes.

Women were generally found to have no say in decision making, were subject to domestic and other forms of physical and sexual violence and harassment in both urban and rural sites, and expressed an increasing sense of physical insecurity. Gender inequalities in health, education, decision making, right of inheritance, food, right of speaking, freedom of mobility, and choice of spouse were common to all sites. In places where mobility has increased, it is seen as a factor of expanded responsibility of having to add to family income. There was also a sense of helplessness among women, even though they contributed, in some cases substantially, to household income.

The PPA revealed that there is both continuity and change in the circumstances and roles of women. Generally speaking, there is continuity with reference to prescribed roles for women and mechanisms of control and, hence, social exclusion, particularly for the poorest women. Two kinds of changes have, however, occurred: one of increasing workload caused by the outward migration of men; the other of the sharing of the burden of household income with women, which has always been seen as the sole responsibility of men. This perhaps has been a single most important addition to women's traditional role—a direct consequence of poverty. Women were found extensively engaged in piece rate home-based work in the urban low-income sites and in domestic employment in rural, poor households, but were paid a pittance for tedious and menial work. Needless to say there was no sense of empowerment experienced by these women. The exceptional change for the better among the poor was reported in Panjgur (Baluchistan).

Two disturbing findings of the PPA, from the point of view of women activists, are that, despite visible expansion of women's organizations working with the marginalized and excluded, the poorest women still remain out of their reach in both rural and urban areas; and that women do not feel empowered by the paid work they do, highlighting the critical relationship between the volume of earning, their control over it, and the sense of empowerment.

WH: From a WPP framework, we are interested in how women are mobilized in new ways politically, and through that, bringing about change. You mention, in the study, one community, Panjgur Baluchistan, where embroidery has become a way for women to earn money and also to wear better clothes and jewelery themselves, because they no longer have to look after the animals and the traditional tasks of managing milk and weaving. The fact that they contribute to the family income seems to suggest a shift in gender relations. What about their nutrition and health? For women in Panjgur, the change you mention as very unusual is—in terms of change in behavior and lifestyles—a sign of this betterment and is expressed in the use of embroidery and jewels. Can this be seen as a form of body politics? What does it mean for their role in the family? Have these changes been translated into women having more decision-making power in relation to men, authority, family, and even beyond the community?

KM: The Panjgur community is an exception, a fact that does not detract from the essential significance of the complexity of place-based politics.

The change that women in one of the communities of Panjgur reported, of their condition being much better than thirty years ago, reflects the changing physical and social realities experienced in this very arid part of Baluchistan, Pakistan's least developed and most rugged province. In this community, women's workload has reduced dramatically because of the introduction of grinding machines in the village and the availability of flour. Repeated droughts have resulted in the reduction of livestock, relieving women of livestock care. Women therefore have much more spare time for cash incomes through embroidery or weaving mats. Given that fine embroidery is a traditional skill that has a market and women's earnings have become socially acceptable, they need not work anymore in people's homes where payment was customarily in kind. With higher incomes women here are better dressed, have more embroidered clothes—up to six sets of outfits, as compared to two to three patched ones, as in the past—and also jewelery.

There has certainly been a shift in gender relations that these women express in terms of their increased 'value' due to their contribution to the family income and their feeling more 'independent.' One sign of independence is that, apart from what they contribute to the household, they can spend more on their clothes and jewelery. More significantly, there is a reduction in domestic violence reported by the women of this particular Panjgur community, which they attribute both to their earning capacity and greater awareness among men and women.

The impact of change in weather conditions, economic and livelihood systems, inroads of technology, and markets has been in this instance positive for women. That women's own agency was instrumental in this particular outcome must also be acknowledged; the belief that such changes can be effected is indeed reaffirmed. The jury, however, is out on its ramifications beyond the community.

WH: In another research project we are doing on women and political conflict in South Asia, there was a very interesting example of women mobilized during peasant struggles over land. Could you say a little more about this process and the role women played in the mobilizing and resistance to the state? Did it extend to taking up more power within the home?

KM: You are referring to the peasant movement that began in parts of Punjab in 2000 in response to the military authorities' decision to change the tenancy status of peasants on all military-run farms. Instead of share-croppers, they would become lessees contracting land for a fixed period of time on cash payment and open to eviction from lands that they have sharecropped for generations since the turn of the twentieth century. The unusual occurrence in the movement was the widespread spontaneous mobilization of women. They besieged police stations to seek the release of arrested activists, pitched tents outside villages and kept vigils to prevent the entry of police and paramilitary forces, led processions, carrying their wooden sticks used for washing clothes, made speeches in public, wrote poetry, gave interviews, appeared in courts to give evidence, and moved from city to city if required—even went to the World Social Forum in Mumbai. All unprecedented, first-time experiences for them. There is no denying the fact that, through the participation, women leaders were thrown up. But whether the involvement has longer-term implications for a change in gender relationships within the family and the peasant organization *(Anjuman Mazaireen Punjab)* is still to be seen. How empowered do they feel? How do they define it? Will they be satisfied going back to their traditional roles? Will they seek new avenues of fulfillment? All are questions we hope that the study you refer to will try to find answers to. That the women have tasted a sense of freedom, experienced mobility, and had their voices heard is undeniable, and the impact on them can be expected to be long lasting.

WH: In terms of your own work in SG, engaged with Pakistani women and particularly rural women, could you explain how SG interacts and works with those women's lives, and how this is—or is not—translated into 'gender and development' policies or other influences of macro-economic and political forces?

KM: SG's strategy is two-pronged: to empower women at the grass roots and take their issues to the policy makers through articulation, lobbying, and various forms of advocacy. SG does not see itself in its individual capacity alone when doing advocacy. It networks with a host of like-minded organizations and takes up campaigns collectively. It is a part of a number of thematic platforms like the WAF, Pakistan NGO Forum, and Joint Action Committees for Peoples Rights and Justice in different cities. It has campaigned for women's political representation, for the repeal of discriminatory legislation, against killing in the name of honor,[5] for equal citizenship rights for women, for peasant's rights, and effective imple-mentation of family laws. It also propagates these issues through its research and publications (one of its strengths, and used widely). SG is invited to official planning/working groups, especially those on women, reproductive health, environment, violence against women, women's shelters, and poverty. It contributed chapters to Pakistan's national reports to the United Nations Conference on Environment and Development and the Fourth World Conference on Women, held in Beijing, and helped in the drafting of the National Policy on Women's Development and Em-powerment (2002). These joint and individual efforts have had varying degree of success. For instance, reserved seats for women in representa-tive bodies have been restored at 33 percent in local government and 18 percent in other legislatures; women's issues are on the national develop-ment agenda; the permanent Commission on the Status of Women has been formed; the government has felt compelled to enact legislation on honor killing; etc. However, on all of the above, the government has fallen short of women's demands. The struggle, therefore, will continue until we have all of women's concerns addressed.

WH: What about your personal struggle? It is not only in SG that you are working, but also in regional and international fora. There are often many snide remarks made about NGO-ization of women's movement, 'jetsetting' stars among civil society that grace the halls of the United Nations and have lost touch with the realities at home. Knowing your work, this is not the case. So how do you see these international activities as supporting the work you do at home? Do you think it worth all the travel and long time away from home? Where would you like to see the center of energy of global movements, including the women's movement in these troubled days with the Iraq War and a second term for Bush: still focused on the United Nations or should it be shifting toward the World Social Forum (WSF) and other forms of mobilizing?

KM: Personally I had been politically active through different groups since the early seventies. But it was the Shirkat Gah–catalyzed WAF and then Shirkat Gah itself that provided the space, direction, and anchorage for me. We started small, working on local and national issues, building on the networks that emerged in the particular climate of an authoritarian political setup. The next step to regional and international networking was a natural one. Initially it was to seek solidarity in extremely oppressive conditions at the time. In Pakistan, the United Nations became important for the same reason. It provided the space to link with others in similar situations, to bear pressure on government to relent, to hold it to its international commitments. I see the international component of my work as essential to what I am doing in the country, and that in turn is meaningful, as long as it is rooted in ground realities of the ordinary woman in Pakistan. My work in Shirkat Gah ensures that and is really the starting point of all that I do elsewhere.

On your question about the NGO-ization of the women's movement and 'jetsetting' stars, there may be some truth in that, but only some. For the stars lose their sparkle if they drift away from the core issues that, in the first place, propelled them to the so-called stardom. However, in this fast globalizing world, international and regional networks/meshworks have gained both relevance and importance. There is a need for strong global movements as developments at the international level increasingly impact lives locally. Re travel, to do so or not has to be determined case by case on its utility to one's strategic objectives and agendas. If I were to respond to all the invitations I receive, or indeed my colleagues receive, we would not have any time for our work at home. One has to make a judgment call.

The efficacy of the United Nations in post-September 11, 2001 and post-Iraq is a moot question. I strongly believe that the United Nations as the only intergovernmental body has to be strengthened, be allowed to play its role, and not be deliberately marginalized. Having said that, one also has to recognize that it is cash strapped and under pressure, particularly from the United States, which wants to bypass it on issues that prick it. It is therefore imperative that we focus on alternate centers of mobilization like the WSF and other regional and thematic forums. The UN conferences gave civil society space to build and foster networks, and if that space is now tight for us, we need to create alternative ones. The women's movement and other social movements have to take charge of the global agenda setting and not wait for the United Nations to take the lead, because I do not see it able to do so unless pressurized in the near future.

Notes

1. This dialogue took place during October 2004 and was completed in March 2005.

2. See for a history and backdrop of the creation of WAF, its strategies, and challenges: Khawar Mumtaz and Farida Shaheed (1987). For an update on WAF, see Shahla Zia (1998).

3. WLUML Web site is www.wluml.org

4. *Between Hope & Despair; Pakistan Participatory Poverty Assessment.* Planning Commission, GOP, Islamabad, 2003. The study has been published in eight volumes, one as a national report and the rest focusing on Pakistan's provinces and administrative areas.

5. Shirkat Gah's research and work on the subject has been published and is available on request: Rabia Ali (2001), Karo Kari, TorTora, Siyahkari, Kala Kali (2002), Hassam Qadir Shah (2002).

Part Two

Women, Place, and
Struggles Related to the Environment

5

Political Landscapes and Ecologies of Zambrana-Chacuey: The Legacy of Mama Tingo

DIANNE ROCHELEAU

Women, Environment, and Social Movements

I cannot write or think about 'Women, Environment, and Social Movements' with a blank slate, in isolation from politics and history and the swirl of current events throughout the world and close to home. The phrase already has a life of its own. The 'baggage' that comes with this topic includes three questions that won't go away.

The first question has to be 'Which women?' Who is writing, whose story is it, and whose experience? On what basis are women linked across domains of experience and expertise (academic, NGO, social movement, and local) and across lines of class, race, culture, nationality and belief? Are we dealing with claims of sameness and sisterhood, stories of differences and otherness, or the contingent connections of affinity and solidarity? On what basis am I linked to specific people, places, and movements, and what are my own feminist politics of place as I write?

The second question is, are we really talking about women only, women and men, or the tangled, gendered, social relations of power that both join and separate all of us? How do women and men, and ideals of masculinity and femininity, relate to environmental social movements? Are women leading men in emerging environmental movements, are they shoulder to shoulder in shared movements against local and external actors, or are women struggling against men's environmental actions

72

and decisions at local and larger levels? How do questions of sexuality and complex gender identities enter into environmental politics and practices?

Third, what is the basis of women's relation to the environment? Is it defined by an essential biological female link to nature, by gendered political and economic interests in resources within the existing social order, or by distinct gendered knowledge, experience, and values within a particular culture?

The 'politics of place' also has a life of its own and raises the key question: what is the relation of people, place, and nature? How are people rooted in place? Is place the same as territory, to be mapped on a geographic grid? Or is it a transitory and relative quality of connection between humans and other beings, their artifacts, technologies, and surroundings? Could it be about a network and not a territory? Are people tied to land through 'blood and soil,' by exclusive ancestral ties? Do they base their rights to be in place on current practice, through labor and physical presence? Can people claim rights to life and livelihood in any habitat based on need, as a basic human right? Do other species have standing—legitimate claims to be in place—on their own, or based on their association with the cultures, economies, and spiritual practices of particular people?

To speak about women, environment, and the politics of place is to walk into an ongoing and complex conversation framed by all of these questions. There is a multitude of ways for women to be in place, to be in relation with other people, assemblages of plants and animals, artifacts, and technologies (Latour, 1993; Whatmore, 2002; Escobar, 2001; Harcourt and Escobar, 2002; Massey, 1994; Rocheleau, et al., 2001). The experience of women and men in the land-struggle movements of the latter part of the twentieth century in the Dominican Republic provides an example of a complex relationship between gender, justice, place, and environment in a 'land-struggle movement' led by an elder rural woman, Florinda Soriano Muñoz, known as 'Mama Tingo' (Ricourt, 2000). The outcome of these struggles had major implications for diversification of livelihoods, landscape, and the restoration of diverse species and cultivars to smallholder agroforestry systems in the hills of Zambrana-Chacuey in the north central part of the country. The people, their fields, forests and gardens, and their way of life were part of the fruits of

Mama Tingo's political labor and her martyrdom in 1974. The story unfolds within the context of a relational web that reconciles networks and territories, men and women, experience and expertise, and insider and outsider in an ongoing story of women's politics of place. To tell that story, let me start by situating myself, followed by brief answers to the questions I raised above, to frame the subsequent place-based tale. I will end with a reflection on the insights from Zambrana-Chacuey.

Rooted in the Landscapes of Home(s)

It is a feminist proposition that we must first see like ourselves, and know where we stand, in order to engage others in honest dialogue, then look back at ourselves and the world around us, to see like others, with their permission and assistance (Enloe, 2004; Harding, 2003; Haraway, 2002). I saw the links between the land-struggle movement, the martyred leader, Mama Tingo, and the landscapes and ecologies of Zambrana-Chacuey in 1992 from a very specific position in a tangled social and ecological web. The early roots of this web spring from childhood and cultures of being-in-relation as a woman, a feminist, and a child of labor movement culture. I encountered the people and the hilly farm and forest patchwork of Zambrana-Chacuey as the granddaughter of an Appalachian coal miner and 'union man,' a miner's camp housewife and gardener maternal grandparents, and two French-Canadian farmers-turned-factory-workers and labor union activists paternal grandparents (Rocheleau, 2004).

During my first fourteen years of life, we moved house several times, yet always maintained close ties to extended family homes through regular visits, pictures, and stories. We did not feel lost or rootless, but rather had a sense of living and moving freely in what I would now call a rooted network, with tendrils that extended from the 'inner-city' streets of Hartford, Connecticut, to the roads and forests of Appalachia and New England.

So an intense curiosity about work and knowledge, bound tightly with a respect for workers and a concern for their conditions; and a sense of mobility, with multiple—and moveable—roots, were part of the invisible baggage that I carried into my academic preparation and, later, into research. My own observations and experience of patriarchy, heroic stories of motherhood and working women, the whispered secrets of women's private lives, and women's knowledge of home and the world ran through my childhood like a subterranean stream of double—no, multiple—consciousness. I loved my grandfathers and great-uncles for their way of making farming and factory lives sing with life, their love of work, their dancing, stories, and hearty laughter, but I also knew they were practicing patriarchs, part of something real that was not good for women, children, themselves, or most other living things. This childhood 'apprenticeship' gradually merged with my own professional field experience in the Dominican Republic and Kenya from 1979 to 1992 and followed me to Zambrana in 1992 (Rocheleau, 2004).

I was primed to see women's situation and oppression in relation to, not in isolation from, labor, class, and agrarian struggles. Gender relations in Zambrana-Chacuey would be filtered through my own experience among family and community members. Rather than an exotic 'machismo' and Dominican men as 'the villains,' I would see men and women in an entangled web of relations, ranging from solidarity, cooperation, and mutual support to oppression and inequality. Patriarchy—and even class relations—meshed with other, more positive relations within a complex context of everyday practice nested within larger political and economic structures. The social movements in the story lived within this web of relationships, tied to a mix of cultures, from home place to global networks.

The Road to Zambrana

In October 1992, I formed a research team with three colleagues[1] and arranged to conduct a four-month study on a farm forestry project in the rolling hills south of Cotui in the center of the Dominican Republic. The Rural People's Federation of Zambrana-Chacuey (a regional grassroots organization formed during the land struggle of the 1970s and 1980s) and Environment Development Alternatives (ENDA)—an international NGO—were collaborating on a farm forestry project, among several other social, health, agricultural, and resource management programs.[2] The Forest Enterprise Project, by all accounts a highly successful initiative, promoted planting of *Acacia mangium* trees for timber as a lucrative cash crop on smallholder farms. ENDA had negotiated with the National Forest Service, a division of the military *(Dirección General de Foresta),* to secure permission for legal cutting of this species with special permits from the project. National laws otherwise prohibited the felling of trees, even planted trees on private property. The Federation and ENDA were in the process of constructing a cooperative sawmill with external funding support. The Federation as a whole had embraced the project and supported the formation of a spin-off subsidiary group, the Wood Producers Association, which quickly became a major economic and political force within the Federation and the region at large. We met with ENDA foresters and community organizers at their Cotui office, and the Federation put us on the agenda for their monthly plenary meeting of the representatives from fifty-nine farmers, women's and youth associations from thirty-one communities (Rocheleau, et al., 2001).

I knew it would be different from previous research sites when we first set foot in the headquarters of the Federation in Zambrana, prior to our presentation at the assembly. The walls were covered with cards from previous meetings of local associations. Each card was covered with words printed in the stark, thick letters indicative of markers: Blackness, Power, Respect, Woman, Together, Solidarity, Knowledge; or Fear, Alone, Poverty, Ignorance, Humiliation. Paulo Freire clearly lived here, in spirit and in practice. Having duly noted the mention of race and the positive association with blackness, neither commonplace in my prior experience in the Dominican Republic, I was struck by a poster portrait of a woman on the wall of cards. She was an apparently African woman, with strong cheekbones and her head wrapped with a scarf in a way that I had come to associate with women farmers I'd known in Kenya. "Who's that?" I asked. "Mama Tingo," they'd said, as if I'd know immediately who *she* was; as if, of course, everyone would know who she was. I didn't, I admitted sheepishly, and there began my first lesson about how people came to be living in these tightly knit networks of smallholder communities in the hills and valleys of Zambrana and Chacuey Districts, between Santiago and Santo Domingo.

The story of Mama Tingo was at the root of the history of the Rural Federation of Zambrana-Chacuey. It was all part of a larger social movement, which was in turn part of a very long history of surviving and selectively taming and negotiating with a long series of political and economic regimes that were hostile to rural smallholders. Her story contradicted popular images of the peasant farmer as a heroic, light-skinned, rural man wresting a living from the land. Women and men of all colors from light to black had labored in the fields for centuries to produce food and cash crops from Dominican soil.

Internationally the environmental politics of place has been connected closely with indigenous people with long histories on the land, often presumed to be linked by a single culture to a specific landscape and ecosystem over centuries, if not millennia. The experience of people in the Dominican Republic, in contrast, has created a profoundly place-based politics among people whose culture is derived from and defined by a historical and continuing mixing of peoples, plants, animals, technologies, and artifacts from across the planet. Throughout the Caribbean, including the Dominican Republic, people have been brought together in place by a long history of encounters, many of them violent or coercive, including the ravages and displacement of enslavement. Yet people have created communities and a profusion of recombinant cultures and emergent ecologies from the combined legacy of Indigenous, African, and European cultures and their various (often divergent) experiences of conquest, colonization, slavery, resistance, resilience, oppression, persistence, innovation, commerce, chance, and choice.

The politics of place, power, and changing human ecologies in this context were and are about more than gender, class, racial, ethnic, or anti-imperial struggles over 'environment' as a collection of resources in a specific location. Environmental movements, as well as rural farmers' land struggles in this region, were about the terms of connection between people and between groups of people, other species, artifacts (houses, gardens, tools), and the surrounding physical world. They were also about the terms of connection between local and larger places, both earthly and spiritual (hence the significant involvement of both the Catholic Church and various Afro-Caribbean religions—*Santería, Palo,* and *Umbanda*—in land-struggle movements). Land, in turn, was not treated simply as 'real estate,' as an exchangeable and interchangeable commodity, but rather as the ground where body, home, community, and habitat are joined in everyday experience as well as in history (Escobar, et al., 2002; see also Grueso, et al., 1998 and Losonczy, 1989 on parallel experience in Colombia). Place is neither a two-dimensional space nor a container, but is rather a nexus of relations (Massey, 1994), a patterned logic and ethos of contingent connections rooted in a particular way, anchored in a given space and time.

Throughout the country in the twentieth century, women were a part of the farm operations: in some regions of the country they identified independently as 'farmers,' while in others (such as the Sierra) women's farm labor was seen as supporting or 'helping' men in the family. In this central part of the country, African heritage was more clearly expressed in the popularity of Afro-Caribbean religious practices, as well as in distinct land use traditions and a flexible gender division of labor. With Mama Tingo watching from the wall, I was on notice that this would be a different perspective on gender, race, land, and politics than I had found in the Sierra communities only fifty miles and two hours away, where I had worked from 1978–81.

We hoped to learn from their organizational and land management experience and to share their insights with others. Over the course of the next four months we visited and interviewed thirty-one groups in sixteen communities (out of a total of fifty-nine groups in thirty-one communities).[3] As we began to study the gendered terms of participation, decision making, and distribution of benefits of this apparently successful community forestry project (Rocheleau, et al., 1996; Ross, 1996), we were increasingly fascinated by the story of the Federation itself and the relational web that had spawned the movement and subsequent organizations. I was especially drawn to the contributions and interests of women, in no small part because of my personal history and evolving professional perspective. I began to look at the commercial farm forestry trends through a critical feminist lens on ecological, cultural, and political grounds (Rocheleau, et al., 2001).

The Federation

As people recounted the histories of their farms and forests and their own life stories, the chronicle of the Rural Federation and the legendary leadership and martyrdom of Mama Tingo always ran just under the surface. The bedrock of solidarity among these groups was the shared sense of place, entwined with the practices of solidarity, affinity, and mutual support across lines of difference (race, class, gender, and political affiliation). The Rural Federation of Zambrana-Chacuey was one of seventeen Federations within the Rural Peoples' Confederation Mama Tingo, named for the charismatic woman farmer who led the movement prior to her assassination in 1974. Most of the farmers we met had acquired (or recaptured) their land through a series of land struggles, using nonviolent civil disobedience (by men and women), in spite of armed soldiers and police, jail terms, and campaigns of intimidation.

The stories about the Federation, past, present, and future, made it clear that this was more than one organization. It was rooted in three separate wings of a very broad movement, each with a different and equally rich version of the Federation's history and distinct hopes and fears for its future direction. The three 'wings' were cooperativist farmers demanding fair terms of trade for agricultural products and inputs; (Catholic) liberation theology groups focused on political, economic, and human rights; and more traditional Catholic Church advocates of basic needs (Rocheleau and Ross, 1995; Ross, 1996).

Women figured prominently in each of these groups, yet also constituted a fourth, invisible force within the broader peasant movement to reconstitute places for viable, just, and democratic communities. Women members of housewives' and farmers' associations, as well as women married to farmers' association members, also played a major role in shaping the landscape as farmers, gardeners, nursery and livestock keepers, and gatherers and managers of fuelwood, medicinal herbs, and water supplies. During the course of the 1980s, they led the Federation in an increasing involvement in development, moving from campaigns for infrastructure and basic services into a long-term sustainable development partnership with ENDA on ethnobotany and herbal medicine, agriculture, forestry, and local enterprise development (Ross, 1996). This partnership eventually resulted in the Forest Enterprise Project and the sawmill.

What came through was the way the Federation formed the center of gravity and the logic of connection in a diverse and robust social network. It wove the warp and weft of different interests and identities together into a relational web that was both strong and flexible, and hence resilient and adaptive. The roots of the Federation (organized in 1974, and formally founded and legally recognized in 1978) extend back through centuries of popular resistance, persistence, and resurgence under a series of regimes that have been hostile to rural farmers and forest dwellers.

The roots of Mama Tingo, the Federation, and the larger Confederation named for her also tapped into the wellsprings of women's parallel cultures of resistance and resilience, and their alternative domains of political and religious authority (invoked from the hearth to the earth to the heavens) developed over centuries. The women of the Federation built upon a foundation of women's distinct experiences within and beyond patriarchal institutions, from colonial empires, religious hierarchies, and mass enslavement to a series of US invasions and occupations and the ensuing dictatorships of the twentieth century.

The history of women in the Zambrana-Chacuey Federation exemplifies the complexity of the Federation and its ability to accommodate difference, its egalitarian ideals, and its contradictions. From the outset the Federation had a base in women's groups and women's politics of place, although that history is often partially forgotten or subsumed under more economic or traditional political explanations, whether from leftist, free enterprise, or nationalist perspectives. One of the Federation founders, Tito Mogollón, also affiliated with the New Dawn Movement, was one of four human rights promoters sponsored by the Catholic Bishop of La Vega in the 1970s. He noted that he and other organizers originally approached women's groups in a nearby community threatened with eviction by the Rosario-Dominicano Gold Mine in 1974. Eventually two women's groups formed the nucleus of two new associations, which grew into the Federation. These, in turn, joined seventeen other, similar regional Federations throughout the country, which together became the Rural Peoples' Confederation Mama Tingo.

The successful, nonviolent land struggle waged by these groups was rooted in symbols and icons that appealed to long histories in place and the rights of rural people to maintain their lands or to regain lands lost to the US-based sugar corporations and the Trujillo regime and its wealthy clients. However, the movement also proclaimed the right and the profound need to create space, through land reform, for displaced and landless people who had migrated from other regions to make new homes and new communities based on a shared sense of purpose, respect, and mutual support. Peasant farmers were responding to what Penny Lernoux has called a 'Green Plague' of sugar plantations, which increased twentyfold from 1900 to 1980 and accounted for 25 percent of all land in cultivation by 1980 (Lernoux, 1980).

In an act of civil disobedience in 1974, near Higuey, to the east, a group called *La Otra Banda* ('The Other Gang') opened a major campaign in the 1970s land struggles by occupying fifteen hundred acres of land in a Gulf and Western Corporation sugarcane field (Lernoux, 1980). Playing upon the name of an infamous death squad, *La Banda,* authorized by President Joaquin Balaguer in the 1970s (Betances, 1995), *La Otra Banda* staged a positive form of 'direct action.' Rather than simply burning the cane or blocking access to others, they cleared the land and planted traditional food crops, underscoring the importance of the *conuco* (the multispecies traditional cropland plot) as a cultural and political symbol. The event and its linkage of culture, politics, and traditional crop species became a touchstone of the Zambrana-Chacuey Federation and many others established in that period. People were not so much claiming ownership as making a statement about the proper use of land, the nature of an agrarian landscape, and their own place in it.

Likewise, Mama Tingo not only led land occupations (or what we could call 'political land reclamation') in Yamasa, where she was assassinated in 1974, she also reasserted a place for women in the land struggle and the creation of 'liberation ecologies.' For some it is the death of Mama Tingo that continues to symbolize her strength and courage. It is perhaps a more feminist interpretation to see her legacy in the relational web that supports the profusion of life (also known as cultural and biological diversity) and the continuing struggles for autonomy and respect in the patchwork landscapes of Zambrana-Chacuey.

Beyond the Federation:
Movements, Networks, Roots, and Power

This chapter is meant as an invitation to reconcile networks and territories through women's politics of place, based on the specific experience of women in Zambrana-Chacuey. Their stories are filtered through a set of very specific encounters with these women and interpretation of their stories, which led us beyond the confines of organizations and movements into the realms of sacred space and everyday connections, between humans and other beings, their technologies, artifacts, and physical surroundings.

Academic and professional perspectives often cast women's power and equality in terms of formal institutional rules and organizational structures. In contrast, women's lives in Zambrana-Chacuey led beyond and beneath those visible expressions of social relations to the web of relationships that predated and gave rise to the Federation. The women of this region did not need permission to join and to govern, or recognition as members and leaders in the Federation to wield power. Many of them had those, often in parallel domains of knowledge and authority that were illegible to more powerful actors (from men at home to government officials). However, the formal recognition of women as members and the relatively equitable structure of the Federation in the 1980s enabled a powerful synergy between women and men and between economic, political, cultural, spiritual, and ecological domains of authority and power.

The experience of women in the Rural Federation of Zambrana-Chacuey raises the issue of legibility and the importance of formal organizational structures and recognizable movements. Some social scientists have challenged the way that the state sees resources and organizations and makes them legible—decodes them—through classification and intervention (Scott, 1999). We also need to examine problems of legibility within the social sciences and within feminist politics. Even social scientists and communities of solidarity may be incapable of seeing beyond classically 'heroic' struggles or direct and formally organized resistance, such as the land struggle described by so many Federation members. The everyday 'negative' resistance of noncompliance and subversive noncooperation has received some attention because of the work of Scott and others. Yet the kind of struggle embodied by women herbalists, midwives, farmers, and political leaders such as many of the women of the Federation still seems to escape many social movement scholars and advocates. The deep well of courage, solidarity, and affinity that has sustained the people of the Federation for generations is the continuing performance, affirmation, and creation of positive alternative cultures expressed in values, landscapes, artifacts, rituals, and daily practice that draw their legitimacy from a domain beyond the control (and even the gaze) of recognized, dominant power.

Federation and Feminist Signatures in the Landscape

The story of this landscape was very much the story of the Federation and the women's politics of place within it. The biodiversity in the landscape was linked to the cultural richness of the communities we studied, and was by then already linked to ongoing processes of urbanization and industrialization at local, regional, and national levels. The Federation had cocreated this regional forest formation, yet the landscape also reflected relations of power within and between households, communities, classes, organizations, and state agencies. The dynamics of this very viable human ecology in a densely populated and intensively used landscape also reflected the visions and labor of generations of women and men and the symbolic presence of Mama Tingo.

Federation members were often tree planters, and many had fostered rich agroforests in areas formerly used as pastures, cropland, or cocoa and coffee plantations. We also documented the positive relationship between tree users (woodworkers and charcoal makers often vilified as deforesters) and planting of a variety of indigenous and exotic timber and charcoal species. As we proceeded with the sketch maps and surveys of tree and crop species, it became apparent that the patio gardens constituted a polka-dot forest, a major component of a regional agroforest. The fact that the patio gardens, the mainstay of these species-rich agroforests, were largely women's domains was an exciting finding for a project focused on gender (Ross, 1996; Rocheleau, et al., 1996). Even more striking was the fact that the seeds of forest past and forest future were basically wrapped around peoples' homes. The highest biodiversity was found close to—not removed from—the focal point of human habitation. This was true for indigenous forest tree species as well as for overall woody plant species diversity, including crops. The Federation had fostered a diverse yet unique regional landscape. Members quilted the patches and ribbons of forest into a distinctive socio-ecological formation, a regional agroforest rooted in community, a shared history of struggle, and visions of a possible agrarian future.

Power

The experience of the Federation as a whole, and women specifically, demands a rethinking of ideas about place, power, environment, and politics and a new vision of women's politics of place rooted in complex ecologies and changing landscapes. We complicate our notions of power, to incorporate 'power with' (solidarity), as well as 'power over' (coercion) and 'power against' (conflict or resistance). In addition to the 'power with' of academically legible social movements, popular organizations, and institutions, we need to consider more entangled and embedded workings of power alongside, power under, power in spite of, and power between. These can be found in the skillful play, ambiguous meaning, and pragmatic affiliations of patron-client relations, as well as patriarchal families and political parties. This expanded vision of complex, and sometimes creative, entanglements with power allowed women in the Federation to imagine and create more just, viable, and humane economies and ecologies and new ways to be at home within them, while still struggling with unequal and unfair distributions of property, political office, and legal authority.

Conclusion

The story of the Federation in Zambrana and the work of women in forests, gardens, and political change provide a lesson in practical political ecology and feminist politics of place—a practical, place-based, feminist political ecology.

The Federation reconciled networks and territories; it created a combined framework linking people 'horizontally' (between people and other living beings) and 'vertically' (between people and other species) with their physical surroundings and, literally, the ground beneath them. In the case of Zambrana-Chacuey, it was also crucial to bring together notions of fixity and long histories in place with the experiences of displacement, migration, mobility, multiple complex identities, flexibility, and fluidity. The Federation resolved this paradox by jumping scales, joining people to each other based on copresence in specific geographic location, and creating networks of people linked across separate spaces by shared interests (women's, farmers', and wood producers' associations) and common values (the Federation and Confederation).

The Federation embodied—literally gave space and material form to—a coalition of distinct networks of people linked to each other in households, extended families, local farmers' and women's associations, and entire communities, each rooted in distinct territories (in a series of multiple and overlapping land areas, from household private properties to communal water points and shared crop plots used by farmers' association members, to administrative boundaries of communities and districts).

The practical and political history of the Federation, the Confederation, and the larger movement both shaped and reflected the resilience of the local groups, and all rested in large part on the power of women and their politics of place within the organization. While it was central to the very definition and identity of the region, the Federation was not to be taken for granted. It was anything but typical.

The people of the area existed within landscapes of cohabitation with a variety of beings-in-relation, a network that entwined culture, politics, and biotic elements. Based on empirical observation and social and ecological analysis, we came to see this landscape as home to a regional agroforest, rather than a formerly intact entity violated and diminished by humans. It is a biotic community (and, arguably, a cyborg forest) forged in the relations of different groups of people with each other and with various other life forms, nonliving landscape features, and changing technologies (see Haraway, 2003, on feminism and cyborgs). The agroforest(s) of Zambrana-Chacuey constituted a cyborg forest, a gendered construct that reflected the political courage as well as the calloused hands and watchful eyes of Mama Tingo, not only in the dramatic land takings, but in the everyday remaking of the regional ecologies of home.

Notes

1. The team consisted of myself and Laurie Ross—then a graduate student at Clark University (Worcester, Massachusetts)—along with two Dominican colleagues, Professor Julio Morrobel (then Professor of Forestry at the *Instituto Superior Agricóla* in Santiago) and Ricardo Hernandez (then a graduate student and local historian in Cotui). We eventually recruited several additional colleagues from the Federation and ENDA to join us in conducting the study.

2. The Federation and ENDA (as of 1992–3) sponsored several other projects including Traditional Medicine for the Islands (TRAMIL), Ethnobotany and Herbal Medicine; Agroforestry for Soil Conservation and Soil Fertility; woodworking, rattan furniture, and metal working workshops.

3. We combined ethnographic, standard survey, and feminist life history approaches, including participant-observation; group interviews; key informant interviews; life history interviews; community and organizational histories; detailed sketch mapping and land-use history with twenty selected households; felt-board land-use simulation games with selected groups and households; and a formal survey with a gender-stratified random sample (forty-five) of the more than seven hundred Federation members in farmers' associations and housewives' associations, respectively.

6

Domesticating the Neoliberal City: Invisible Genders and the Politics of Place

GERDA R. WEKERLE

This chapter examines the roles that women play in developing alternative visions of life in the neoliberal city in their focus on reproductive labor and consumption. It outlines the ways in which women's activism challenges neoliberal urbanization and corporate globalization through the politicization of everyday life and their engagement in a practical place-based activism. Using the examples of women's mobilization around community food security, I argue that urban women in cities of the global North use food and urban garden struggles to reappropriate and domesticate the spaces of the neoliberal city. As Goodman and Dupuis (2002: 17) put it, "food . . . emerges as an arena of struggle, as well as a realm of connectivity" in the city. These food movements rooted in a politics of place also pioneer noncapitalist development strategies of relocalization (Starr and Adams, 2003) aimed at delinking everyday life from the global economy. Through the creation of alternative forms of social consumption and production, these localized food systems "propose an alternative that challenges the dominant logic underlying the global food and agriculture system—the logic of industrialization" (Hendrickson and Heffernan, 2002: 362).

While much attention has been devoted to critical responses to globalization that involve contestation and reform and globalization from below through popular movements, a third response—relocalization/delinking strategies—has received less attention. This involves the creation of local alternatives and local economies that are unconnected, or not as directly connected, to the global economy (Starr, 2000). As Starr and Adams (2003: 25) note, "The most significant area in which local production is being defended and developed is the food system." Such precedent-setting initiatives also experiment with new forms of democratic participation that open spaces for dialogue among diverse cultures in the multicultural city of the global North.

This chapter also raises questions about the invisibilities of gender dynamics in the neoliberal city that are perpetuated by metanarratives of globalization and neoliberal urbanization. The dominant narratives of the global city are presented as degendered, yet are articulated and implemented as the expression of particular forms of masculinity that frame the city as a growth machine and economic engine for capital accumulation. Counterposed to these are alternative narratives of livelihood, sustainability, justice, and democracy, which mobilize social movements and inspire an active claiming of urban space. Yet even the feminist literature may inadvertently contribute to the gendered bifurcation of narratives of the neoliberal city. As Gibson-Graham (1996: 78) points out, the feminist empirical studies of women's lives in cities portray men and women as using and inhabiting different urban spaces, with women portrayed as occupying multiple yet subordinate roles in capitalist production. In these narratives, immigrant women and women of color are often presented as central figures in movements that challenge the logic and impacts of globalization in the neoliberal city. These are not always feminist movements or explicitly focused on women's equality. Rather, they are frequently unmarked women's movements, framing their activism as work on behalf of the community or for the public good.

As globalization and neoliberal urbanism have become dominant scripts in structuring theories and research on cities, this has often meant that alternative discourses and practices are rendered invisible. Master narratives of global economies are privileged; theories of place and the local, as well as noneconomic, forms of subordination are minimized (Fainstein, 1999). In large part, spatial inequalities, social polarization, and the deterioration in the everyday life experiences of urban dwellers and workers play a small part in the metanarrative of neoliberal urbanism. At the same time, narratives of neoliberal urbanism render invisible or secondary the reappropriations and resistances that locals continue to forge in the neoliberal city.

Some authors have directed our attention to the ways in which urban restructuring is both racialized and gendered in the North American city. As Neil Smith (2002: 435) suggests, "neo-liberal urbanism . . . comes with a considerable emphasis on the nexus of production and finance capital at the expense of questions of social reproduction." In critiquing the current battles over public space and social order in North American cities, Smith (1997: 126) has coined the term *revanchist city* to describe processes that seek to "reinstate certain kinds of class, race and gender privileges." While the revanchist city argument highlights the ways in which marginalized groups are excluded in the neoliberal city, it also focuses primarily on the exclusion of men of color and homeless men. Its limitations lie in the reliance on theories of political economy. By focusing primarily on class, corporate power, and policies of the state, this tends to overstate the economic domination and oppression of marginalized urban communities. It ignores the ongoing and emergent sites of resistance that are often rooted in place. By emphasizing change, neoliberal urban theories further tend to render invisible the continuities of daily life in North American cities and the subaltern strategies of resistance organized around access to food, shelter, and livelihood. Counterposed to the stories of women as marginalized and dominated in neoliberal cities are the narratives of reappropriation and domestication of space that convey a different dynamic.

Food as a Politics of Resistance

While the focus of attention in the globalization discourse has been on the privatization and control of public space (Smith, 1997; 2002), less attention has been directed toward a counter-trend: the appropriation of public space by ethnocultural communities and transnational migrants who make new claims on rights to place. An important shift is the renewed focus on local production. It is only recently that we have begun to document how poor people, and particularly new immigrants in North American cities, develop strategies of survival and livelihood, in part by utilizing the public spaces and resources of the city in various forms of self-provisioning. The community food security movement, which works to build a more democratic food system around community needs, offers a counternarrative to that of the neoliberal city as a growth machine: the city as a productive garden. As Hendrickson and Heffernan (2002: 362) point out, local food systems have the goal "to connect all actors in the food system in a sensible and sustainable way that sustains the community, is healthy for both people and the environment, and returns control of the food system to local communities." At the same time, these movements to relocalize food have generated a global movement of access to healthy and nutritious food that connects individual food consumers, households, and local communities to regional, national, and transnational networks that challenge the global food system.

I will focus specifically on two examples of community food security initiatives in Toronto, Canada, a city known for the density of its food security networks (Wekerle, 2004). The food security movement operates at multiple sites and scales, including agencies of the local state, places where food is grown, community agencies, regional links between farmers and consumers, and coalitions that span the scale from the body to the household, neighborhood, city, and globe. In Toronto, it is often women who have provided the leadership in this movement to socialize food (Field, 1999: 203). They serve as founders and directors of non-profit agencies; women constitute the majority of volunteers; and women city councillors have been key supporters of food security initiatives.

Toronto is a first world city—the largest in Canada, with a population of 2.5 million. It is also described as the most multicultural city in the world. Successive waves of immigrants have created many large ethnocultural communities, now numbering in the high hundreds of thousands. Recent financial pressures and the downsizing of the public sector have meant that NGOs are called upon to fill the gaps in the social safety net. This has been apparent in greater civil society involvement in the creation of community gardens and food security programs, and in the management of public space.

The local state has taken a proactive role to work in partnership with NGOs (Wekerle, 2004). The Toronto Food Policy Council, a municipal agency established in 1990, has played a key role in network building, policy development, and political advocacy. In 2004, the city of Toronto allocated more than $1 million to community food security programs, including school breakfast programs, community kitchens in city community centers, a community gardening program, and funding for food animators to do community development work in low-income neighborhoods.

FoodShare is the best known and most active of dozens of food security NGOs in the city. It is a nonprofit agency started and led by women that was funded in its early years by the municipal government and now is primarily self-funded. It focuses on advocacy work as well as service delivery. A visit to Lima, Peru, inspired FoodShare to transfer to Toronto what it learned about women's survival strategies from Latin American cities (Field, 1999). This included the creation of community kitchens where women cook together and forging direct links between farmers and urban consumers. A commercial incubator kitchen, where women create food-related jobs, is open seven days a week, twenty-four hours a day. Out of this has grown a catering service run by low-income and immigrant women that caters events for many nonprofit organizations in the city. It also offers food skills training for unemployed low-income women and youth.

FoodShare has organized and supported community gardens where culturally specific and organic food is grown throughout the city. Recently, it has developed an urban farm and farmers market in the downtown core on the grounds of a mental health center, providing jobs to patients. The Good Food Box program reaches neighborhoods throughout the city and connects city residents to farmers in the wider region. Volunteers gather weekly at the warehouse, Field to Table, to pack boxes of fresh produce for four thousand households per month. This supports local farmers and organic growers. The roof of the Field to Table warehouse, in an industrial district, has been turned into an organic rooftop garden for growing herbs, salad greens, and plants sold to community gardens throughout the city. Reflecting on these various projects, two women active as leaders in FoodShare conclude, "These initiatives remind us that personal action in everyday activities is still inherently political" (Moffatt and Morgan, 1999: 234).

The community food security initiatives that have become prominent features of urban life in North American cities (Gottlieb, 2001; Hassanein, 2003; Wekerle, 2004) are first world city examples of the processes described by Arjun Appadurai (2001) in Mumbai, where local movements of poor people develop economic alternatives and precedents for policy change through organizations rooted in democratic practices.

The food security and community gardens movements in a city such as Toronto are examples of place-based activism that reclaim public space for community use, develop alternative food systems based on nonprofit and cooperative models, and mobilize civil society through volunteers and nonprofit agencies. Through interlocking networks and coalitions that operate at multiple scales, an agency like FoodShare is able to disseminate its own project successes widely and draw upon and learn from successful models elsewhere. For example, food security activists in Toronto have visited their counterparts in Belo Horizonte, Brazil, a city well advanced in its support for food security.

How do I situate myself in relation to the struggles around food and gardens in Toronto? Over the past fifteen years, I have been a participant, supporter, and observer within the community gardening and food security movements in Toronto. In 1990, I founded an advocacy group to promote community gardens in the city and have remained active in local and North American community gardening networks. Over the years I have been involved in various volunteer and advisory capacities to FoodShare, the city's Food and Hunger Taskforce, and an urban farm project developed by the city and other agencies. My students at York University have organized new community gardens and volunteered and conducted research for food security agencies. In my own research, I have documented immigrant gardens in the city—a project that became a two-year exhibit at a major museum in Toronto.

I also have had a long association with the neighborhood park that I describe below. The opportunity to be engaged and to engage my students with an activist community focused on food security has allowed me to see on the ground the connections between theories of neoliberal urbanism, subaltern struggles, civil society, and the state. They have highlighted women's abilities to forge movements for change from the materials of everyday life. The many initiatives around community food security give life to alternative narratives of globalization and have given me a better view of the possibilities for re-embedding the environment and creating local economic alternatives.

Creating a Big Back Yard in the Heart of the Global City

In a downtown residential neighborhood that has historically been a reception center for successive waves of immigrants to the city, a Wal-Mart store, symbol of the reach of global capital and the American Empire, faces a neighborhood park with its typical Toronto amenities: large shade trees, children's play area, an ice hockey rink/tennis court, and basketball hoop. Not typical at all are the two brick community bake ovens sited next to the hockey rink and basketball court. These introduce a surprising domestic note to the traditional public park. Closer inspection reveals other anomalies: tied to the wire fence surrounding the ice rink are a grapevine and tomato plants; a split-rail fence—typical of a rural farm—encloses basil, other herbs, and a stand of wheat; and naturalized areas of native plants are scattered throughout the park. The squat red brick building that typically serves as a rink house in the winter has been made into a parent-child center and café, complete with kitchen and wood-burning stove. There are also temporal changes. Every Thursday the park hosts an organic farmers market, selling meat and produce grown by farmers in the region and connecting them with city dwellers. This safe and nutritious food competes with the large corporate-owned supermarket across the street. As Hendrickson and Heffernan (2002: 363) note, initiatives such as the farmers market create "the potential to reorder time and space and thus to reconnect food and people spatially and temporally. . . . This local food system depends on eaters reconnecting time (as season) with place."

The story of how this public park became part of a local food system has been documented in local newspapers and other media. But it is also a story of how a group of neighborhood women politicized consumption and reproductive labor by appropriating public space in the center of the city. Ten years ago, like many inner-city parks that have problems with drugs, crime, and youth gangs, this park was neglected and people were afraid to use it. Yet it was the only green open space in a community with ten schools, many recent immigrants from Sri Lanka and Latin America, retired workers from Southern Italy, and new middle-class in-migrants who are gentrifying working-class housing. In an effort to improve the park, a group of mothers living in the neighborhood raised funds for a better play area for their children. They wanted to plant flowers to make it more attractive. (In 1993 the city had removed the last flowerbed from the park because of lack of funds.) Because city workers controlled uses in the park, including all plantings, the local mothers engaged in guerilla gardening tactics, carting in soil and planting flowers at night.

In transforming the park from a public space that no one cared for, residents began to refer to it as 'The Big Backyard.' Neighbors started to move plants from their home gardens. They tore up the grass and created small beds of flowers and herbs close to the high-traffic areas. With the support of park staff, these plantings have expanded into large beds of herbs and vegetables tended by local residents and volunteers. These changes have shifted the constructions of urban nature in the park. From simply trees and grass or a place to walk dogs, the park has become a productive landscape that combines visual beauty, organic produce, and native plants that remind park users of what was there before urban development.

After seeing a film about community bake ovens in rural Portugal, the mothers' group wanted to build its own communal oven in the park. Outside brick ovens in rural areas were very common in nineteenth-century Canada, but few remain. This was a precedent—inserting food production and consumption into a public park designed solely for recreation. After lengthy negotiations with the city and raising money for materials, a local resident built a traditional, wood-fired brick oven. Located in the center of activity, the bake oven has become the focal point of the park and a symbol of community solidarity. The oven is fired twice a week for bread baking and pizza. They utilize fresh herbs and vegetables grown in the park. School classes come to bake bread. Local youths, with limited options for employment, bake bread and sell it from carts they have constructed. In 2003, 28,481 portions of food were served in the park. About 1,750 additional hours of part-time paid work was created (Friends of Dufferin Grove Park, 2004a). Learning to bake bread and using fresh herbs that grow in the ground at your feet is educative; it concretely challenges the commodification and standardization of food that comes from factories and is sold through large corporations. Because of high demand, there is now a second bake oven, and the precedent of the bake oven at Dufferin Grove Park has stimulated demand for ovens to be built in five other parks in the city.

An NGO—the Friends of Dufferin Grove Park—was created. Every Friday night, a community dinner is cooked in the park bake ovens using produce from the farmers market. This is sold at a low price. As Hendrickson and Heffernan (2002: 363) note in their case study of another city, "Producing food this way brings the process back to the heart of an authentic personal relationship and re-embeds food production within a community." Introducing the growing of food and food production to a public park is an experiment in community building and in challenging the corporate domination of the food system (Friends of Dufferin Grove Park, 2004b).

Despite its very local function, the Dufferin Grove model of community control over its local park has impacts beyond its locality. Many newspaper articles have been written about the changes in the park. The park was awarded a prize by the Parks Institute in the United States and is featured as a success story on the Web site of Project for Public Spaces in New York. The Friends of Dufferin Grove Park Web site (www.dufferinpark.ca) connects local residents and disseminates park practices more widely. The Friends of Dufferin Grove Park have also set up its own research arm—The Centre for Local Research into Public Space—to tell its own stories, rather than becoming the subject of research by others. An initial project is research on legislation related to public space in the city and monitoring parks department policies and budgets.

The changes that a group of inner-city residents, many of them mothers with a diversity of ethnic and class identities, has been able to make in this small neighborhood park have engaged the imaginations of the city and of community development workers in other cities. Starting with control of the material base of the park—the land itself, a small building, and the ability to build an oven to produce food—these local residents have been able to leverage the interest in food production and consumption into better nutrition, local jobs, and changes in city policies on public space. The communal bake oven, associated with poor rural areas of Europe and the developing world, has been brought into the center of the global city, challenging the corporate symbol of the shopping mall and the supermarket and restoring to public visibility the acts of producing and eating food. By focusing activities in the park around gardening and food, organizers have created a space of tolerance for diverse class, gendered, and racialized identities. In particular, neighborhood women have politicized consumption and reproductive labor and made it the focus for organizing.

These changes have not occurred without conflicts over turf. Use of scarce space is continually being renegotiated. The city periodically tries to regain its control over the spaces of the park, most recently claiming the need for storage space for the ice-making machine, the Zamboni. But the community has good media contacts and is organized to rebuff these attempts, naming its kitchen the 'Zamboni Kitchen' because it is located in the space appropriated from the machine. 'Mothers' values' and the domestication of the park space are sometimes seen to be in opposition to the activities of young males who play basketball and use the ice rink or the retired men who want to play cards undisturbed. As the park gains a reputation beyond the neighborhood, it attracts more users, many of them from outside the neighborhood. Already local real estate agents use the attractiveness of the park to sell houses in the neighborhood to middle-class buyers, thereby increasing gentrification and pushing out more low-income residents. This poses a challenge to the social construction of the park as a multicultural and cross-class home space. Perhaps the most pernicious threat is the very success of the park itself. It has now become a complex community activity center serving a range of local and nonlocal users. Although the park has received foundation grants and project funding, these are not stable, and the many activities that take place in the park are coordinated by unpaid volunteers. While achieving a measure of community control over a neighborhood space, the downside of a neoliberal governance strategy that downloads responsibility for essential services to the community is the ongoing struggle to raise funds and avoid burnout.

The two civil society examples that I have chosen to highlight—a park that has been domesticated and turned into a big back yard and a warehouse that has become a farm, a kitchen, a food distribution center, and much more—illustrate the ways in which women activists in a first world city have taken the initiative to meet one of life's most basic needs: access to nutritious and culturally appropriate food. They have politicized food, using it to leverage jobs and community development and to do popular education about the globalization of food systems and locally controlled alternatives. Each of these projects has also become a training ground for democracy, engaging people across class, race, ethnicity, and age in shared work. Through engaging in a practical place-based politics, both the Friends of Dufferin Grove Park and FoodShare have also 'jumped scales' (a term coined by Neil Smith, 1993), from the individual body, household, and neighborhood to the local state, regional, national, and global scales. Yet I do not want to suggest that these projects directly challenge corporate globalization. In Starr and Adams's (2003: 42) words, they play a critical role insofar as "they engage in a highly adaptable framework of insurrectionary experimentation."

Neoliberal Urbanization, Gender, and the Politics of Place

These mobilizations of place remain on the margins of current debates on the strategic role of cities in globalization. The academic literature on neoliberal cities focuses our attention on specific actors, scales, and narratives and renders others invisible. While several writers on neoliberal urbanism and scalar politics end with questions about the openings for "more progressive, radical democratic reappropriations of city space" (Brenner and Theodore, 2002: 376), local struggles and place-based movements are devalued as having little relevance for understanding the dynamics that shape cities. Indeed, place-based movements are frequently portrayed as parochial, defensive, and even conservative. David Harvey (2000) labels local loyalties, identity politics, and a focus on difference "militant particularism," which he considers a defense of class privilege and impotent in creating change.

Central to the narratives of the neoliberal city is the concept of scale. This is deeply gendered and associated with masculinist discourses of global competitiveness articulated at the scale of city, nation, and global capital flows. A feminist politics of scale, on the other hand, is portrayed as based on the active and strategic use of multiscalar political strategies that acknowledge the interlocking and mutually constituted relationships of the body, household, neighborhood city, national, and global scales (Marston and Smith, 2001). In the work on community food security, we have seen that women connect everyday life to the macrostructures of global capitalism, primarily through creating alternative structures that politicize the work that women do. For example, Dufferin Grove Park challenges the association of the household scale with processes of social reproduction and consumption by socializing food and reappropriating public space as a commons for food production, consumption, and income generation.

As Sallie Marston (2000) suggests, social movements create new political opportunities through forging linkages across and among scales. Erik Swyngedouw (1997) argues that we need to focus on the struggles through which scales are produced in sociospatial power struggles. He urges greater attention to the ways that social movements contest the rescaling and glocalization processes and the ways in which movements seek to jump scales and link them. According to Swyngedouw (1997: 142), "Clearly, social power along gender, class, ethnic or ecological lines refers to the scale capabilities of individuals and social groups."

In the neoliberal literature, the focus of attention has tended to be on the state, developers, entrepreneurs, and public-private partnerships (Tickell and Peck, 1996; Fainstein, 2001). As Saskia Sassen (1998: 82) notes, this focus on global economic activities represents the male gendered power dynamics associated with men of power. The scale capabilities of women, racialized minorities, and the poor in cities of the global North are only beginning to be examined. In the two examples I have drawn upon from Toronto's food security movement, the appropriation of space as a meeting place and material resource has allowed the development of strong community ties and experiments that run counter to the model of corporate globalization. These experiments have been disseminated widely through Web sites, media accounts, and involvement in regional, national, and transnational social movement networks.

There is an upsurge of activism, organizing, and social movement activity, particularly on the part of women, people of color, immigrants, and low-income urban residents in North American cities. This place-based activism is documented in newspapers, on Web pages, in case studies, and in books on grassroots struggles against globalization in cities of the developing and developed world (Kaplan, 1997; Naples, 1998; Rowbotham and Linkogle, 2001; Wekerle, 2000; Escobar and Harcourt, 2003). Yet these mobilizations of place remain on the margins of current debates on the strategic role of cities in globalization.

Women's urban survival strategies and the production of urban space and place through lived experience became a theme in women's urban activism in North American cities over the past decade (Naples 1998). In the 1990s, urban feminist research shifted away from a spatially bounded notion of place to a view of "places as constructed from alliances and oppositional struggles to lines of power" (McDowell, 1993: 313). This describes popular mobilizations in Latin American cities where grassroots women have mobilized to confront economic restructuring and poverty (Lind, 1997; Rowbotham and Linkogle, 2001). Militant mothers in many cities responded to structural adjustment programs by developing neighborhood organizations to provide communal kitchens, healthcare, and childcare and to demand state provision to meet neighborhood needs. There has also been considerable debate about the meaning of these grassroots responses to social need that emerged out of necessity (Lind, 1997). Community women often became trapped as "unpaid managers of social reproduction" or low-cost service providers. In particular, there are questions about the transformative potential of these subaltern strategies to influence policy or power relations rather than remaining as institutionalized and localized strategies of survival.

A growing body of literature addresses the linkages between marginalized women within cities of the North and South, particularly in the 'borderlands' that transnational migrations create in global cities (Sassen, 1996). To take just one example, recent work by feminist geographers (Gibson, et al., 2001; Katz, 2001; Pratt and Yeoh, 2003) calls into question the framing of migrant domestic workers as victims of globalization. This work reframes the meanings of transnationalism from the standpoint of the lived experience of these women. Pratt and Yeoh (2003) argue that we must pay attention to the concrete specificity of daily experience and the ways transnational subjects negotiate scales and difference. They call for "grounded, multisite, multiscale research" (Pratt and Yeoh, 2003: 164). By connecting transnational migration, place making, and the forging of a transnational feminist politics, these studies provide us the materials to craft an alternative globalization narrative.

The movements of women organized around a practical politics of place suggest that neoliberal globalization in cities is incomplete, fragmentary, and contradictory. In cities of the global North, movements of urban women are at the forefront of challenging restructuring and its impacts on daily life and livelihoods and in constructing and reconstructing urban spaces. They emphasize the social construction and defense of place, belonging, and new forms of democratic participation. Arturo Escobar urges us to direct our attention to noncapitalist development strategies, to everyday forms of resistances, by which "people actively continue to create and reconstruct their lifeworlds and places" (Escobar, 2001: 155). Instead of viewing the defense of place as an example of NIMBY-ism or tribalism, Escobar reminds us that resistances are often rooted in places, specifically urban places, and in defense of place and its construction. In the formulation of a counternarrative to the neoliberal city, women's urban movements can be framed as "place-based struggles that might be seen as multi-scale, network-oriented subaltern strategies of localization" (Escobar, 2001: 148).

Looking through the 'politics of place,' we see that women's day-to-day life and activism in Toronto has involved the reappropriation of space and domains through food and the domestication of public space. Organized women have used the politics of place and identity both to meet survival needs and to move beyond survival to engage in a wider democratic politics that includes the city, region, national, and transnational scales. Instead of dismissing the politics of daily life, participants in women's urban movements have given it a high priority. The reasons for this include the importance of the material conditions of daily life, including livelihood, but also an understanding that movements around livelihood contain possibilities for a transformative politics (Rowbotham and Linkogle, 2001).

My thanks to Maria Dolors Garcia Ramon for inviting me to deliver a paper on women and the neoliberal city at the International Seminar on Gender, Public Space and the City organized by the Department of Geography, Autonomous University of Barcelona, in 2003. My appreciation to Roger Keil for his comments and to Wendy Harcourt and Arturo Escobar for their insightful editorial suggestions.

7

Women and the Defense of Place in Colombian Black Movement Struggles

LIBIA GRUESO AND LEYLA ANDREA ARROYO

Introduction

The Colombian Pacific is a vast rainforest area, stretching from Panama and Ecuador and between the westernmost chain of the Andes and the Pacific Ocean. It is known as one of the 'hot spots' of biological diversity in the world. Afro-Colombians, descendants from slaves brought to the region beginning in the sixteenth century to mine gold, make up about 90 percent of the population, with indigenous peoples from various ethnic groups accounting for about 5 percent of the region's population of close to a million. About 60 percent of the people still live in rural settlements along numerous rivers. Although the region has never been completely isolated, two factors have brought watershed changes in recent years: the radical neoliberal opening of the country to the world economy adopted by the government after 1990; and the granting of collective territorial and cultural rights to the black communities in 1993 (the so-called Ley 70, or Law 70), following the drafting of a new national constitution in 1991. Three processes have been of paramount importance in this regard: First, the increased pace of capitalist extractivist activities, such as the rapid expansion of African palm plantations and illegal coca cultivation in the southern part of the region; second, the growing concern with the destruction of biological diversity, leading to conservation and alternative development projects; and third, the rise of important ethnic movements, particularly the social movement of black communities, with which this chapter is concerned.

This chapter examines the aims and problems facing black women's organizing within the wider context of the social movement of black communities of the southern Colombian Pacific, particularly the network of organizations known as the Process of Black Communities (*Proceso de Comunidades Negras,* or PCN). This movement is explicitly constructed in terms of the defense of territory, place, and ethnocultural identity. It should be mentioned at the outset that the network has not been focused on building a women's movement; but it has been through their practice as activists that women have been able to craft an organizing space as women. They have done so by making progressively visible women's role in the defense of territory, place, and identity through everyday practices, from growing food and caring for health to organizing. By creating avenues to increase their access into the public spaces of organizing and decision making, women have started to address issues of gender inequality within the community. In the process they have developed strategies to simultaneously achieve their goals as women and as leaders of the black community.

Both authors of this chapter have been immersed in black organizing processes for more than fifteen years. They have contributed specifically to women's organizing through their involvement with women's collective economic, cultural, and political projects. The authors have been involved in the articulation of a women's perspective through their own political practice within the black organizing process as a whole. In doing so, they have played a pivotal role in the strengthening of a Black Women's Network of the Pacific (*Red de Mujeres Negras del Pacífico*) and its articulation with ethnoterritorial organizations, particularly PCN. Their basic stance is that only through a shared project can appropriate solutions be found for both the problems facing the black communities as a whole and those affecting women in particular.

Territory: The Space for Life

In the view of the organizing processes of the black communities of the Colombian Pacific, the control of the territory is the centerpiece of the struggle. Over the years, the movement has developed a sophisticated conception of the territory. The territory is seen as constructed by the communities on the basis of the 'use spaces' (*espacios de uso*) of the ecosystems that sustain the life project of the community. The territory is the space where the social matrix is woven generation after generation, linking past, present, and future in a close relationship with the natural environment. The traditional use of territories and resources, based on kinship, is the process that legitimizes the right over those spaces. Within this conception, 'land' is not possessed as property; what is possessed is the long-standing right (*derecho ancestral*) to the use of various noncontiguous spaces, the locations of which are determined by the dynamics of the relation between people and between people and the environment. This traditional distribution of use of spaces is attuned to natural dynamics and defines gender and generational roles and responsibilities.

Production activities, in this worldview, are based on existing natural resources; hunting, agriculture, fishing, mining, and timber extraction constitute the basis of the rural economy. Tasks geared toward the social well-being—such as health, food, housing, education, and recreation—depend largely on the intimate knowledge of the environment and its uses. This knowledge and tasks determine the spatiality of the life project; within this spatiality, women and men have traditionally had complementary tasks according to their respective long-standing knowledge and roles. The territory is permanently constructed and reconstructed through these kinship and gender-based tasks. Generally speaking, whereas men take on those tasks that require greater physical strength and time away from the familial environment, women are in charge of those productive aspects that allow a permanent return to the domestic space, thus insuring the socialization and integration of the family, including the care of children and the elderly. There is also a gender division within the activities devoted to the well-being of the community. Women and men healers, for instance, both meet health needs, but with specialties defined by the knowledge of specific plants and according to the group or health problem to be treated, be they pregnant women, newborns, or adults with diverse maladies.

The construction of identity is associated with the spatiality of productive activities. The inhabitants of a river basin often belong to two or three kinship groups; last names may signal the place of origin or a given specialty. Since women remain in the river settlements, they are the referent for belonging to a place, and this belonging is strengthened through their descendants. It can thus be said that the territory is equally appropriated by women and men through culturally specific practices that differ markedly from those in the rest of the country. These practices are increasingly threatened by capitalist groups and even by government programs that are not based on the local cultural dynamics. Given its strategic location and its biological importance, the region-territory of the Pacific has become hotly disputed and, indeed, has been turned into one of the main sites of armed conflict in Colombia.

From Cultural Practice
to the Defense of Place and Rights

The defense of the territory—with all the social and cultural complexity it entails—is a continuous objective of the organizing process. As reference points for territorial belonging, women play a prominent role in the socialization of cultural practices and values; if men demarcate the territory in their mobilization for production, women consolidate it through the construction of cultural identities. When, for instance, knowledge of animals and plants for food and healing is lost, there is a loss of the value of the territory as a space for life. Changes in food practices have caused new dependencies on extraterritorial markets and practices. The territory thus ceases to be the basis of the life project at the same time money becomes an essential means for food and health. A vicious cycle is established by this shift from territory to money as the basis for daily life, as this change implies greater extraction of resources and degradation of the ecosystem, loss of knowledge and practices, and closure of alternatives. The massive migration of young women to the cities to work as maids and domestic workers is an indicator of the loss of the territorial basis of the communities. While many of these women retain a close attachment to their territories, when they return they bring with them new cultural habits and dependence on money, thus contributing to deleterious changes, such as the replacement of local herbs by processed condiments, midwives by doctors, wild game for processed meat, and so forth. Oral traditions start to disappear, and children no longer have the same tie to the territory. The territory begins to be transformed into a reservoir of timber, gold, fish, and other resources for sale.

It is for this reason that the organizing process is evermore conscious of the need to strengthen and recover the everyday productive practices that have characterized the communities. This is seen as the basis for their larger socioeconomic and political project as black communities within the scope of the nation. This is why the defense of the territory as a cultural habitat renders this movement into a politics of place. The black and indigenous communities advance their struggle by positioning the region vis-à-vis the state in ways that envision culturally and environmentally sustainable alternatives. In this process, the communities oppose the state's developmentalist agendas; however, even if based on long-standing practices and cultural rights, the struggle is not a rigid defense of tradition—or even of blackness as such—but rather a real possibility for building an alternative social reality based on more democratic values not only among humans but between humans and nature (see Grueso, et al., 1998; Escobar, 2004, for a detailed analysis of the movement).

The defense of one's own perspective of the future thus entails a view of development that incorporates those gendered cultural practices that foster the conservation of the natural environment. This principle supposes a critical position regarding the women in development programs implemented by NGOs and the state to the extent that many of these programs are intended to create a market culture through conventional credit and employment programs. Often times, these programs enter into contradiction with the local women's organizations with whom they work. Often times, these organizations—such as black women cooperatives in towns such as Guapi, Tumaco, and Buenaventura—have ties to ethno-territorial organizations; they rely on cultures of solidarity that often clash with the individual- and market-driven projects of the external organizations. Program evaluations by these organizations frequently refer to 'difficulties' in running the programs, since women act out more on the basis of need than efficiency, solidarity rather than profit. From the perspective of the movements, however, it is only characteristics such as these that can guarantee in the long run the permanence of territory, culture, and place, and it is these same features that external agencies often overlook.

The Challenge of Inequality

Unlike what happens in the socioproductive space, the political and familiar spaces are characterized by a lack of gender complementariness. At the domestic level, women are fully in charge, including the administration of resources, but without allowing them to participate in decisions regarding distribution. There is little support and no effective communication among couples. While men can establish other family units in their extensive traveling of the territory associated with productive activities, it is women who hold the direct responsibility for children, home, and the home garden. This brings added pressures onto women, placing at risk their pivotal role in the maintenance of the territory. At the political level, the lack of complementariness is reflected in the difficulties faced by women in having access to public spaces of analysis, planning, and organizing. In order to have access to these spaces and recognition, women have to make a double sacrifice of their own spaces and time without having the support of men for domestic tasks. Once they enter the political space, however, women contribute as much as men; even more in some aspects given their talents, say, in administration or for negotiating inside or with outside actors. Given this situation, black women have been developing strategies to achieve their goals as women and as leaders of the black communities.

Black Women in the Context of the Social Movement of Black Communities, According to Some Leaders[1]

While the important role played by women in the organizing process around Law 70 of 1993 and thereafter is undeniable, women activists soon started to reflect on the low political profile given to their role. What follows is a collection of these reflections from 1997. An indigenous (nonblack) leader, for instance, put it thus:

Black women have been active politically and have fulfilled an important role, even if somewhat restricted. Women have been absent from high positions; in the few cases where they have been present, this has been individualistic. In many sectors, the participation of black women has also taken the form of occupying bureaucratic posts, which is not real participation since it does not rely on a clear identity as blacks. As long as black women do not define themselves as such, they will be subjected to being defined by others: men, their own organizations, external organizations. Black women will have to develop their own political project by reflecting on the situation of the country with themselves as point of departure, thus providing orientation for action not only for them but for everybody. The orientation provided by men has been more self-interested and individualistic, and women can overcome this problem. Women can more easily carry the banners of their ethnic group and interethnic relations.

An activist of popular sectors said:

Women have participated in two ways: according to conventional rules, in traditional clienteleistic political organizations dominated by men, with women contributing to gather votes for male leaders and waiting for his political favors; more recently, there has been a form of participation that already includes a gender discourse, even if sometimes in these cases women too can be co-opted. Women need to think of a political project as women. Many men consider that the gender perspective is an affair of women, and this needs to be corrected. Some ethnic elements, such as polygamy, are troublesome; many men do not allow their women to join political activities, and these things have to change. The validity of a women's project will depend on their ability to articulate their own demands, not only vis-à-vis men, but in relation to society as a whole.

And this is how three male leaders of the PCN saw the participation of women:

There is high degree of women's participation in PCN, even if a political proposal of black women does not exist. Black women do not need a specific political project. The traditional sexual division of labor of black communities does not correspond to the Western category of gender, which is a Western discourse. There is a particular situation of black women shaped by ethnic and cultural relations. For us it is basically a cultural issue: it is not a struggle of one or the other, but of the black people as a whole. Gender is determined by culture; we have to gain more clarity about where gender relations are going. In fact, women of PCN have not assumed their leadership from a gender perspective, or with gender as the fundamental struggle, but on the basis of a broader cultural principle, that of the construction of a future society that encompasses women and men. We certainly have contradictions and things that need to be solved, and we have lots of problems to face and do not need to add one more. We understand that black women have their demands, and they have to do with their role as centerpieces of the family, a role that needs defending, and women need to take this defense on. But to think about a women's struggle outside the ethnic and cultural process would be like to defend blackness just because it is black.

Finally, from a woman leader of the PCN:

There are two levels of organization: the first is operational, as support for organizing activities in rural areas, helping with the logistics of activities, including buying supplies and so forth, which women do with children and young men and women on the basis of their cultural roles. Second, there is the more explicitly political level; although there are fewer women at this level, once they take on their authority they show greater confidence in the debates. The participation of women and men in rural communities is facilitated by experience and extroversion. Age is a factor in leadership. Among the younger leaders, under forty, there are more men than women. Women oftentimes have to attend to domestic obligations, while men attend their political responsibilities first and foremost, even if their cultural commitments are shown in other ways. In the rural areas, it is impossible to raise the issue of women or youth, since there are no other categories than children and the elderly, besides adults. In urban areas it is altogether different, because there the struggle for power means adopting external cultural categories. There is no need for a project of black women since we are black before we are women or men—to be black does not mean skin color but a historical legacy, a culture; we cannot say 'here is one' (men) and 'there is another' (women). We need to convey the role that each actor fulfills in the ethnoterritorial project. Any political project must make explicit the role of women. The political project needs to evaluate traditional values and practices; to be sure, it must open itself up to supracultural rights, and it has to propose ways to change sexist practices, including those that might even be condoned by women. The transformation of these practices needs to originate with women and should take as a point of departure the culturally established gender relations and how these are reflected in the political domain.

The Political Participation of Women
from the Perspective of the Network of
Black Women of the Pacific[2]

Women's organizing processes in Colombia have usually started under the tutelage of the state. In the Pacific, women's organizations developed around social programs for education, housing, cooperatives, and the like; and in the context of women's capacities for community development and the search for improvements to the situation of marginalization of black communities as identified by the state. The ethnic and territorial struggles and organizing have modified this dynamic; women have shifted from participating in social service provision to action and reflection for women's rights, and form these to the rights of the black communities. Contrary to the statements of the leaders in 1997 (quoted above), women today take on a more active stance in the conceptualization of their role in the process of validation of their rights as members of black communities and as black women. The Network of Black Women of the Pacific is an instance of this process, although this does not mean that they have overcome completely the lack of awareness about their rights as blacks and as women. In its analysis of the political situation of black women, the Network takes the following principles as its point of departure:

> First, we want for all black women to harbor the Pacific in their hearts and minds, that is, for all women to have the political awareness of the ethnocultural and territorial rights of the black communities, so that we can all face the threats that hang over our region and our communities. Second, we wish for all black women to understand and embrace the problematic and aspirations of the Black Community as a people, a *pueblo,* and for us to express and mobilize our needs and interests as black women from within the Black Community (Rojas, 2000).

Given that the political principles of the PCN constitute the framework for alliances with other political actors on matters regarding ethnic and territorial rights, the Network of Black Women of the Pacific has defined and assessed the problematic of women from the perspective of these principles, in those areas in which their actions have to do with black communities. The politico-organizational principles of the PCN can be summarized as follows:

- *"The right to being black,* to a black identity, from the perspective of our own cultural logic and particular way of seeing the world, from our view of life in its manifold social, economic, and political dimensions—a logic and view of life that are in contradiction with the logic of domination against which we struggle.
- *"The right to the territory* (as the space for Being). We cannot be if we do not have a space to live according to what we think and wish as a way of life. Our view of the territory is that of the habitat, that space in which black women and men craft their beings in a harmonious relation with nature.
- *"Autonomy* (the right to the exercise of Being), understood in relation to the dominant society and other ethnic groups and political parties, stemming from our cultural logic and what we are as a black people.
- *"The construction of our own perspective of the future.* That is, to construct our own view of social and economic development, based on our cultural vision, traditional production practices, and social organization; the vision of development that has been imposed on us reflects other interests and visions; we have the right to give society our worldview as we wish to construct it."[3]

In this way, culture and identity are established as the organizing principles of both everyday life and political strategy. As a frame for identity, blackness is not seen as something given but under constant construction and well beyond skin color; blackness is seen more in cultural than racial terms, as an ethos and commitment to life and resistance to domination.

The following table summarizes the analysis made by the Network of Black Women of the Pacific and its commitment to the struggles as black women and as members of the black communities. The table also shows their critical assessment of internal and external obstacles to be overcome in relation to each of the principles. This exercise clearly identifies problems and perspectives to address them from their perspective as women.

Table 7.1 Black Communities' Organizational Issues

Problems identified in relation to the politico-organizational principles of the Process of Black Communities (PCN)		Strategies to overcome problems from the perspective of the Black Women's Network	
Principle	Problem from Black Women's Perspective	Action Objective	Line of Action
The right to a black identity It means recognition, appreciation, and acceptance within the communities and in the rest of society, as black people with a distinctive culture It means self-recognition and self-valuation as black women; it implies the need to raise the consciousness of their ethnocultural and gender territorial rights as a distinctive ethnic group	• Racial, social, ethnic, and gender discrimination • Low self-esteem and personal undervaluing as black women • Loss of ethnic identity • Relations of subordination and submission as black women assumed as almost natural • Victim of physical and psychological abuse and domestic violence • Responsibility for the home and the upbringing of children • Loss of values in the relationships among black women: competition • Low esteem or even rejection of her phenotypic characteristics as black woman: hair, nose, lips, voice, feet, and so on • Lack of prominent black women in past and present history as role models • High rate of school drop-out among children because of associations of feminine role • Gender identity and roles that reinforce low self-esteem, low leadership capacity, low development of personal and intellectual potentials in black women • High levels of illiteracy among black women • High rates of maternal morbidity and child mortality; limited access to and low quality of health services • Victims of forced displacement	• To raise the level of recognition and appreciation of black communities as a specific population group differentiated from the rest of Colombian society • To promote awareness of the situation of discrimination and undervaluing of black women and girls, as well as of the cultural obstacles that prevent their full development and affect their personal dignity	• Incorporation of ethnic and gender rights perspectives into projects and programs that advance the Black Women's Network (*Red de Mujeres Negras*) and those arranged with other institutions • Documentation, information, and analyses of human, economic, social, and cultural rights of black communities and their impact on women, girls, youth, and the elderly • Design and implementation of a plan of education about ethnocultural and territorial rights of black communities, and about the rights of women and children • Information and training about gender and ethnic biases in the upbringing and development of black girls and women

(continues)

Table 7.1 continued

Problems identified in relation to the politico-organizational principles of the Process of Black Communities (PCN)

Principle	Problem from Black Women's Perspective	Strategies to overcome problems from the perspective of the Black Women's Network	
		Action Objective	Line of Action
The right to the territory (space for being)	• Low social and political participation of women in the community's decision-making sphere	• To promote women's access to participation in ethnoterritorial decision-making processes, and in the implementation of decisions that affect their lives	• Adoption of measures to ensure fair qualitative and quantitative levels of participation of black women in ethnoterritorial organizations and in work groups concerned with territorial use, management, and defense
To develop and strengthen their capacities as women to be a part of the decision-making processes that affect us as a distinctive ethnic group, ensuring our permanent affirmation vis-à-vis the 'other'	• Cultural obstacles that prevent or restrict women's participation	• To strengthen women's capacity to participate in decision-making and leadership spheres	• Encouragement of black women's organizations for dealing with the state and civil society organizations
	• Low level of knowledge and abilities for the exercise of politics, especially in decision-making spaces	• To promote and strengthen women's organizations for effective networking with other community-based groups, as well as with state agencies and NGOs	• Dissemination of information to stimulate participation of women
	• Their participation takes the form mainly of claims for better life conditions for the family, education, health, water, and income. It does not include claims to assert ethnic rights	• Raising consciousness about and encouraging reflection on cultural limitations that curtail black women's political participation	• Strengthening of links, sharing of experiences, development of joint projects, reinforcement of solidarity, and appreciation and respect among black women's organizations
	• Their involvement in processes of organization is of an operative quality, and their presence is low and attitude passive in problem evaluation and design of solutions		• Qualifying black women's participation through capacity building and practical experience
	• They are very rarely elected to represent the community or the organization in activities that imply travel outside of the community, and when they manage to travel, they never do it unaccompanied		
	• Women can more easily discuss 'political' issues among themselves and in domestic spaces		

(continues)

Table 7.1 continued

	Problems identified in relation to the politico-organizational principles of the Process of Black Communities (PCN)	Strategies to overcome problems from the perspective of the Black Women's Network	
Principle	Problem from Black Women's Perspective	Action Objective	Line of Action
The right to own our vision of the future It means to develop our own life project within a framework of recognition and respect for difference, and the redefinition of the relationship between the Black Community, the state, and the rest of society	• Internalization of a concept of development based on 'having' and 'doing,' and in which 'being' a community and a black woman is denied • Low levels of ethnic and gender identity that would allow for an identification of needs and interests of the community and black women, which are necessary for the design of their own development programs	• To encourage discussion and reflection among black women on the characteristics and implications of the neoliberal development model for the Pacific and for women • To promote and strengthen incorporation of women's interests and needs in the design of the Life Project for the Black Community (*Proyecto de Vida para la Comunidad Negra*) as a political proposal of the PCN	• Identification of and support for women's production projects that are environmentally and culturally sustainable and that favor territorial ity and ensure food security • Elaboration of ethnic-sensitive educational proposals for the socialization and upbringing of children in the domestic and school environments, and that favor gender equity and recognition of own ethnic and territorial worth
The right to be a part of and participate in the struggles of black people throughout the world This is related to the recognition, currency, and experience of our ethnic and gender rights at the national and international levels	• Very low knowledge of the struggles of black people throughout the world and of the movements for recognition of ethnic rights and women's rights • Very low appreciation and recognition of black women's contribution to the construction of Colombian national identity	• To promote reflection and appropriation of ethnocultural and territorial rights and their impact on women's lives • To raise consciousness and to inform about the organizational processes and the mobilizations against all forms of exclusion of black peoples in Colombia and throughout the world	• Information and capacity building for qualified participation of the PCN in the Continental Afro-American Network (*Red Continental Afro-americana*) and the Binational Colombian-Ecuadorian Committee (*Comite Binacional Colombia-Ecuador*), as well as invigoration of The Latin American Peoples' Global Action (*Accion Global de los Pueblos Latinos*) and its impact on black women's situation • Design of strategies for the participation of black women's organizations in the campaign against forced displacement and for ethnic rights

Final Thoughts:
Women, Gender, Politics of Place,
and Displacement in the Pacific Today

Place-based women's struggles in the Pacific confront the market-led model of neoliberal globalization by opposing the accompanying cultures of consumption, food dependence, and erosion of autonomy in other basic elements of well-being. For instance, as they gain awareness of the effects of the erosions of some basic foodstuffs and herbs in the maintenance of nutrition and health, women assume the defense of territory with greater determination. This is a very clear example of the ways in which women engage in strategies of deglobalizing food, and to this extent the defense of what is one's own *lo propio* is the healthiest antiglobalizing strategy. We want to make clear that to speak about the globalization of the cultures of the Pacific as a pervasive strategy is, despite the inroads of the process, to overlook the cultures of resistance by the communities to development and globalization. In the very failure of development projects one finds the negation of a complete cultural colonization, and one sees place-based strategies of anti-globalization in motion.

In the Pacific, the gender issue is seen in terms of a) the impact of racism and exclusion on both women and men; b) the role of women and men in opposing them; c) the respect for their differences; and d) the overall strengthening of communities in the appropriation of their culture and identity as a people. It is important to take into account, however, the differential impact of certain processes on women and men. In recent years, the armed conflict that prevails in other parts of the country has spilled into the Pacific, bringing about massive displacement of communities; today, there are over three million internally displaced people in Colombia, a disproportionate number of them Afro-Colombians and indigenous peoples (Escobar, 2003). Women and children are also disproportionately affected, with black women being the target of particular forms of sexual and racial violence. They often have to take on responsibility for their families in the cities to which they are displaced under culturally and economically difficult conditions. Not infrequently, armed groups utilize a strategy of seducing young women in order to gain a foothold on river communities. Coupled with forms of sexual violence, this means that black women have become again enslaved bodies, this time in favor of those who wield the power of the weapons.

Paradoxically, it is women who nevertheless are able to maintain greater mobility in the occupied territories, which allows communities to maintain a certain presence in their territories and to repopulate them after the armed actors leave the area, when this happens. This means that women's roles in the defense of place have become even more important in the context of war; their roles include resistance to displacement, leading efforts to return, and effective reappropriation of spaces when return becomes feasible. Not infrequently, the actions of women have become a veritable option for the survival of communities and the defense of place. This is an aspect of the politics of place that sadly is becoming increasingly common in the Colombian Pacific and elsewhere.

Notes

1. These narratives are from interviews with one of the authors (Libia Grueso), collected for a training workshop for women and men leaders of Afro-Colombian organizations held in Cali in 1997 (Grueso, 1997).

2. The Network of Black Women of the Pacific is a regional organization that groups together rural and urban black women, women's cooperatives and organizations around basic needs and women's rights. It emerged in 1992 and includes about seventy organizations throughout the Pacific.

3. This is a partial statement of the principles. For a full statement, see the Proceedings of the Third National Assembly of Black Communities, Puerto Tejada, September 1993.

8

Women Displaced:
Democracy, Development, and
Identity in India

IN DIALOGUE WITH SMITU KOTHARI[1]

WH/AE: In our discussions you have spoken of your 'journey of conscience' over the last thirty years as you have witnessed the agony and disruption of communities and their cultural and knowledge systems being displaced in conflicts over natural resources. Can you elaborate on this in relation to how you see modernity, development, and globalization impacting on place?

SK: Firstly, there is a continuing assumption among political and economic ruling elites that their interventions in the name of development or democracy are what communities and countries need, that they are inevitable, even just. Often in the language of the planner and the politician, you encounter the phrase that some must sacrifice so that others may flourish, that this is in the public interest, it is in the national interest. Who is this public? Whose nation is it? Was the sacrifice inevitable? Were less disrupting alternatives considered?

It is this arrogance of the development enterprise that has caused enormous violations of people's relationship to place. These development interventions or other political, economic, and cultural developments have created the loss of meaning and connection to place. Place is under siege in these violent processes of development. By place I mean both the site of subsistence, the site of cultural, ancestral and kinship relations, and the site of security and affirmation and renewal. This is not a blanket defense of these systems—some of which have persistent elements of

115

social and cultural violence—but a need to recognize the almost total lack of recognition of the ecocultural and political rights of those whose lives and livelihoods are so brutally disrupted when the development juggernaut rolls into people's lives. What are consequently devalued are the voices and ideas and visions based on the historical evolution of knowledge systems and experiences of people located in place. The present phase of economic globalization has only intensified some of these processes as more and more of the fertile and plural fabric of nature—that is, 'the place' that continues to sustain a staggering diversity of human cultures and of life itself—is appropriated and violated.

WH/AE: You have been very vocal about peoples' movements and resistance to this violence in their lives. Over the past three decades and more, you have been involved in and with people's movements. What changes have you seen? Has there been a change in understanding of social justice? What do you see as the key issues for your movement work in India in relation to place-based political concerns?

SK: Given the plurality of histories, contexts, and struggles, it would be unjust to generalize. Both within and between movements there are significant differences—historical, ideological, cultural, etc. So while the movements of the lowest caste groups in India (the Dalits) have sought political recognition and cultural revitalization at new, preferably urban sites, other Dalit communities see their priorities as seeking control over resources and politics at their ancestral rural sites. Or, for indigenous and tribal peoples, the range can be from the assertion of autonomy, sovereignty, and self-rule in place, to seeking better wages and living conditions in new settlements to which they have been forcibly or voluntarily moved. Or, for millions of traditional fishworkers allied together in the National Fishworkers Federation, the struggle is to resist corporate-led and largely state supported mechanization, thereby retaining control over their traditional fishing grounds. In other instances, women have spearheaded struggles to defend land and forest, as well as urban livelihood and shelter. Place, then, is both site of historical and cultural meaning and site of relatively new settlement or resettlement. Social justice, then, is not just the struggle for rights but also for the very redefinition of what constitutes development, knowledge, democracy, and dignity.

WH/AE: How do you see movements and the democratic process?

SK: Most movements in India have consistently struggled to redefine democracy from the way it was formulated and constructed in the post-Independence period. How can 542 members in India's Parliament represent one billion people? How can people who belong to thousands of diverse, culturally and ecologically rooted contexts find their voice in that system? The response of those in political power is to decentralize the state process to more and more localities/local elites. While this has undoubtedly created new political spaces, it has only been a partial flowering of democracy and a partial, often constricted space for people's political participation. Their own politics of space does not find avenues of expression in most governmental fora, which, despite the hype, is just the central authorities and institutions cloning a similar system in decentralized contexts whilst largely retaining their power over the basic direction of development and democracy.

Democracy is widely propagated as representative, but in reality, in most countries, it is a highly restricted and shallow political process. And for the underprivileged, the excluded, and the discriminated it is even less accessible. We need to recognize and acknowledge that for a vast majority of the world's people, particularly for the indigenous and peasant communities and most minorities and most women, the representative democratic process is limited; indeed, the process is often antagonistic and insensitive to the democratic inspirations of the people. There is growing sophistication among movements as they simultaneously engage themselves in asserting autonomy and self-rule and creatively engage electoral and representational politics. Regimes, on the other hand, have become much more sophisticated in dealing with dissent—from co-optation and pacification to low-intensity engagement toward exhausting and mainstreaming elements of the movement. It is this dialectic that we need to be more sensitive about.

Take the post-September 11, 2001 rhetoric on democracy. In the United States, a sizeable population has been manipulated to believe that the invasion of Iraq, or even the drive to control the world's resources, is in the defense of democracy; it is to protect the American way of life. How democratic is it when your construction of democracy and your belief in the 'good life' is built on invasion, neocolonialism, and loot? Democracy, in this context, has largely been reduced to a sophisticated manipulation of the minds and aspirations of a majority who now equate democracy primarily with the availability of choices in the marketplace and the charade of choosing between two relatively similar political parties.

WH/AE: Where do you place women in this process?

SK: Because of historical, social, and economic structures, women have been marginalized and discriminated; and, given the largely patriarchal state and community and family structures, they are even further removed from active and sustained participation in democratic processes, both in public and private places. When patriarchal states decentralize, they continue to be insensitive to the deep history of discrimination against women across class, caste, and ethnicity. This is also why women have played such central roles in the new social movements, particularly in livelihood struggles, often challenging men in their own families and communities. Increasingly, also, women in social movements see the limits of representative democracy and seek to democratize society and democratize movements in very different ways, working from the ground and tackling livelihood and economic relations as a central axis in family and community and in local and regional processes.

WH/AE: You have been significantly active in the ecological movement, nationally and globally. What roles have women played in these mobilizations?

SK: For us in India, a country where almost 70 percent of the population depends on natural resources for their survival, the most serious crisis is the exploitation, destruction, commodification, and privatization of natural resources. Some undoubtedly benefit in this process, but given that majorities are ecosystem people and are small, marginal, or landless, and given that these resources are still inequitably distributed, this crisis makes most rural livelihoods even more fragile. The vulnerability increases as the commons are also invaded or privatized.

The direct loss or erosion of their livelihoods is rarely recognized, let alone compensated. When compensated, it is in cash and is an insult, since it is minimal and reduces complex relations in place into a grudgingly recognized economic value. There is also the problem of the viability of the ecological system as the commons are appropriated by interest groups that are invariably opposed to the place-based livelihoods of local communities. This has also systematically alienated and displaced women who now have to cope in an even more vulnerable situation. In this era of intensification of economic globalization, the logic of competing for limited financing for development and of maximizing exports to meet balance of payments requirements has also adversely impacted the livelihoods and security of women as more and more of the natural resource base is privatized and restructured. In all these situations, women have been victimized the most, and have played a central role in the defense of land, forests, rivers, and coastal areas.

WH/AE: Can you give us some more examples?

SK: There are numerous examples—from the defense of forests three centuries ago to the Chipko (Hug the Trees) movement, to the struggle against large dams in the Narmada valley. As a more detailed illustration, let me narrate the story of the struggle in India's Koel and Karo valleys, which I have written about elsewhere. In the mid 1970s, over a decade before the historic mobilization in the Narmada valley and the subsequent formation of the *Narmada Bachao Andolan* (Movement to Save the Narmada), a remarkable struggle of tribal (*adivasi*) communities took root in a cluster of valleys in the hilly, resource-rich, southern part of eastern state of Bihar. The state has since been bifurcated into the predominantly tribal southern state of Jharkhand and the northern state of Bihar. This democratic struggle against a hydroelectric project on the Koel and Karo Rivers has been one of the most sustained struggles for identity, justice, and place—a struggle that has contributed hope and inspiration to a wide cross section of people's struggle throughout India.

The project, targeted to generate 710 mW of electricity, composed of two dams—one each on the Koel River and its tributary, the Karo River— linked through a 34.5 kilometer-long transbasin channel. Planned as far back as 1955, officials have sought to displace 7,063 families from 112 villages in the predominantly *adivasi* districts of Ranchi, Gumla, West Singhbhum, home to the predominantly Munda *adivasis*. Community estimates suggest that the actual displacements will be of about twenty thousand people, nearly two-thirds *adivasi;* sixty-six thousand acres of land will be submerged, of which thirty-three thousand acres is under cultivation, and the rest is forest land over which the *adivasis* have traditional rights; and 152 *sarnas* (sacred groves, places of traditional religious worship) and more than three hundred *sasandiris* (sacred groves) will be inundated.

When initial construction started, the local people launched a peaceful Satyagraha (Gandhian nonviolent resistance) at the dam site and on its approach roads. Soon after, they came together in an organization, the Koel Karo Jan Sanghathan (KKJS), the Koel-Karo People's Organisation. As the movement gathered momentum and facts about the full extent of the impacts of the projects became clearer, it became evident that the scale of displacement would be much more severe and extensive than officially acknowledged. A powerful slogan took root at this time: 'We will give our life, but not the land.'

The united response of the villagers in not allowing any land acquisition brought the project to a halt. Some of the most creative strategies of resistance evolved during this period. Dayamani Barla, an activist of the KKJS says, "Developmental intervention has resulted in reducing the tribal population in this area by 30 percent. The participation of the *adivasi* women in our struggles has been more than that of men. They are more vociferous, as they have to bear the major brunt of the economic and cultural destabilization."

Adivasi women in the villages facing the threat of displacement by the proposed dam clamped a people's curfew. They equally participated with men in blocking any project-related vehicles, machinery, or personnel inside their villages. Women ploughed up the roads and sowed seeds. Volunteers stood as watch guards to see that no one trampled upon their sown fields. Organizations involved in the struggle could not take any decisions or make any settlements without consulting women's groups. Given that production and reproduction are so linked to place—and in tribal India, women are central to this process—it was no surprise that they were some of the most militant peaceful defenders of nature and culture. The resistance and defense of place was so strong that even India's then Prime Minister P. V. Narasimha Rao, who was to inaugurate the project on July 6, 1995, had to cancel his visit. The project was suspended soon thereafter.

In late 2000, the newly elected government of Jharkhand—ironically the state came into being after over a half century of *adivasi* struggle that argued that internal boundaries in India had been drawn based on dominant languages and tribal culture, and language had been marginalized in this process—sought to revive the project. The local communities reignited their collective resistance. A public expression of solidarity was planned for February 3, 2001, in response to the police destroying a people's barricade, an emotional symbol of their decades-old struggle. It was to break this sustained unity that the police, without provocation, opened fire on the gathered assembly. Nine people died and at least twelve others were seriously injured. The police claimed that they had to resort to firing 136 rounds, because some people in the crowd had attacked them with stones and bricks.

The struggle in the Koel and Karo River valleys and villages is a struggle against development policies that have privileged the needs of industries and urban centers over those of the local communities, policies that have been made predominantly by those who have little comprehension of the importance of place and of the critical issues that this discussion and this book raise. As I mentioned earlier, the place-based interests of local communities have come into sharp conflict with the national interest of states and of national and global capital and their remote-controlled, extractive governance. State and central governments have sought to keep the channels of extraction open, and toward this end it has resorted to numerous strategies—from financial incentives to engendering the community rivalry and conflict—to manipulate and divide the *adivasi* population. The biggest threat to the tribal people is the large-scale alienation from their land through large projects such as mines, industry, animal sanctuaries, new townships, highways, military cantonments, and army firing ranges, all in the name of national development and national interest. Displacement disrupts collective identity, which itself is integrally linked to the geographical place where the communities have historically resided. When people are displaced, the very cohesion and interdependence of community life is broken. Alienation, emotional distress, and immiserization inevitably result. The processes of economic globalization that have placed additional pressures on resource-rich Jharkhand have compounded these conflicts of interest.

As also discussed earlier, Koel-Karo is also the site of another critical contestation—of electoral democracy that most often privileges privilege, and of the efforts to build direct democracy rooted in place. The latter has been no stranger in Munda areas where consensus-based local governance has historically been part of a sophisticated political and social system.

The Jharkhand region has witnessed a long history of repression and state high-handedness. Over two hundred years ago, the first acts of resistance to British colonization occurred in these areas, and some of India's most sustained struggles—from the Santhal rebellion to the struggle led by Birsa Munda—are part of the collective history of those in the movement in the Koel and Karo River valleys. Women have been at the forefront of most of these movements. The mobilizations have strengthened collective solidarity and self-confidence as people have moved out of their homes and participated collectively in marches, Satyagraha, and collective social activity. These processes are part of an evolved, people-centered politics that has suffered periodic setbacks, but has emerged again and again to assert a place-based vision of cultural and ecological plurality and justice.

WH/AE: If you were to synthesize the lessons from struggles like those in the Koel and Karo valleys for the 'politics of place' process, what would these be?

SK: The experiences of the Koel-Karo movement illustrate that the politics of place are more than gender, class, and ethnic struggles over environment as a collection of resources in a specific location. Women's environmental movements, as well as ethnic, tribal, and rural farmers' struggles, are about the terms of connection between people and between groups of people, other species, and the surrounding physical world. They are also about the terms and connection between local and larger places, both earthly and spiritual. Places, in turn, are not treated as real estate, as exchangeable and interchangeable commodities, but rather as the ground where body, home, community, and habitat are joined in everyday experience, as well as in history.

WH/AE: Beyond a concern with the democratic process within movements, what else do you consider critical in your work and analysis of movements?

SK: Another way of seeing the multiple dimensions of women's struggles—partly illustrated by the Koel-Karo struggle discussed above—is how contemporary movements are responding to the politics of boundary making at five different levels:

1. Boundary of the Indian Nation-state;
2. The internal political boundaries within the Nation-state;
3. Boundaries between urban and rural spaces;
4. Boundaries within the community; and
5. Boundaries within the family.

Most Indian women negotiate the politics of place in these five arenas, often simultaneously. So negotiating and challenging patriarchal, family, and community structures can be a simultaneous engagement, whilst challenging the state's politics of identity and development. A women and the politics of place framework, therefore, offers a fundamental intellectual and political challenge within these arenas made more challenging by the increasingly public roles that women are playing in providing leadership to these struggles.

The increasing realization of identity, place, and boundary—including the importance of language and the neglect that the community feels culturally, economically, and politically—has created widespread resistance, encouraging numerous instances of creative engagement with power in its multiple dimensions. There is a sharper realization of the multiple identities that are encompassed within a single individual. There is also a widening realization of identities related to place—centered on livelihoods, cultural relations, and community. Interestingly, the standardization evident in the dominant thinking and practice of development, identity politics, and democracy is creating both the contradictions and the opportunities.

For example, in Kashmir and northeast India, we have witnessed a history of challenges to the country's national boundaries and the critical roles that women have played within these mobilizations. Despite massive efforts to subjugate or manipulate the urge that lies at the base of these struggles, many of these movements are still active. Similarly, within the country, the move to redraw the internal boundaries of the state—based on the recovery of cultural, economic, and political control, and not on dominant language—is critical in many struggles. There are also struggles in areas that have been economically neglected. All of these mobilizations are encouraging women to challenge and redefine traditional boundaries.

WH/AE: You speak about displacement, one of the themes of the Women and the Politics of Place framework. Can you elaborate on what this means in the Indian context?

SK: Since independence in 1947, planned development programs and projects have displaced 20–30 million women from their sources of subsistence and meaning. A majority of those involved in the development business do not understand—or do not want to acknowledge—that it is not just people who are displaced, but also cultures, languages, complex knowledge systems, and symbolic and cosmological universe. This developmental and policy apathy and its reductionist, arrogant sensibility is powerfully manifest when development planners and practitioners argue that cash compensation is an adequate way of assuaging the brutal disruption of people from place.

Of course, once displaced, there are numerous situations where women have been compelled to cope during and after migration, but it is important to recognize that these coping strategies are brought into play after an often brutal process of alienation, discrimination, and exploitation. Undoubtedly, women make good domestic or construction workers or secure other forms of employment, most at the bottom of the employment chain. In many cases, at their new sites of work and residence, they have established remarkable networks of affinity groups as well as collective efforts that seek to expand their rights in their new settlements and work places. New relationships are being continuously forged; new roots are being formed giving meaning to the new places that they inhabit. Despite this, however, there is no denying the need to address the root causes of displacement, migration, alienation, and discrimination.

WH/AE: The place of women in local governments is often quoted as a success of the women's movement in India. How do you see this? Has this given new opportunities for leadership?

SK: The politics of leadership is very complex, particularly in the context of the issue of multiple boundaries discussed above, as not all leadership is contingent on representation in local governments. Nevertheless, within representational governance, a decade ago, the women's movement had a significant victory when it secured an amendment to the Indian Constitution that guaranteed them one-third representation in local governments. Simultaneously, the lowest caste groups also secured one-third representation. Today, several hundred local governments are not only headed by women but by women belonging to the lower caste groups—a phenomenon unthinkable only a couple of decades ago. There are currently efforts underway to extend this representation to all elected bodies, and it is a matter of a few years when a third of all representative governments will be comprised of women. Thirty-three percent women, including women from historically discriminated and oppressed groups, entering local politics is deepening the democratic process, however you look at it.

There are significant challenges, particularly with the capacity and awareness of those being elected to engage with the content of democracy and development. But for the moment, women are entering local politics and social life with greater confidence and determination, and they are changing democratic space as they take greater control of family, local governments, social movements, and local and national politics. Few places in the world are witnessing such dramatic changes, as women are slowly but surely becoming an active political force in places where historically they had little or no representation.

All this needs more thorough discussion, as we do need to make a distinction between 'empowerment' through top-down policy processes versus the recasting of power through struggles at the base of our societies. In the former there is continuing condescension by those in power who are still largely reluctant to cede power. In many local governments, women may just be fronting for their more powerful male relatives. It is the efforts to alter the very dynamics and structures of power that are being waged at numerous sites that are bringing important lessons for cultural and political struggles.

WH/AE: The World Social Forum (WSF) seemed to be one place where that was evident. You were closely involved in the third WSF at Mumbai in January 2004. How do you see that process and its impact on democratic processes in India, and in relation to your current work in northeast India? What has been the specific role that women have played in these movements? Have they played a major role? How do you see women's specific role as agents or, indeed, as victims in the rise of what you have called political fundamentalism?

SK: I am glad that you have asked me the latter question about political fundamentalism. As you know, the politicization of religious fundamentalism has been on the rise the world over. In India, Hindu nationalism has established new roots and has secured a wider political foothold; this process has often been nurtured in the growing climate of social alienation, economic insecurity, community fragmentation, contentious religious nationalisms within and outside the country and a weak state unable to firmly contain these forces and defend our plural, multireligious and multiethnic ethos.

Hindu nationalism has its own political mobilizations that seek to work on a grossly distorted and simplistic discourse of tradition and of Hindu purity being under threat. It validates a patriarchal, chauvinist sensibility that legitimizes the subjugation of women and of lower caste and class groups; and, more importantly, selectively draws on tradition to reinforce a reactionary politics of place. So we do need to make a clear distinction between, on the one hand, religious and chauvinistic assertions and mobilizations that seek to exclude and, on the other hand, the wider struggle for dignity and justice.

The plural, therefore, also coexists with the reactionary and can justify exclusion and discrimination, as well as justify norms and institutions that sustain old as well as legitimate new conservative hierarchies of power. The challenge, as we see it in our national alliances and at the different sites of progressive struggle, is to sustain the plural in ways that respect the autonomy of collectivities to nurture their own life ways, whilst internally working out a sustained and creative engagement with universal normative frameworks; for instance, the Indian Constitution or the Universal Declaration of Human Rights with its amendments that are now becoming more sensitive to the more nuanced and complex issues of sovereignty, self-determination, and identity.

There is a more difficult issue, however. Millions of women have little or no space to actively participate in the cultural, social, economic, and legal journeys of their families and communities. They are compelled to seek their validation within existing fundamentalist and patriarchal structures. Millions of educated women actively participate in, legitimate, and find security in chauvinist and fundamentalist institutions and parties. A real or an imagined 'other' further impels them to validate cultural and political processes that undermine a just and plural alternative. Negotiating through this thicket of conservatism is a painful and slow process undermining the huge gap that exists between progressive laws and ground reality and underscoring the massive challenges that still lie ahead. One of the central dilemmas for a politics of place is working with the modernization process in ways that continue to enhance women's dignity and rights whilst simultaneously seeking to redefine the very content of modernization.

On the World Social Forum, the Mumbai event was historic. It is the first time, even for the Social Forum, that such a wide diversity of movement groups across the center-left and left ideological streams collaborated and participated in staging the event.

But the real challenge is how that spirit can be sustained. When activists return to their home sites, the exigencies and priorities are primarily defined by local compulsions. Similarly, I feel that we have overestimated the progressive change resulting from global civic engagement. The primary engagement still has to be at the local and national levels. The task of engaging with, challenging, and transforming deeply entrenched local and national power is the primary site where a politics of place needs to be sited and strengthened.

WH/AE: One final question. In one of our earlier meetings, you spoke about the importance of politics being validated. In our project, 'women and the politics of place,' where would you see us finding our validation: from intellectuals, from the social justice movement, or from the women's movement? Can we relate to 'the grassroots women' legitimately in this sense? If not, how do you see us (and yourself) as 'mediator' and 'translator' of these struggles, if at all? What are the political consequences—potentialities and limitations of this role?

SK: As it has evolved so far, the politics of place process has primarily been an intellectual engagement by activist scholars. Our collective process has been enriched by our own individual engagements in a diversity of social and political movements. It has also been a valuable building of an affinity group that has challenged and affirmed each other.

In turn, I believe, it has helped me to understand my sphere of activities and my life better, contributing in the process to sustaining my political work. Validation from larger constituencies is indirect. Further validation and challenges will come when the book is published, translated, and disseminated. The analysis and insights of the POP (politics of place) process also need to be shared in larger publics, which will also provide the necessary modifications and enrichments to this individual and collective journey. The limitations will only be a consequence of how individually and collectively we are successful in taking these ideas and perspectives to wider audiences that, in turn, can inform and influence our future work.

It is important, however, that we do not overstate the importance of this exercise. It is a modest effort to synthesize our collective thinking and learning and to share that with a wider audience. At a fundamental level, therefore, it is an exercise of engaged political scholarship both holding a mirror to the world we live in and celebrating the diverse efforts to build a saner, just, and dignified future.

Note

1. This dialogue took place 'face to face' in October 2004 and was completed in February 2005 by e-mail.

Part Three

The Diverse Economy:
Women, Place, and Alternative Economies

9

Building Community Economies: Women and the Politics of Place

J. K. GIBSON-GRAHAM

Women and the Politics of Place (WPP) is a project of narrating and theorizing a globally emergent form of localized politics— one that is largely *of,* if not necessarily *for,* women—with the goal of bringing this politics into a new stage of being. What is truly distinctive about WPP is the vision of a *place-based,* yet at the same time *global,* movement (Osterweil, 2004c). Indeed this distinctive vision is what first attracted us to the project, for we were already imagining and fostering an economic politics with the same locally rooted, yet globally extensive structure. Rather than 'waiting for the revolution' to transform a global economy and governance system at the world scale, we were engaging with others to transform local economies *here* and *now,* in an everyday ethical and political practice of constructing 'community economies' in the face of globalization.

WPP can be seen as an offspring of second wave feminism, a movement that arguably gave rise to a distinctive understanding and practice of politics, one that is hinted at though not quite captured in the phrase, 'the personal is political.' Whereas formerly politics was seen to involve large groups of people or small numbers of highly influential individuals organizing to gain power or create change, second wave feminism initiated a politics of local and personal transformation—a "politics of becoming," in Connolly's terms (1999: 57). Feminism linked feminists emotionally and semiotically rather than primarily through organizational ties. Without rejecting the familiar politics of organizing within groups and across space, individual women and collectivities pursued local paths and strategies that were based on avowedly feminist visions and values, but were not otherwise connected. The movement achieved global coverage without having to create global institutions, although some of these did indeed come into being. Ubiquity rather than unity was the ground of its globalization.

WPP builds on that ground, extending the idea of a politics of ubiquity by emphasizing its ontological substrate: a vast set of disarticulated 'places'—households, social communities, ecosystems, workplaces, organizations, bodies, public arenas, urban spaces, diasporas, regions, occupations—related analogically, rather than organically, and connected through webs of signification. If *women* are everywhere, *a woman* is always somewhere, and those 'somewheres' are what the project is about: places being created, strengthened, defended, augmented, or transformed by women. It is as though the identity category, woman, were to be addressed through contextualization or emplacement, and the feminist question had become, what might a politics of the emplacement be? Not a politics of identity per se, but a politics of the coproduction of subjects and places. A politics of becoming in place.

In the political imaginary of WPP, place takes on a specifically political meaning. Shedding its connotations of anticosmopolitan localism (see Chapter 14), place emerges as the site of political activism and social transformation (see Chapter 12) rather than primarily as a 'home ground.' Women are associated with place not because they are home-based or placebound, but because of their inaugural and continuing role in shaping a new politics. Over the course of more than three decades, feminists have inserted issues of the female person and body—the place 'closest-in'—into political discourses and struggles in their domestic settings, in their communities, and in the national and international political arenas, thereby enlarging the domain of the 'political' (see Chapter 1). And while global women's movements have devoted much energy to 'engendering' global development processes through international conferences and commissions, feminists have not fixated on the global as the ultimate scale of successful activism (see Chapter 2). In confronting imperial globalization, they are continuing their orientation to the local, daily, and bodily, recognizing that transforming the world involves transforming sites, subjects, and practices worldwide. That this place-oriented activism may involve them in global movements (of migrant workers, for example) is not a contradiction, but simply a confirmation that places are constituted at the crossroads of global forces.

One of the inspirations for the WPP project has been the desire to assert a logic of difference and possibility against the homogenizing tendencies of globalization and the teleological generalities of political economy (Harcourt and Escobar, 2002; Dirlik, 2002). The vision is that women are both threatened and mobilized by the contemporary wave of globalization, and that they are already everywhere engaged in constructing and revitalizing places in response to the exigencies and possibilities of their everyday lives. What the project hopes to do is foster this tenacious, dispersed, and barely visible 'movement,' creating connections (networks or 'meshworks'), sharing information and inspiration through academic and nonacademic channels, and developing local experiments into a collective knowledge that will spawn and support more projects and ideas. Representing this movement and connecting its participants, the project will create a recognized (self-)identity for something that already exists, thereby empowering and expanding it.

For J. K. Gibson-Graham, the language of place resonates with our own ongoing attempts to bring into view the diversity of economic practices, to make visible the hidden and alternative economic activities that everywhere abound. If we can begin to see these largely noncapitalist activities as prevalent and viable, we may be encouraged to actively build upon them to transform our local economies (Community Economies Collective, 2001). Place signifies the possibility of understanding local economies as *places* with highly specific economic identities and capacities rather than simply as *nodes* in a global capitalist system. In more broadly philosophical terms, place is that which is not fully yoked into a system of meaning, not entirely subsumed to a (global) order; it is that aspect of every site that exists as potentiality. Place is the 'event in space,' operating as a 'dislocation' with respect to familiar structures and narratives. It is the unmapped and unmoored that allow for new moorings and mappings. Place, like the subject, is the site and spur of becoming, the opening for politics.

In our own work we have been pushed to bridge the separations that define and distinguish places. Continuing to think and write together after graduate school, we have had to constantly negotiate the deep and watery distance between the United States and Australia, and perhaps more importantly the social distance between two different continents, nations, communities, and life trajectories. To pursue our work of rethinking and reenacting economy, we have tried to span the gap between the academy and activism, engaging in place-based action research involving both university and community-based researchers/ activists. Our action research projects have aimed to recognize and value the distinctive economic capabilities of localities and to build upon these strengths through nourishing communal economic practices and constructing alternative economic institutions. Along the way we have become increasingly communal in our own practices of production and in our sense of ourselves. In 1992 (after fifteen years of working together) we adopted a joint persona, J. K. Gibson-Graham, to honor and encourage our small, collective, authorial enterprise.

In the rest of this chapter we outline the different aspects of our ongoing project of building community economies in place, highlighting the affinities and overlaps that have brought us to identify with WPP. We see our project as having four principal elements. The first involves deconstructing the hegemony of capitalism to open up a discursive space for the prevalence and diversity of noncapitalist economic activity worldwide (see Gibson-Graham, 1996). The second requires producing a language of economic difference to enlarge the economic imaginary, rendering visible and intelligible the diverse and proliferating practices that the preoccupation with capitalism has obscured; we see this language as a necessary contribution to a politics of economic innovation. The third is the difficult process of cultivating subjects (ourselves and others) who can desire and inhabit noncapitalist economic spaces. To frame this cultivation process we step aside from the familiar structural vision of capitalism with its already identified and interested subjects, developing a vision of the 'community economy' as an ethical and political space of becoming. In this communal space individual and collective subjects negotiate questions of livelihood and interdependence and (re)construct themselves in the process. Finally, there is the actual practice of building community economies in place. Here we offer two examples of women's activism, one from Kerala province in India and the other involving Filipina migrants working with NGOs with whom we are currently pursuing a collaborative project of action research.

Envisioning a Diverse Economy

Much of our earlier work has been oriented toward destabilizing the epistemological certainties that justify a particular global narrative and authorize a globally mobilized anticapitalist politics as the one true path to economic empowerment and transformation (Gibson-Graham, 1996; 2002). This has involved repeatedly querying what seem to us grandiose representations of world-scale capitalist penetration and dominion. By undermining the looming capitalist eminence in the foreground of representation, we have attempted to make room for a vision and a self-knowledge of local initiatives—especially noncapitalist economic ones—as powerful and efficacious, not simply a prelude or second best to a global movement or organization.

Arturo Escobar has argued that the project of making the invisible visible, or seeing "different economies always on the rise," requires a different "politics of reading on our part as analysts, with the concomitant need to contribute to a different politics of representation" (2001: 158). To read a landscape we have always read as capitalist, to read it as a landscape of difference, populated by various capitalist and noncapitalist institutions and practices, is a difficult task, for we must contend not only with our colonized imaginations but also with our beliefs about politics, understandings of power, conceptions of economy, and structures of desire. We are all subjects of a capitalist order—in the sense that our understandings *and* our emotions, our personal ambitions *and* our visions of collective possibility are organized around a visceral belief in the hegemonic presence and power of capitalism.

As one way of creating fissures in the imposing edifice of capitalism, we have been elaborating a vision and language of the 'diverse economy.' A language of economic diversity brings to light what exists in the shadows, disclosing the noncapitalist economic activity that is (everywhere) available to build upon, once we become able to name and see it. This more inclusive economic language harbors heretofore hidden economic identities that can prompt identification and self-recognition, calling into being collective and individual subjects who can imagine and perform alternative economies.

In undertaking this project we are up against something powerful and pervasive—if not capitalism per se, then its prevalent representations.

In both mainstream and left discourse, the economy is understood as essentially *capitalist,* the productive economic subject is restricted to the positions of wageworker or *capitalist* entrepreneur, and places are either incorporated or incorporable into *capitalist* space. To the extent that economic discourse has a place for economic difference, it locates it in a *capitalocentric* field in which capitalism is the norm and noncapitalist economic relations or entities are understood with respect to capitalism as either the same as, complements to, opposites of, or contained within capitalism.

Yet alongside the hegemonic capitalocentric discourse of the economy, there are many counter-discourses of economy that have arisen from alternative strands of economic thinking (for example, classical political economy, economic anthropology, feminist economics, sociology, and geography) and from working class, third world, and social and community movements (for example, the feminist, socialist, cooperative, and local sustainability movements). These counterdiscourses offer abundant resources that we can draw upon in constructing a language of economic diversity.

The most controversial, yet most successful counter to dominant economic thinking has been spearheaded by feminist activists and economists, who point to the huge amount of labor (much of it performed by women) expended on unpaid and nonmarket-oriented activities such as housework, childrearing, volunteering, and care for the elderly and infirm (see, for example, Beneria, 2003; Brandt, 1995; Delphy, 1984; Elson, 1995; Folbre, 1987, 2001; Henderson, 1991; Matthaei, 2001; Waring, 1988).[1] Empirical work on this topic has established that in both rich and poor countries 30–50 percent of economic activity is accounted for by unpaid household labor (Ironmonger, 1996; Luxton, 1997). There is now a call for the system of national accounts to be revised so that the total measure of economic performance, gross economic product, includes both gross market product *and* gross household product (Ironmonger, 1996: 38–9).

A second challenge to the hegemony of the 'capitalist economy' is presented by the vast literature on the informal economies of both 'less-' and 'more-' developed nations. The pressure to recognize that livelihoods are sustained by a plethora of economic activities that do not take the form of wage labor, commodity production for a market, or capitalist enterprise has largely come from the global 'South,' although there is increasing evidence of the variety and magnitude of noncapitalist transactions and nontransacted subsistence practices pursued in the developed economies of the 'North' (Williams, 2004; Emery, 2004).[2]

A third language of economic difference comes, perhaps surprisingly, from Marx. In *Capital,* Marx foregrounded capitalism against the background of feudal, slave, and independent production as well as the nonexploitative relations he identified with communism. Unfortunately his language of economic difference has been translated into (or misinterpreted as) a historical stage theory of economic evolution in which capitalism is situated near the pinnacle of development and all other forms of economy represented as precapitalist or as (now discredited) postcapitalist alternatives. This means that we are still under the sway of a systemic conception of economy in which only one economic 'system' can exist at a time.

Indeed, despite the proliferative energy that continually gives rise to new economic languages, these tend to remain "non-credible alternatives to what exists" (Santos, 2004: 238), subsisting in the shadows of mainstream economic thinking. Although feminist interventions, for example, have successfully expanded conceptions of the economy to include as legitimate contributions both paid and unpaid labor and market and nonmarket transactions, within the hegemonic framing this vast sea of nonmonetized economic activity is still situated as merely supporting the 'real' economy and as ultimately dependent on the determining dynamics of capitalist growth. The idea of independent economic dynamics within household economies, the voluntary sector, or neighborhood economies is rendered virtually unthinkable. And the idea of basing a development project on the nonmarket sector is theoretically and practically speaking 'out-of-bounds.'

It is clear that there already exists a substantial understanding of the extent and nature of economic difference. What does not exist is a way of convening this knowledge that destabilizes the received wisdom of capitalist dominance and unleashes new creative forces and subjects of economic experimentation. Our intervention is to propose a language of the *diverse economy* as an exploratory practice of thinking about economy differently in order to enact different economies. The language of the diverse economy expands our economic vocabulary, widening the identity of the economy to include all of those practices excluded or marginalized by the theory and presumption of capitalist hegemony. Within this language, relationships are contingently rather than deterministically configured; economic value is liberally distributed rather than assigned to certain activities and denied to others; and economic dynamics are potentially proliferated rather than reduced to a small number of governing laws and logics.

Our objective is not to produce a finished and coherent template that maps the economy 'as it really is' and presents (to the converted or suggestible) a ready-made 'alternative economy.' Rather, our project is to disarm and dislocate the naturalized dominance of the capitalist economy and make the space for new economic becomings—ones that we will need to work to produce. If we can recognize a diverse economy, we can begin to imagine and create diverse organizations and practices as powerful constituents of an enlivened, noncapitalist politics of place.

We begin constructing our language by convening some of the radical diversity of economic relations and conceptualizing them in terms of three practices:[3]

- Different kinds of *transactions,* which includes different ways of negotiating commensurability
- Different types of *labor* and ways of compensating it
- Different forms of *enterprise* and ways of producing, appropriating, and distributing surplus.

Our current representation of what we have called the diverse economy is shown in Table 1. In this table, what is often seen as the *economy*—that is, formal markets, wage labor, and capitalist enterprise—is merely one set of cells in a complex field of diverse economic relations that sustain livelihoods in communities around the world. Below we briefly explore each of the columns, highlighting practices and forms of organization that are usually ignored.

Transactions

In its singular, normal, and lawful guise, 'the market' is usually identified with capitalism and, as such, is imbued with expansiveness, authority, and force. Yet, seen in the context of the plethora of transactions that make up our economic world (shown in Table 1), it seems absurd to think that such a small part of the transactional whole, and one that is so aridly abstract in its theorization, has such power to colonize and obscure.[4]

Formal market exchange accounts for only one set of practices by which the goods and services that sustain livelihoods are transacted. Goods and services are also produced and *shared* in the household; nature provides abundant goods that are *taken* as well as stewarded; individuals and organizations *give away* goods and services; some people rightfully or illegally *steal* goods; and goods and services are *allocated* by the state, and traded within and between communities according to

Table 9.1 A Diverse Economy[1]

Transactions	Labor	Enterprise
Market	Wage	Capitalist
Alternative Market	*Alternative Paid*	*Alternative Capitalist*
Sale of public goods	Self-employed	State enterprise
Ethical 'fair trade' markets	Cooperative	Green capitalist
Local trading systems	Indentured	Socially responsible
Alternative currencies	Reciprocal labor	firm
Underground market	In kind	Nonprofit
Co-op exchange	Work for welfare	
Barter		
Informal market		
Nonmarket	*Unpaid*	*Noncapitalist*
Household flows	Housework	Communal
Gift giving	Family care	Independent
Indigenous exchange	Neighborhood work	Feudal
State allocations	Volunteer	Slave
Gleaning	Self-provisioning	
Hunting, fishing,	labor	
gathering	Slave labor	
Theft, poaching	Surplus labor	

Note: 1. The table is organized as columns and is not intended to be read across the rows. Note, for instance, that noncapitalist enterprises (bottom row) are engaged in market transactions (top row).

traditions of *ritual exchange*.[5] What is clear is that there is a huge variety and volume of nonmarket transactions and that they are a significant (and possibly the dominant) form of transaction that sustains us all.

If we examine the formal market itself, we see a variety of socially, naturally, and governmentally constructed contexts for commodity exchange. Markets are naturally and artificially protected, monopolized, regulated, and niched, and in all these cases transactions are governed by context-specific, contingent social relations rather than abstract and universal logics. Moreover, since markets are often conflated with capitalism, it is important to recognize that not all commodities transacted in formal markets are produced by capitalist firms employing free wage labor; they may be produced by worker collectives, slaves, independent producers, or feudal serfs.

In addition, there are many 'alternative' market transactions in which goods and services are exchanged and commensurability is socially negotiated and agreed upon: transactions that take place in the informal and underground markets in which goods and services are traded according to very local and personalized agreements; the exchange of commodities between and within producer cooperatives where prices are set to enhance sustainability of the cooperative; the ethical or 'fair' trade of products where producers and consumers agree on price levels that will sustain certain livelihood practices; local trading systems and alternative currencies that foster local interdependency and sustainability; and the marketing of goods and services produced by the state and 'sold' under conditions where profit is not the prime arbiter of viability. Barter is another prevalent form of transaction in which goods deemed to be equivalent in value by their producers or traders are exchanged without recourse to money.

Labor

The most prevalent form of labor the world over is the unpaid work that is conducted in the household, the family, and the neighborhood or wider community, predominantly by women. Other forms of unpaid labor include the work of self-provisioning or subsistence (for example, gardening, gathering, hunting, fishing, and making clothes). To include all of this work in a conception of a diverse economy is to re-present many people who see themselves (or are labeled) as 'unemployed' or 'not economically active' as economic subjects; that is, as contributing to the vast skein of productive and transactional activities that sustain social existence.

The usual image of wage labor is of workers who sell their labor power to a capitalist employer in return for a monetary wage set at a level that allows them and their dependents to buy the commodities necessary for subsistence. There are, however, many other forms of labor that are 'paid.' Worker cooperatives employ a labor force (themselves) that is paid a living wage at a level decided upon by the cooperators. Self-employed workers are in the position of paying themselves a wage, setting (within the constraints of the success of their business) their own wage level and benefit entitlement.

Other people work in return for payments in kind (sometimes mixed with monetary payments): A share farmer works on someone else's land in return for a proportion of the harvest. A live-in migrant domestic servant works in someone's home in return for room and board and a small allowance of spending money that does not amount to a living wage. A pastor performs caring labor in a community and is supported by in-kind payments—access to a house, car, gifts of food, and a small stipend. Residents of a community offer their collective labor to others at times of high labor demand (harvest, house renovation, or moving) in return for a reciprocal claim on labor at another time.

Forms of Organization/Enterprise

The diverse economy comprises many kinds of enterprise in which ownership and production are differently configured. We are concerned with highlighting the ways in which enterprises organize the production, appropriation, and distribution of surplus; that is, the diversity of their class relations.[6] The notion of surplus rests upon an accounting distinction between the labor that is necessary for the producer's subsistence and the labor that is surplus to the requirements of the direct producers and can be used to support other persons and activities.[7] This accounting distinction enables a view of a major source of social wealth (whether in the form of surplus labor, surplus product, or surplus value) and provides an analytical frame for highlighting the different ways this wealth is collected and dispersed.

Many producers have no control over what happens to their surplus—it is appropriated by nonproducers who claim right to the wealth produced on a variety of grounds. In capitalist firms, workers can be seen to have relinquished the right to their surplus as part of the wage contract, and the surplus is appropriated by their capitalist employers (or board of directors of the capitalist firm). Similarly, in feudal agricultural enterprises, access to land for subsistence is granted on the condition that farmers perform surplus labor on their landlord's land or produce surplus product, which is appropriated by the landlord. Slaves produce surplus labor that is appropriated by their owners or those who lease them from slaveholders. In all these cases the capitalists, landlords, and slaveholders/lessors have first claim on distributing the appropriated surplus, which in the case of the modern capitalist firm goes to cover taxes, interest, dividends, advertising and management costs, investment in expansion (that is, capital accumulation), bribes, personal wealth enhancement; indeed, any expenses in addition to those devoted to reproducing the production process (productive capital and labor power).

In addition to the exploitative form of class relations where nonproducers appropriate surplus, there are nonexploitative enterprise forms in which workers appropriate their own surplus. Independent, self-employed producers are in charge of producing, appropriating, and distributing their own surplus and setting the distinction between their wage (the necessary labor payment) and their surplus. In worker cooperatives, cooperators set their own wage and produce a communal surplus that they collectively appropriate and distribute.

One should remember that not all capitalist firms are driven to distribute their entire surplus to expansion or the consumption fund of shareholders and managers. Difference *within* the category of capitalist enterprise is as important to recognize as the difference between organizational forms or class processes.[8] Increasingly there are 'alternative' capitalist firms who distinguish themselves from their mainstream capitalist counterparts, in that part of their production process, their product, or their appropriated surplus is oriented toward environmentally friendly or socially responsible activity. State capitalist enterprises employ wage labor and appropriate surplus, but have the potential to produce public goods and distribute surplus funds to public benefit. Nonprofit enterprises similarly employ wage labor and appropriate their surplus, but by law are not allowed to retain or distribute profits.

By distinguishing all these different ways in which social wealth is generated and deployed, we are able to represent an 'economy' as something more extensive and less concentrated than our usual, commonsense understanding of capitalism. Elaborating a vision of the 'diverse economy' is one of our strategic moves against the subordination of local subjects to the discourse of (capitalist economic) globalization.[9] It prompts a recognition that 'things could be otherwise' politically, based on the recognition that they are already 'otherwise' discursively. What is visible, intelligible, and measurable has a different imaginative and social status than what is sequestered in the obscure realm of the unthought and unseen. If the elements of a diverse economy can be endowed with credible existence, they can become candidates for political projects of strengthening and building different economies here and now.

The intellectual project of widening the horizon of the economy and locating the diverse practices that occupy the economic landscape is one step toward repoliticizing the economy, exposing its singular capitalist identity as a regulatory fiction (Butler, 1990). But what kind of economy might we put in place if we were truly engaged in building alternatives that were not necessarily or predominantly capitalist? To begin to think about this is to embark upon another kind of language politics, one that involves what we have called the 'community economy.' But rather than the proliferative fullness we see in the diverse economy, the community economy is an emptiness—as it has to be, if the project of building it is to be political, experimental, open, and democratic.

Community Economies/Communal Subjects

What might it mean to build a community economy if we refuse any positive blueprint that tells us what and where to build? Blueprints for economic development have, to date, been dominated by the naturalized universal of the capitalist economy (as the model of economy, as the only true, viable, self-regulating economy, as something that effaces its particularist origins in the West, in certain forms of market, in certain types of enterprise). Or alternatively they have attempted to prescribe socialism, understood as capitalism's opposite, with central planning and state ownership supplanting the disavowed markets and privately owned industrial property associated with the capitalist 'other.'

Underpinning the complex set of strategies, policies, and beliefs that constitute development discourse (whether it is aimed toward building capitalism or socialism) is a particular ontological framing of the economy that is rooted in the experience of Western European and North American industrialization. The relationships between production and consumption, investment and growth, proletarianization and material well-being, competition, technological change, and efficiency that characterized these experiences have been reified as logics of economic functioning and placed outside of discourse onto the terrain of reality. Here they are worshipped as universal principles (sometimes represented as natural 'laws') of economic evolution. Different attempts to produce economic development ignore these laws at their peril, it seems.

Our stance involves both resisting the attractions of any blueprint or vision of lawful development *and* proposing the *community economy* as a new and different kind of universal that might guide the process of building different economies. Unlike the structurally configured economy with its regularities and lawful relationships, the community economy is an acknowledged space of ethical interaction and self-formation. Anything but a blueprint, it is instead an empty and unknown terrain that calls forth exploratory conversation and ethical and political acts of decision.

For the minimalism and 'emptiness' of the abstract community economy we are indebted to Jean-Luc Nancy (1991a: 74), who theorizes community starting from a presubjective recognition of the interdependent coexistence that is entailed in all 'being'—something he calls "being-in-common" that constitutes "us all" (Nancy, 1991b). Recognition of economic being-in-common is a precondition for a politics aimed at building and extending community economic practices.[10] In approaching the task of signifying the community economy, however, we must keep in mind the ever present danger that any attempt to fix a fantasy of common being (our sameness), to define the community economy, to specify what it contains (and thus what it does not) closes off the space of decision and the opportunity to cultivate ethical praxis. The space of decision as we have identified it is the emptiness at the center of the community economy; it constitutes the community economy as a *negativity* with potential to become, rather than a *positivity* with clear contents and outlines. The practice of the community economy is a fluid process of continual resignification, rejecting any fantasy that there is a perfect community economy that lies outside of negotiation, struggle, uncertainty, ambivalence, and disappointment, rejecting the notion that there's a blueprint that tells us what to do and how to 'be communal.' Indeed it is a recognition that there's no way *not* to be communal, *not* to be materially implicated one with another, that recalls us to the political task of 'building a community economy.'

As with the discourse of economic difference, the practice of the community economy can be seen as already existing and widespread. It is interesting, for example, to note the many alternative economic movements that are explicitly about resocializing economic relations and infusing them with ethical values and political intent. One has only to think of the fair trade networks that connect third world producers with first world consumers, so that, in the buying and selling of coffee or bananas or craft products, the act of commensuration is *not* disembodied but is ethically negotiated in a quasi face-to-face manner (mirroring the once vital socialist trading blocs). Or the farmers' markets and farm share arrangements and local buying campaigns of community supported agriculture that have sprung up in cities around the industrialized world to bring fresh produce to consumers at (higher) prices that allow farmers to stay in business. Here we see attempts to eliminate intermediaries and increase the proportion of surplus available to the producer. We can also look to employee buyouts of firms in the face of corporate abandonment in the United States and worker takeovers of factories in the face of economic crisis, as in Argentina today. Here workers are becoming owners, self-managers, and appropriators of surplus, learning to make decisions about allocating the value they produce. We can look to the anti-sweatshop movement that raises awareness about rates of exploitation and below-subsistence wage rates in industries producing commodities on which we all depend. Or to stockholder movements that use their financial clout to promote ethical investments and police the enforcement of corporate environmental and social responsibility. Or to the living-wage movements in North American cities and newly invigorated discussions across Europe and the United States of a Universal Basic Income (Van Parijs, 2001). Even mainstream economic policy has become interested in promoting social entrepreneurship in which nonprofit enterprises provide social services at affordable rates and commit to employing community members who are excluded from capitalist labor markets (Amin, et al., 2003). In all these movements, economic decisions (about prices of goods, wage levels, bonus payments, re-investment strategies, sale of stock, and so on) are made in the light of ethical discussions conducted within various communities of 'us all.' In some cases these communities are geographically confined to the 'local'; in others they are international in scope and span the 'global.'

Movements that are resocializing economic relations provide us with many opportunities to identify sites where ethical economic decisions can be made, where we can begin to perform economy in new ways. These movements involve the coming into being of novel economic subjects who can desire and enact alternative economic relationships. Their example recalls the centrality of the ethical economic subject to the politics of constructing a community economy. If our action research practice is concerned to actually build community economies in place, we are necessarily involved in a micropolitics of self-transformation, cultivating ourselves and others as subjects who can identify with and undertake community economic projects. In this connection the economic activities and subjectivities of women come to the fore as salient and exemplary on a number of grounds—not only because women as economic subjects are targeted by the contemporary mainstream development agenda, but also because they are actively engaged in the hidden and alternative economic activities of the diverse economy, because their traditional economic pursuits often acknowledge sociality and interdependency, and because women worldwide have become economic activists in place-based movements to defend or enhance livelihoods and environments (see, for example, Chapter 10).

Women as Subjects of Economic Development and Activism

Alongside buoyant beliefs in the efficiency and benefits of globalization, a haunting uncertainty has arisen surrounding the question of *who* the local agent of development in the age of globalization might be. Somewhat paradoxically we have recently seen heightened interest in the central role of women in development. While nearly invisible within global and national scale debates about leveling the playing field and joining the global economy, at the local level women in poor urban and rural areas have become the targets of market-led approaches to economic development. Women have been recruited into microcredit schemes and microenterprise development projects upon which the hopes for poverty reduction and economic growth are pinned. And in new debates that trace the success of development agendas to the 'social capital' of certain communities, women's work in nurturing social ties and building and maintaining aspects of civil society is foregrounded as key.

The pioneering achievements of the Grameen Bank in Bangladesh were one of the many factors encouraging international development agencies to shift their economic focus to women. Direct improvements to a poor community's livelihoods could be achieved, it seemed, by facilitating women's access to small amounts of credit that they could use to support home and community-based microenterprises. With the new microcredit and microenterprise focus, neoliberal, market-led, internationalist orthodoxies were married with longstanding local community traditions of revolving credit networks and women's involvement in informal sector production and trading. The ongoing success of these microfinance schemes relies upon the self-regulating power of the women's borrower group to provide collective and corrective surveillance of individual women's economic habits (Rankin, 2001). As more of these schemes have been monitored, there is growing concern that some of their impacts may have undermined the trust and supportive networks (the social capital) that enabled them to be established in the first place.[11]

Clearly it is women's economic identities as existing or potential entrepreneurs that are called forth by these policies. And, as Rankin (2001) argues, it is to women as rational economic subjects, for whom individual gain is paramount, that the appeal for involvement in the schemes is made. Both these aspects of identity are linked to a vision of the economy as essentially capitalist, and the feminine subject as desirous of becoming a capitalist entrepreneur. This is a vision that denies the diversity of women's economic commitments and involvements and ignores the multiplicity of economies and subjects that coexist in economically distinctive places. Importantly, it is a view that disregards the many different opportunities and directions for local economic transformation.

Viewing the recent gender-focused interventions by international development agencies within a 'diverse economy' frame, we can see that these schemes seek to strengthen or establish women as self-employed workers in small enterprises that are modeled upon capitalist enterprise. The 'development dream' is that, through good fiscal management and innovative product development, some of these micro-enterprises will become fully-fledged capitalist enterprises, and the economic benefits will then flow to the wider society.

At the base of the development dream is faith in the incredible productive capacity of capitalist enterprise to generate wealth that can then 'float all boats,' supporting higher standards of living and increased levels of well-being. What is rarely a part of this dream, however, is the mechanism by which these benefits will be distributed (let alone redistributed) to all *beyond* those who actively participate in the capital investment or labor markets. The 'us all' that constitutes the majority of society not directly participating in these markets (where some 'return' can be expected) is left out of the picture. The ethical dimensions of surplus generation, its distribution, and its role in building society are not up for discussion in mainstream development discourse, despite ample evidence that the disparities wrought by capitalist development are not disappearing, either within many national economies or on a global scale.

In contrast, the project of building and strengthening community economies assumes that the production and distribution of economic benefit cannot be left to chance. It involves a vision of the economy as an ethical space of negotiated interdependence rather than a self-regulating structure automatically producing (via the invisible hand) increased social well-being through the unbridled pursuit of self-interest. In an environment where the development apparatus is explicitly engaged in producing the entrepreneurial subjects of a capitalist order, it is necessary to pursue an alternative 'politics of the subject,' cultivating 'interests' in community economies and capacities to construct them. Not surprisingly it is primarily in the process of building economic alternatives that alternative subjects and capacities emerge.[12]

Women Building Community Economies in Place

Below we examine two projects in which women are taking decisions to build new kinds of economy—economies in which social interdependence (economic being-in-common) is acknowledged and fostered and new kinds of community are produced. Each story attests to the power of place as a site of economic diversity and potential rather than a colonized node in a capitalist world. Each shows women as activists building and strengthening their community economies. And each highlights the constitution of communal subjects through the project of building a community economy in place.

Filipina Migrants Building the Community Economy

The international migration of Filipino workers for employment is a central economic strategy for the government of the Philippines, where migrant remittances currently constitute the major source of foreign exchange, exceeding direct foreign investment. Officially reported remittances amounted to more than $US 7 billion per year for the past three years and are projected to reach more than $8 billion in 2004 (Mellyn, 2003; Domingo, 2004).[13] Since this amount exceeds foreign aid for development, the Philippines government, like the governments of other migrant-sending nations, is beginning to consider the development potential of migrant remittances.

Migration is also an important individual and family strategy, with younger workers (the majority of whom are women) leaving home to seek work, primarily in domestic service or merchant seafaring jobs. Conservative estimates place the current number of Filipino overseas migrants at 7.5 million, roughly 10 percent of the population. If the remittances of each of those migrants reach on average five people, then well over half of the 76 million Filipinos are directly affected by flows of migration and migrant remittances.

At the turn of the twenty-first century, there were almost one hundred fifty thousand Filipina domestic workers in Hong Kong alone (Villalba, 2001). The bulk of these women's remittances go to their families to expand their consumption and raise their standards of living. But some of them have begun to question the exclusive use of their savings for family consumption, recognizing that such use condemns them (and eventually others) to continued migration for employment. Although supporting their families is important to them, many also want something additional from the migration experience: ". . . we wanted to be recognized in our home town, to make a difference in our place, and to make something of ourselves. Some of us even thought of bringing change in our community" (Filipina migrant, quoted in Villalba, 2001: 81).

An opportunity to 'bring change to the community' is currently being provided by an innovative NGO called the Asian Migrant Centre (AMC). Rather than pursuing the usual NGO strategy of providing services to migrants, the AMC has instead taken up the project of fostering economic activism among them. This has involved a two-pronged initiative: 1) supporting the unionization of domestic workers, and mobilizing their political activity around issues in the host country involving wages, benefits, working conditions, and immigration policy, and at the same time 2) fostering savings groups to marshal funds for investment to create businesses in the women's home communities. From the perspective of the AMC, migration is a temporary experience that can be instrumental not only in transforming family and individual futures but also in creating sustainable economies in women's localities of origin (Gibson, et al., 2001).

Savings groups are made up of five to twenty women who are usually able to save about 5 percent of their wages (approximately HK$200 per month) (Gibson, et al., 2001). They work with NGOs based in the Philippines to develop investment and business plans, often involving local community and family members in various capacities. One of the organizations pioneering community enterprise development in collaboration with the AMC is Unlad Kabayan, an NGO that is currently fostering projects in eight provinces of the Philippines. With the assistance of Unlad, migrant savings groups are investing in organic chicken farms, rice milling, ube (aromatic yam) processing and confectionery making, a general store, and a coconut coir manufacturing plant, among other businesses. The hope is that such enterprises will reduce and eventually replace the need for continued, cyclical out-migration.

We are engaged in a collaborative action research project with Unlad, the local government, and members of the community to develop a number of enterprises in the coastal town of Jagna on the island of Bohol. Potential projects involve a group of porters at the local port who are researching the feasibility of a trucking business that could connect upland farmers with urban markets; women who have received sewing training and are investigating the possibility of producing and hiring out ceremonial robes, such as togas for school graduations or wedding and bridesmaids dresses; and various primary producers who are interested in value-added production of locally identified products, such as virgin coconut oil for the local and export markets.[14] The project participants (including migrant investors, the research team and NGO staff, and local collective entrepreneurs) are committed to establishing businesses that accord with values other than profit maximization and to cultivating subjects other than the self-interested individual—investors, workers, and managers who are capable and desirous of constructing a community economy in place. What that involves is continually negotiating the goals and relationships of each enterprise, taking into account their impacts on social well-being and ecological sustainability, and their potential for increasing the surplus available for building the community economy.

To understand the current and potential success of the AMC, Unlad, and the women migrants, it is important to recognize the micropolitics of self-formation that accompanies the women's involvement in savings groups for alternative investment. Women migrants who participate in savings groups are making the decision not to consume their wages in Hong Kong, and thus are drawing a boundary between their necessary and surplus labor, taking the decision to reduce consumption in order to constitute a surplus available for other things. They are also deciding not to distribute their entire surplus to their families' consumption fund, but instead to reserve a portion for community-oriented investment.[15] Through the lens of class analysis we can see that these women constitute a new class position for themselves as independent appropriators and distributors of their own surplus. While they may inhabit simultaneously the class position of exploited and indentured laborer (a portion of), whose surplus is appropriated by their employer, their new independent class position is nonetheless empowering. Moreover, the distribution to community enterprise projects adds a communal class identification to their independent and indentured ones (Gibson, et al., 2001; Gibson-Graham, 2004a). Thus they are redefining themselves not only as self-appropriating (of their surplus) but also as ethical subjects of a community economy.

Women Building the Community Economy in Mararikulam

Mararikulam is one of the poorest areas of the coastal Indian province of Kerala. Yet in this district, literacy rates are above 90 percent, infant mortality is low, and life expectancy is greater than seventy years—indicators that are close to what we would expect in a wealthy country (Franke, 2003: 8). Currently Kerala is engaged in what they call the "Mararikulam experiment"—an adventure in generating local income and employment for the poorest of the poor, inspired by the Mondragon experience in the Basque region of Spain. At the heart of Mondragon's success in generating local employment and increasing standards of living is a strong base of worker-owned industrial cooperatives in which the workers appropriate the surplus they produce (rather than it going to the capitalist or to the board of directors of a capitalist firm). The cooperatively produced commodities are marketed locally, nationally, and internationally. And the industrial co-ops are supported by 'second degree' cooperative organizations that function to redistribute a proportion of the surplus generated toward creating more co-ops, including not only more industrial co-ops but also co-ops providing education (from preschool through university), housing, health care, and social security (Gibson-Graham, 2003a).

Mondragon provides an inspirational model of a community economy built around the generation, marshaling, and distribution of surplus. But any examination of the Mondragon experiment must be struck by the contingent conditions prevailing in the Basque region that presented those cooperators with their particular challenges. This place-based model cannot be transported to any site in the world and expected to work without modification. In each site the particular and contingent conditions will present their own challenges, shaping the decisions made and pathways followed. The insight that surplus *is* generated and that wealth *can be* shared equitably and democratically is what Mondragon teaches us.

The Mararikulam experiment is not only following and adapting the Mondragon model, but also building on decades of struggles for social justice in Kerala and most recently the province-wide 1996–2001 Kerala People's Plan Campaign that lifted literacy levels and engaged people in planning processes through innovative grassroots initiatives carried out in each village (Isaac, et al., 1998). In the spirit of self-reliance associated with Mahatma Gandhi, and as part of this experiment, over fifteen hundred neighborhood savings groups made up of twenty to forty women are transforming themselves from credit associations to production cooperatives.

The exclusive emphasis on women's involvement is a way of addressing issues of gender equity and women's empowerment in Kerala, developing women's productive power to enhance their social and political power. The first step has been to generate capital by organizing women to redefine some of their meager earnings as a surplus to be saved and invested rather than as a part of the necessary consumption fund. Even very small amounts, when saved by seventeen thousand women, have yielded enough to capitalize a number of small cooperatives (Franke, 2003: 9).

This is where the Mararikulam experiment is both building on and going beyond the development approach of the Grameen Bank of Bangladesh, which has demonstrated the benefit that savings and small-scale loans can have on women's livelihoods. In Mararikulam the lending structure is organized and controlled by elected committees of the women's neighborhood groups, not an outside bank bureaucracy. Members of the savings group are linked not just via the social monitoring of saving and loan repayment, but also as potential worker-owners in a collective income-generating enterprise. The usual projects that target savings and microcredit involve women working alone in self-employed microenterprises; and the level of marketing, technological, and quality control support is minimal, thus increasing the vulnerability of the exercise and diminishing its chances of growing beyond a certain small size. Rankin (2001) has also pointed out the dangers of programs that rely on collective disciplining of individual repayment behavior resulting in an undermining of other aspects of the community economy such as traditional sharing practices. In the Mararikulam case, the emphasis on microcooperative enterprises attempts to address the individualization of these initiatives. Moreover, the small co-ops are supported by a centralized marketing and capital management corporation that provides services to all the microenterprises across the larger community.[16] Purchasing these services involves a distribution of surplus generated in the small-scale enterprises, but it is a distribution that ensures the likelihood of success of the microcooperative and the sustainable generation of an income for the poor women involved.

The goal of the Mararikulam experiment is to generate up to twenty thousand jobs "paying enough to bring households above the poverty line" (Franke, 2003: 8) by creating a big federation of small co-ops. The initial co-ops started by producing soap, an ideal product not only because it can be made using coconut oil, an abundant local product, but also because Kerala consumes more soap per capita than the rest of India. At a meeting held in 2002, thirty thousand women took the Mari soap pledge, to buy Mari soap rather than imported brands, in a conscious act of resistance to corporate globalization as well as an affirmation of local self-reliance.

By 2003 the second stage was underway, with co-ops producing semiprocessed foods, umbrellas, school notebooks, school bags, and kits. The third, more ambitious stage will develop Mararikulam's food producing potential, including fish farming and processing the ocean catch of fish, shrimp, and mussels. It will also develop more technologically advanced employment in the manufacture of coir (coconut fiber) products such as geotextiles and packaging. Here they will become exporters, producing food and manufactured products beyond the local capacity for consumption.

The basic idea of the Mararikulam experiment is that local 'wealth' can be collectively marshaled to bring people out of poverty. Local governments and the worker-owners themselves supply more than 40 percent of the investment funds for this experiment, with additional funding coming at this stage from provincial and international agencies. Rather than relying on the promise of a trickle-down of benefit from the development of capitalist enterprise, the women of Mararikulam are taking matters into their own hands, deciding to use their own savings to leverage funds from community-based organizations to build self-reliant worker cooperatives in which they are the first receivers and distributors of their own surplus. Through constructing the capacity to generate surplus in cooperative enterprises that are collectively supported by community-wide organizations,[17] the women of Mararikulam are maximizing the chance that benefits will be widely shared and constituting themselves as communal economic subjects in the process.

A Concluding Thought on the Politics of Place

What is encouraging and inspiring to us about these stories of women who are building community economies in place is not just the evidence of local success, though this is indeed remarkable and hopeful. Much more broadly, however, we believe that we are witnessing the emergence of a new economic politics—one that is place-based, yet globally distributed in localities and regions on every (populated) continent (Gibson-Graham, 2004b; Osterweil, 2004c). A number of factors have conspired to delay the widespread recognition of this emergent politics, not least of which is the tendency to privilege the global as important and transformative while denigrating the local as contained and co-opted—especially where economic politics is concerned. Another factor of course is the global/local binary itself, which makes it difficult to perceive the two poles coexisting in one political form. And yet this is indeed what seems to be happening—a *globally* emergent politics of *local* economic construction, based on widely shared values of autonomy, self-sufficiency, and community. We can recognize this politics in the 'movement of movements' and the World Social Forum, in the popular fascination with the experience of the Zapatistas and the Argentine unemployed workers' movement, in the explosion of books, articles, videos, and Web sites covering these movements, as well as local economic projects that are less well known. It seems something is happening simultaneously on the local and global scales.

At the beginning of the chapter, we spoke of the way that second wave feminism has shaped and motivated our place-based economic politics. Feminism became a global movement not because it was globally organized, but because women are everywhere. And of course not only are women everywhere, but so are economic practices, resources, relationships, and organizations. What this suggests to us is the globally transformative potential of place-based initiatives, as economies are (re)constructed locally, and participants are linked across distance through mutual learning, ties of cooperation, and local identifications with a global 'movement.' It is this new global politics that WPP is helping to bring to (self)recognition, and that offers the possibility of far-reaching change.[18] We are excited to be living in these terrible times.

Notes

1. Cameron and Gibson-Graham (2003) provide a review of this literature.

2. From a capitalocentric perspective, these activities are often seen as remnant social or cultural practices rather than (an arguably growing) part of contemporary economies.

3. Clearly more dimensions of difference could be added; for example, property and resource ownership.

4. Indeed North comments that "it is a peculiar fact that the literature on economics . . . contains so little discussion of the central institution that underlies neo-classical economics—the market" (North, 1977, quoted in Callon, 1998: 1).

5. While the vast extent of the literature on gift giving and ritual exchange has focused on these practices in 'traditional' societies (see, for example, Gudeman [2000] for an overview), recent research in 'the West' has highlighted the huge significance of gift giving, sharing, and obligatory allocations between extended kin and other networks (church groups, locality-based communities, etc.) (Community Economies Collective, 2001; Godbout, 1998). Feminist Genevieve Vaughan (1997) theorizes a parallel economy of generosity existing alongside the "exchange economy." She sees giving as an extension of mothering and as a practice that resists calculations of commensurability.

6. Attempts to recoup and develop Marx's economic analysis of surplus production, appropriation, and distribution have rekindled an interest in an antiessentialist economic language of class (as opposed to a language of social distinction) (Resnick and Wolff, 1987; Gibson-Graham, Resnick, and Wolff, 2000, 2001). This language is nonsystemic and offers the possibility of theorizing the complex coexistence of multiple class processes in the constitution of contemporary societies and subjects. It is also nonlinear in that it is released from a teleology of economic development, where feudalism gives way to capitalism, capitalism to socialism (or to the end of history). In other words, it allows a reinstatement of history and contingency in the domain of economy. It denaturalizes dominance, making capitalist dominance a historical and theoretical question rather than a natural feature of capitalism. We are interested in developing and bringing this class language to a position of more prominence in an alternative (counterhegemonic) discourse of economic difference.

7. Hindess and Hirst (1975: 26) clarify this point when they state, "surplus labour . . . exists in all modes of production because the conditions of reproduction of the labourer are not equivalent to the conditions of reproduction of the economy."

8. A failure to be attentive to this difference blinds us to the potential for there to be 'good' capitalist firms/employers and encourages myopia when viewing the downside of communality or socialism.

9. For the most part, economic diversity has been framed in the familiar terms of market vs. state (this is what gives us the Third Way and the Social Economy as 'the' alternatives), or in the evaluative hierarchies of traditional and modern, backward or developed that permeate and perpetuate the project of capitalist development.

10. Such a politics of course always confronts the dangers of posing positivity, a normative representation of the community economy, in which certain ethics and practices are valued over others. For instance, the language of the diverse economy recognizes the contemporary prevalence of slavery as a mode

of economic organization, indentured labor as a form of remunerated labor, and theft as a mode of transaction. All are sites in which the sociality and inter-dependency of economic relations is not hidden but is violently and coercively present. It is difficult to imagine the place of these practices in a discourse of community economy that can counter the hegemonic hold of capitalism on the ideas of freedom and democracy. And yet theft is often the only resort of the poor for economic survival, and when it involves reclaiming what has been unlawfully taken, as in common land, resources, or intellectual property, it may be construed as a legitimate mode of economic redistribution. Likewise indentured labor per-formed in one national economy might generate savings that can be used to start community enterprises in another. On what basis might we exclude or include such activities in the practice of building community economies?

11. "Ethnographic studies have shown that in some microcredit pro-grammes group members vigorously monitor one another's consumption pat-terns to ensure cash reserves are devoted foremost to loan repayment. In prac-tice, the groups can thus generate an environment of hostility and coercion that polarizes, rather than unites, their members" (Rankin, 2001: 32).

12. When unemployed workers in Argentina took over abandoned factories after the economic crisis of 2001, the obstacle they encountered was not the state or capital—which were after all in disarray—but their own subjectivities. They were workers, not managers or sales reps or entrepreneurs, and as one of them said, "If they had come to us with fifty pesos and told us to show up for work tomorrow, we would have done just that." Instead, for lack of an option, they found themselves recreating Argentine manufacturing. Just as they had formerly constituted a capitalist economy through their identifications and daily practices as workers, so they are now constituting an economy and sociality of 'solidarity' as members of the unemployed workers' movement (MTD). That this requires "a struggle against themselves" is one of their principal tenets and observances (Chatterton, 2005: 26, quoting Colectivo Situaciones). For the MTD, combating capitalism means refusing a longstanding sense of self and mode of being in the world, while simultaneously cultivating new forms of sociability, visions of happiness, and economic capacities (Colectivo Situa-ciones, 2004: 13). It is as though they had taken up the challenge of economic subjectivity that Foucault identified many years earlier, and made it the touch-stone of their movement:

> The political, ethical, social, philosophical problem of our days is not to try to liberate the individual from the economy . . . but to liberate us both from the economy and from the type of individualization that is linked to the economy. We have to promote new forms of subjectivity through the refusal of this kind of individuality, which has been imposed on us for several centuries. (Foucault, 1982: 216)

13. Mellyn (2003) estimates that this amount would be doubled if unregu-lated remittances were taken into account.

14. This is a project Katherine Gibson is involved in with Australian National University (ANU) colleagues Deirdre McKay, Kathryn Robinson, and Andrew McWilliam, and doctoral students Amanda Cahill and Jayne Curnow (Australian Research Council Grant No. LP0347118 "Negotiating alternative economic strategies for regional development in Indonesia and the Philippines").

15. This transformation often involves internal conflict and conflict with the agendas of family members:

> Because I am the youngest in the family I only supported my father and mother. . . . I told them before I come here in Hong Kong from working in Singapore, "I only have to send you 1,500 pesos every month." Because I said "I want to save my income." So I am not planning on staying in Hong Kong for long, for many years. So I want to come back home in a few years. (Gibson, et al., 2001)

16. The marketing firm works on establishing brand loyalty (for example, the Mari soap pledge discussed in the following paragraph), and will also "arrange economies of scale where practicable, will oversee product quality to facilitate out-of-region markets, will assure consistent health and safety standard in all the local units" (Mararikulam Experiment Project Web site, page 2).

17. Indeed the construction of local health care clinics is part of the accompanying project of improving public health, health care, and nutrition.

18. This does not mean that other types of politics are no longer necessary or appropriate, or that women in place do not have to negotiate the realities of global power. Rather it is an acknowledgment that there is more than one political way forward, and an attempt to discern the outlines of an emerging political imaginary (Graham, 2002; Gibson-Graham, 2004b; Osterweil, 2004c). For a longer discussion of the politics of place as it relates to the politics of empire, see Gibson-Graham, 2003b.

10

Place-based Politics and the Meaning of Diverse Economies for Women and Young People in Rural Finland

LIISA HORELLI

For the past twenty years, Nordic women have been conducting a place-based politics through the creation of networks for social cohesion with significant impact on diverse economies and the infra-structures of daily life. This chapter presents two case studies of place-based politics in rural Finland, highlighting the interrelations between networks for social cohesion and diverse economies. While these instances of place-based politics resonate with the vision of this book, they have to be analyzed in their specificity.

Place-based Politics as Networking for Social Cohesion

Citizens of the industrialized world are increasingly living in network societies. Castells (1996) states that network societies are characterized by global flows of information, finance, and technology and that these subordinate localities and places. Localities are increasingly seen as part of regions forced to compete with one another in order to become an attractive space for desired flows. The winners are those who have the know-how to take advantage of the opportunities of globalization. One of the strategies that has been applied in this competition for economic survival is the building of regional development networks (Kostiainen, 2002). The actors in these *networks of competitiveness* are usually 'big

158

players, such as enterprises, public institutions, financial agents, and universities (Cook, et al., 2000).

In this view, the losers are those unable to cope with the negative impact of globalization, and who lack control over local decisions. The negative effects can be felt not only in developing countries but also in many Western nations, especially in the everyday lives of children, young and elderly people, and women. Consequently, there is a great need for creative social, cultural, and economic responses to these challenges. In fact, several citizen groups, particularly among the women's movement in Europe and elsewhere, have striven to find new solutions as they mainstream gender and intergenerational equality in planning and development (Horelli, 1998, 2001, 2002a). *Mainstreaming equality can be defined as the application of a set of gender- and age-sensitive visions, concepts, strategies, and practices in the different phases and arenas of the planning and development cycle* (see Horelli, 1997). The vision embedded in some of these efforts has been the creation of supportive *networks for social cohesion.*

The context of the Nordic women differs greatly from that of women in developing countries. The Nordic welfare society, which enables women to both work and raise children, is a long lasting project of the women's movement. The state is not considered an enemy but a guarantee that enables women to have an education and access to politics and the labor market (although with a 20 percent lower salary than men). In fact, until recently, the only area that had not been appropriated by women was local and regional development. The latter has been a separate, male domain, mostly dealt with in the cabinets of power.

At the beginning of the 1980s, the Nordic women's movement around housing and planning strove for 'a new everyday life' by creating a vision and a model of implementation that were based on the integration of work (production), care (reproduction), and dwelling (home, environment, and community). The central concept in this approach was the *collaborative creation of an intermediary level* between the private households and the public and commercial world of enterprises (The Research Group for the New Everyday Life, 1991; Horelli and Vepsä, 1994). The intermediary level is a new structure in the housing community or in the neighborhood comprising activities around the care of children and elderly, local production, and work, as well as local participatory planning and management of spaces. Examples of implemented intermediary levels can be found among cohousing settlements and working communities. Originally, the intermediary level referred only to a structure in the neighborhood, but it was soon expanded to include the housing area, village, or small town. It was then called the *infrastructure of everyday life,* meaning environmentally friendly housing, services, employment, mobility, and other participatory activities that support local residents. As the European women's movement (in the form of the EuroFEM-Gender and Human Settlements network) started to participate in the European Union (EU)-funded regional development, in the 1990s, these concepts were expanded to mean supportive regional and interregional structures (Gilroy and Booth, 1999; Horelli, 2002a).

Networking for social cohesion derives its meaning, on the one hand, from the opposition to the currently dominant principle of competition among the 'big players,' and, on the other, from the collaborative construction of infrastructures of daily life that might enable supportive cultures that enhance the survival of those groups that are dependent on their locality or region (Horelli, 2004).

The so-called holistic economics has played a seminal role in the creation and maintenance of the infrastructure of everyday life since the early 1980s. Hazel Henderson (1996) describes holistic economics as "a cake with four layers." It is based on the economy of nature, on top of which lie social and public economies. The icing of the cake comes from the market economy. The two basic layers, which make half of the cake, are informal and nonmonetized, whereas the other layers are monetized and part of the formal economy. Each layer has a different logic and markets for economic and social transactions, remuneration of labor, organizational forms, and assets.

Cameron and Gibson-Graham (2003), who criticize the "deification of economy" as the governing instance of society and the treatment of the economy as a bounded entity, are also critical of the risk of feminizing the economy by adding a separate sphere or counting in women's unpaid labor. Cameron and Gibson-Graham (2003: 152–153) prefer to speak about *diverse economy,* which brings forth the coexistence of different kinds of transactions, ways of performing and remunerating labor, and modes of economic organization. Diverse economy is a discursive intervention that can be redirected to social transformation (see

Chapter 9). Although the EU's structural and regional policy is based on the contradictory principles of both competitiveness and social cohesion, it only recognizes the market economy and measures (regional) competitiveness in terms of new jobs and enterprises.

As global capitalism has transformed the conditions for balancing power through the interplay of the state, enterprises, and civil society, there is an urgent need to strengthen movements that promote global civil societies, such as the Global Marshall Plan, the ecosocial market economy movement (Fitzpatrick, 2001; Malaska, 2004), and women's movements in defense of place. The present could be an auspicious moment for diverse economies, given that the market economy is affecting its main advocates, the Western industrialized countries. The massive transfer of jobs to China and India has already forced many actors to rely on the informal economy in Europe.

I argue that networking for social cohesion is a vital contribution to the economy in its expanded form, and that the recognition of the diverse economy is fruitful for individuals, communities, and economies themselves, as it allows marginal groups to survive in their localities. In what follows, I present two case studies on the politics of place in rural areas of Finland, and discuss the interrelations between networks of social cohesion and diverse economies.

Place-based Politics of Women and Adolescents in Rural Finland

North-Karelia (one hundred seventy thousand residents) is the easternmost region of Finland, which has a 300 kilometer-long border with Russia. The region is sparsely populated with vast areas of forests and lakes. Currently, the formerly agrarian region has many well-functioning clusters in forest and metal industries and several high-tech centers. Most municipalities provide residents free access to Internet and training for e-citizenship skills. The unemployment rate in North-Karelia is high, around 18 percent, and especially alarming among young people, who are increasingly moving to more prosperous parts of the country. Women in Finland are better educated than men; irrespective of this, they are less well paid than men because of the vertical (exclusion of high status jobs) and horizontal segregation of labor markets. Thus North-Karelian women work as teachers, nurses, and social workers, but not as entrepreneurs or engineers. EU-funded development initiatives have provided women and young people with opportunities to stay in the region and to have a say in its future.

My own involvement in these projects has been twofold. I have assisted the women and young people in codesigning their projects and applying for funding. As an action researcher of the Finnish Academy (the main grant-giving institute in Finland), I also have conducted thematic research on two cases that illustrate place-based politics in the form of networking for social cohesion.

Constructing a Network of Women's Resource Centers in North-Karelia

In 1977, the European Commission issued a call for proposals under one of their innovative pilot programs, RECITE II. RECITE II had a special subsidy for the "integration of women into economic and social life" through the creation of women's resource centers. Six interregional networks of women's resource centers were funded, each consisting of three to seven centers. Thus a supernetwork of thirty women's resource centers covers Europe from north to south and from east to west. One of them lies in North-Karelia (Horelli, 2002a).

Mirja Erlund, the inspiring source and chairperson of the entrepreneur-women of North-Karelia, was asked to join the Recite network of Italian, French, Spanish, and Portuguese partners that presented a proposal for the RECITE II pilot program. She managed not only to mobilize Karelian grassroots women behind the idea of founding a regional women's center but also to get funding from the Regional Council and the city of Joensuu, the capital of North-Karelia with fifty thousand residents. During the life cycle of the first project (June 1, 1998–December 31, 2000) the Karelli Resource Center was created and several smaller ones were started in surrounding municipalities.

The Karelli Resource Center, which consists of a five-room apartment with a kitchen in a three-story building at the center of Joensuu, has facilities for work (with appropriate information technology), lecturing, dining, and art exhibitions. The center started as an association, but turned into a limited company at the end of the project. The new company has a double organization, one official and another consisting of several local and thematic teams of volunteers and professionals. They mostly work on a voluntary basis and sometimes as paid workers of the resource center or of the recently founded cooperative, Napakka.

According to the external evaluation, the first project resulted in forty jobs, twelve new enterprises, twelve development projects, and one service cooperation. Some two hundred women were trained and mentored in business and development. International contacts—face-to-face and virtual—were formed with the southern partners as well as with the Russians and women from the Baltic countries. Altogether more than three thousand persons were mobilized in the first phase (Horelli and Sotkasiira, 2001). The informal and invisible activities comprise a large spectrum, such as mentoring, baking Karelian pies, harvesting berries and mushrooms, organizing events and parties, and so on (see Table 1).

Karelli has gradually become a recognized actor with multiple roles on the regional, national, and even international levels. Karelli is

- A physical and social meeting place open to everybody
- A network of diverse actors (women entrepreneurs, local and regional developers, grassroots, unemployed)
- A provocative mode of acting in which the soft (reproductive and voluntary work, handicrafts) is integrated with the hard (production and entrepreneurship)
- A symbol for women's entrepreneurship and regional development
- A functional and cultural intermediary level with a formal organization linked to informal groups or meshworks

The project and the resource center met immense obstacles during their trajectory, such as the financial and administrative bureaucracy of the European Union as well as intercultural and language problems that prevailed within the international partnership. The pressure to take a stand on femininity and feminism raised anxiety among some women, who were afraid of being ridiculed by men.

The evaluation disclosed that the project had an impact on the intrapersonal level, as many women had an opportunity to share their experiences dealing with self-confidence, sexuality, personal endurance, and well-being. The project also had an impact on the interpersonal level resulting in increasing networks that form the basis for a support-ive culture. In different parts of North-Karelia, meshworks were mobi-lized and, through Karelli, connected to formal networks around re-gional development. The region has now a potential pool of female development planners who are ready to manage almost any type of proj-ect, but in a different mode from the traditional one in terms of the rationality (of care) and the application of creative tools. Even trans-national networking has become routine. The exchanges have resulted in many voluntarily shared ecological and social initiatives.

The impact on the structural and symbolic levels can be seen in the new organizational, cultural, and even economic structure that Karelli provides as an intermediary. These active women have become visible and are no longer laughed at in the general discourse.

In addition, the new mode of integrating reproductive and produc-tive issues in regional development has been recognized in the Regional Council, which has invited the representative of Karelli to become a member of its executive committee. Even one of the priorities of the new structural program for the region is called the "Creation of infra-structures for everyday life." The latter has enabled women to develop project proposals that have brought forth diverse economies and oppor-tunities to stay in the region. Currently, the Finnish government has taken an interest in disseminating the results and in applying the Karelli approach in other parts of the country.

The Creation of the North-Karelian Youth Forum

The North-Karelian Youth Forum project (Nufo) was also part of my five-year-long action research funded by the Finnish Academy (Horelli, 2003). The research methodology consisted of applying techniques to mobilize and nurture the emerging network, traditional data gathering (questionnaires, interviews, participatory observation, psychological tests), and analytic approaches (content analysis, network analysis). The research questions asked, among other things, *how could the network(s) be mobilized and nurtured? What is learning-based participatory net-working like? What are the outcomes of the network at different levels or from varying perspectives?*

Although the Regional Council had been aware of the youth prob-lem for a long time, it had never had projects with young people. It took nearly three years to negotiate a special project to create supportive local and regional networks for and with adolescents. In Autumn 2001, Nufo was granted five hundred thousand euros from the European Social Fund and three municipalities (Joensuu, Kitee, and Lieksa). This made it possible to hire three young women and one young man to coordinate and manage the project for two years. They began to mobilize the network, in consultation with the steering committee and me. The steering committee was comprised by a variety of regional actors, such as representatives from the Regional Council, the municipalities, some schools, citizen organizations, and two adolescents.

The vision of the project, created with the participants, crystallized as 'a joyful North-Karelia with survival opportunities for young people.' The aim of the project was to create with adolescents and adults a supportive network to provide arenas of empowerment and opportunities to meet face to face and virtually. The objectives also implied possibilities for work and local initiatives through subprojects, enjoyable events, and having a say in the region's development.

The project was a success story as the networking managed to bring in new groups of participants of varying age and both sexes. More than five thousand people were involved with the project. Eighty percent of them were young people, slightly more women than men in the age range of 15–25. No significant gender differences were found in the amount of involvement, except that girls did not enter certain fields, such as information and communication technology (ICT) or skateboarding. The results revealed that 'activism' can be of varying sorts, ranging from drama, music, writing, politics, skateboarding, ICT, and environmental protection to organizing different kinds of events. As one of the participants put it,

> "We were a small group which founded this first action group that later on produced the Mopo-musical, then the Growth-project . . . and music events and others. It is a kind of 'save the world' work. We also founded an Internet café where four to five unemployed persons are working, subsidized by the municipality." (Laura, 17 years)

The young people's endeavors succeeded in creating small improvements in many parts of the region, such as spaces for playing music and drama, motorcycle workshops, Internet cafes, as well as mobilizing parties and other platforms for action. The adolescents themselves found that a transition from 'complainers into agents' took place.

"If the Forum had not been constructed, maybe we would still complain here in Lieksa. It (Nufo) has mobilized us." (Maija, 16 years)

The young people also thought that the Nufo-network was a mediator between the world of adults and the opportunities for action and joy. One of them put it thus:

"Nufo is, to me, a kind of catalyst that speeds up issues. I think that it is really cool that it exists. It is a kind of foundation that helps to spur on. And many towns still lack Nufos. I can't understand how dispersed people who want to have a say can do anything. If somebody gets an idea here, she knows where to find support." (Sirkka, 18 years)

In fact, the platforms for action eventually evolved into political spaces (Eyerman and Jamison, 1991), which enabled young people to articulate their ideas. These usually took place through a chain of events starting with a participatory workshop in a school that mobilized one hundred students and some adults, who later on continued to develop their ideas in local or thematic teams. New associations were sometimes founded, such as 'Save Spaces for Rock Music,' which succeeded in getting spaces and opportunities to perform their music publicly.

However, the voices of adolescents are frail and in need of constant nurturing. At the end of the project, the Regional Council was convinced to put up a new structure, a Regional Youth Forum with two representatives from each of the nineteen municipalities of North-Karelia. It has a yearly budget of fifty thousand euros to initiate development projects, which the young people themselves can choose. Currently, new adolescents-managed projects have started and the Nufo approach is being adopted by the municipal youth workers.

As conscious networking among young people was new in the region, a special emphasis was laid on capacity building of all the participants—young and old—in the use of creative consensus-building methods. The EuroFEM Toolkit (Horelli, et al., 2000)—which is a collection of tools and stories taken from women's projects across Europe, from southern and northern contexts—was of great help, as it enabled the participants to make a diagnosis of the context, to dream up their visions, conceptualize the process, and invite political acceptance.

The analysis of the process and results of Nufo allowed action researchers to propose a schema of the learning-based network model of development. It comprises only a core idea (in this case the construction of innovative arenas of empowerment for and with adolescents), the contextual analysis, the collective envisioning of the future with the participants, and a few shared principles of implementation (see Figure 1). The latter gradually crystallized into strategies of implementation that consisted of continuous organizing of meaningful events, participatory networking, capacity building, application of ICT, informing and marketing integrated to all interventions, application of art and creative methods, and ongoing monitoring and self-evaluation (Horelli, 2003). The chosen set of strategies encouraged participants to create and reproduce nodes providing a supportive infrastructure of everyday life. Central in successful networking is the gender- and age-sensitive coordination, which means constant negotiating and interacting with different partners.

Comparison of the Two Types
of Networks for Social Cohesion

The two cases are embedded in the same cultural context that makes the creation of social cohesion difficult because of the individualization of everyday life. They differ slightly in terms of their social basis, scientific approach, and actors. The North-Karelian Youth Forum was mainly situated in the life world—that is, in the practical, everyday life of adolescents—whereas the women's resource center project struggled both with the life world and the system (public and private institutions; Habermas, 1984). Nufo's background derived from the gender and intergenerationally sensitive collaborative planning (Healey, 1997; Horelli, 2002b), whereas the women's project had its roots in the network approach to planning and development. The actors of Karelli were mostly active women representing themselves as individual persons, but also private and public organizations. The Nufo actors were 'ordinary' young women and men, as well as adults, mainly from semipublic organizations and institutions.

Figure 10.1 A Model for a Learning-based Network Approach to Development

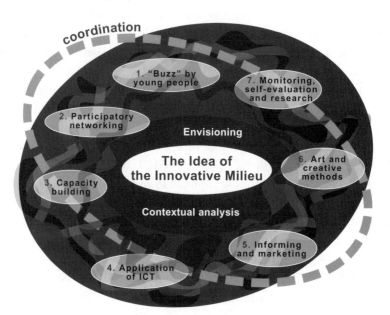

1–7 = STRATEGIES

Examples of nodes constructed during the implementation of chosen strategies:

1. Events, projects, employment, local initiatives
2. Local and regional forums, teams, linking of behavior settings
3. Seminars, workshops, self-evaluations
4. www.ponu.net
5. Marketing as part of all activities
6. Music, art, theater, roleplaying
7. Monitoring, self-evaluation and research

Both projects shared similar goals, namely the promotion of local and regional infrastructure for everyday life that would allow the participants to stay in their region, although the official purpose was the integration of women and young people into social and economic life. The main result of Karelli was the creation of the networked resource center, which later became a limited company. Several jobs, enterprises, development projects, and other informal initiatives were also created. Nufo did not achieve 'hard' results, but it had a multidimensional impact on the intra-personal (increasing self-confidence and agency), interpersonal (net-works and trust), symbolic (improved image of adolescents as competent persons), and structural levels. The infrastructure for the adolescents was described in Figure 1, whereas that for the women consisted of a mixture of increased activities around dwelling, care, and local production, as well as the network of meeting points linked to the resource center.

Table 1, modified from Cameron and Gibson-Graham (2003: 154), shows how the transactions of both the women's resource center and Nufo stretch from the market to the alternative market and nonmarket spheres. The economic organizations represent capitalist enterprises, pub-lic organizations, and alternative cooperatives and associations with a social and environmental ethic. Also, communal, noncapitalist formations are provided by both initiatives and various forms of labor remuneration.

The place-based politics of both projects has influenced mainstream thinking concerning the participation of young people and women in local and regional development. Not only have the doors been opened to new groups, but their 'softer' mode of acting has had an impact on youth policy and on development work itself, at least in the region.

Discussion

I have argued that networking for social cohesion in Nordic context is a version of place-based politics that enables marginalized groups to remain and survive in their localities. The framework of gender and intergenerational mainstreaming in planning and development con-tributes to feminist theorizing by integrating three types of knowledge: a. feminist concepts around equality; b. domain specific concepts that, for instance, concern housing, mobility, and diverse economies; and c. theories of change. The latter are closely affiliated with procedural the-ories of planning concerning methodologies for participatory processes. An example of domain specific knowledge is the substance theories of planning in the housing area. Hence, the collective construction of an infrastructure of everyday life that might bring forth a supportive culture of survival in the region (a gendered utopia of content), integrates all

Table 10.1 The Contributions Made to the Diverse Economy (based on Cameron and Gibson-Graham, 2003: 154).

Transactions	Labor	Organizational Form
Market	*Wage*	*Capitalist*
• Business training market • R & D market • Catering service market	• Manager of the resource center (RC) • Worker in the RC	RC as a limited company A restaurant enterprise within the RC Jobs at the training center
Alternative Market	*Alternative Paid*	*Alternative Capitalist*
Local trading system (under development) • Exchange of services Barter • Direct and equivalent exchange of services	Cooperative • Worker in the (Napakka) cooperative Self-employed • Pie-bakers and collectors of berries and mushrooms In kind • Work of the thematic and local teams of the RC in return for training and business opportunities	Environmental and social ethic • Local and regional women's resource centers (RCs) • Local development teams of women, adults and young people Cooperative • Service exchange cooperative (Napakka) Public organizations • Local youth centers
Non-Market	*Unpaid*	*Noncapitalist*
Flows within local and thematic teams • Members of the RC sharing tasks • Members of the youth associations or teams sharing tasks Gifts • Members of the teams and associations offer to help each other in the work	Volunteer • Volunteer-provided mentoring for young people and unemployed women • Performance of music and drama by young people	Communal • Women's resource centers (RCs) • Service cooperative ((Napakka) • Platforms of empowerment for young people

three types of knowledge. To conclude, I discuss the mechanism of change of networking for social cohesion and the latter's relationship to diverse economy.

The Mechanism of Change

A decade-long research project on the participation of children, young people, and women in local and regional development has shown that, as long as participation takes place within the paradigm of top-down planning, only minor advances take place (see Booher and Innes, 2002). Similar results have been obtained in the evaluations of the EU structural programs from a gender perspective (Horelli and Wallin, 2003). However, the learning-based network approach to development, and especially its version focused on social cohesion, enables planners to transcend some of the traditional gender- and age-related barriers to participation, because the position of the participants is more dependent on their personal know-how than on age or gender. The network approach also represents a different way of doing development, since it provides more space for improvisation and creativity.

The North-Karelia case studies showed that change takes place through planned and improvised chains of events that become part of the implementation strategies, which in turn produce nodes and links in the infrastructure of everyday life (see Figure 1).

A great challenge in the Youth Forum was balancing the tensions between the system and the life-world, instrumentalism and interactionalism, autonomy and interdependence. The young network coordinator and local managers had to 'wear different hats' in order to be able to both support the adolescents and navigate within the demands of the local and EU bureaucracy. Also the women activists learned to access and negotiate with the policy networks. Conscious networking requires sharp analysis of the situation, competence to produce credible and viable visions, and the know-how to apply a set of analytic, expressive, conceptual, organizational, and even political techniques (see also Kickert, et al., 1997).

A main technique used in both projects was the ongoing visualization of the networking process, which otherwise might have remained too intangible and fuzzy. The emerging nodes and links turning into a viable infrastructure of everyday life were regularly mapped on paper as 'amebas.' Their connections and position as hubs (well-connected nodes, like the resource center; Barabási, 2002) were discussed within the local teams. The ways of acting and producing results were described by schemas and models like the one shown in Figure 1. This increased the participants' critical understanding of what was happening, which in turn reinforced the supportive culture under construction.

Networking for Social Cohesion as Part of Diverse Economy

The contributions of the networking for social cohesion as part of the diverse economy can be made more visible by displaying them on a table. Table 1 allows participants and decision makers to see the multidimensional and complex structure that has been built into the region (see also Pietilä, 2004). In addition, the table demonstrates that the boundaries between the different types of transactions, remuneration, or organizational forms have been blurred in the sense that the same activity or organizational form can be included in several boxes. Similar results have been obtained from some British neighborhood renewal programs for fighting pockets of poverty, as well as from a comparative study on local development in six different European countries (see Lehto and Oksa, 2004).

There is increasing criticism against the co-option of women as mannequins of neoliberal economic development (Gibson, 2002). The conscious and careful managing of diversity in terms of both people and economy is, however, a necessity if sustainable results are desired. It is important to monitor and evaluate the quality and even quantity of diverse economies, despite criticisms of the accounting approach to economic activities (Cameron and Gibson-Graham, 2003). Thus it is possible to find out whether "the positive social values and self-directed structure of the invisible economy prevail in all sectors of goods and services provision" (Brandt, 1995; cited in Cameron and Gibson-Graham, 2003: 153). Evaluation is a way to make visible the significance of diverse economies also in terms of producing better concepts and improving the impact of the development process on the supportive value of culture. Recognizing networking for social cohesion as part of a diverse economy might reinforce the sustainability of the local and regional culture.

There is a great need for new indicators, as the existing ones, such as the gross national or domestic product (GNP or GDP) and even the

Human Well-being and Ecosystem Well-being Indexes, are far from satisfactory (Prescott-Allen, 2001). Nor do green and gendered budgets recognize the diversity of economy. The third column of Table 1 reveals that only the capitalist market economy provides allegedly legitimate indicators of successful development, namely jobs and enterprises.

Kostiainen (2002) points out that success in regional development is a polyphonic process. Success lies in the strategies of multiplicity and determination of doing things in parallel, in many fields, and in the fusion of cultures. Therefore, the outcomes of interacting network agents are collective constructions. Social and economic transactions in alternative markets could be recorded in terms of the quality and number of created cooperatives, associations, resource centers, and platforms of empowerment (Davies, 2002). However, noncapitalist activities in the form of "social surplus produced and distributed on the basis of ethical principles to collectively decided-upon ends" (Cameron and Gibson-Graham, 2003: 153) are still waiting for viable ways to be recognized. The transformation toward fair markets should also be reflected in the use of language. The currently dominant objective of development, the competitiveness of a community or a region, could be replaced by 'vibrance' or 'conviviality,' which implies both well-being and economic survival for young people and women. This could be an appropriate outcome of the intersection of politics of place, diverse economies, and alternative approaches to planning.

11

Placed-based Globalism: Locating Women in the Alternative Globalization Movement

MICHAL OSTERWEIL

Introduction

When I first began my ethnographic research on the Italian Global Justice Movement—what in Italy is known alternatively as *'il Movimento No Global,' 'il Movimento Dei Movimenti,'* or *'il Movimento New Global'*—I was not completely prepared for what I would find. Ironically, one of the things that had drawn me to study and engage with this movement in the first place was its complexity and the fact that there seemed to be no clear ideological commonality among its various components. In fact the Global Justice and Solidarity Movement (GJSM) was famous (or infamous) among critics and advocates alike for its extreme hetero-geneity and for not having an overarching ideology or clear set of demands. (One need merely look at the range of issues present at one of the protests where participants range from environmentalists to anar-chists, NGO workers, and a vast variety of others to get a sense of this diversity.) As someone who identifies as an activist herself, specifically one who has often been frustrated by the simplifications 'politics' seems to require of social movements, I was intrigued by the possibility these new movements posed.

However, when I began to speak to individuals, attend events, and read various articles and essays about and from the movement, I was overwhelmed by the extent of heterogeneity and complexity I actually encountered, as well as by what seemed to be at stake. Based on my previous observations of 'the Global Justice Movement,' especially in the United States and through the media, I had expected there to be a much more obvious orientation to the global aspects of neoliberalization. I thought I would find groups primarily focused on demands to 'reduce third world debt,' 'think and act environmentally,' 'oppose the International Monetary Fund (IMF),' and so on. But when I asked self-identified movement participants to explain the significance of *'il Movimento Dei Movimenti,'* they did not point so much to the *issues* of neoliberalism or globalization, nor to the transnational institutions like the IMF, World Bank, World Trade Organization, or even the Group of 8 (G8). Instead, they tended to speak at a different register, emphasizing the overall 'newness' of this movement's politics, including who were its main actors, their targets, and even the very nature of what was considered political.

Reflecting upon some of my earliest encounters with the Italian *movimento,* the significance of this newness, as well as the movement's overall complexity, begins to make sense.

Ethnographic Encounters:
Is this Movement a "Woman"?

One of the moments that stands out in my mind is the first time I attended a meeting of the Bologna Social Forum (BSF). The BSF is one of many local forums that sprung up throughout Italy leading up to and following the violent and massive protests at Genoa in July 2001, where over three hundred thousand protestors from all over the world (but mostly Italy) converged to oppose the undemocratic policies of the G8. These local forums were initially based on the model of the World Social Forum (WSF) in Porte Alegre that began as a global initiative in 2001. The idea of the social forums is to create open spaces to think and work through positive (social, political, and economic) alternatives to neoliberal capitalist globalization and the regimes of violence and war that sustain it, specifically and deliberately outside of the traditional representative political sphere. Remarkably—and before most other countries had begun to experiment with them—almost every city in Italy had set up a forum. Although they varied from place to place, overall they provided a space where organizations, movements, and even individuals without a particular institutional affiliation could work—to strategize, plan, and act—together in a way that was inclusive of the wide variety of oppositional realities, without subsuming them under one centralized structure.

In the middle of this particular meeting of the BSF (my first), Federico—one of the leaders of the then *Disobbedienti*—opened his remarks with a strange statement: he declared, *"Io credo che questo movimento sía una donna!"* (I believe that this movement is a woman.) He then went on to explain what he meant: this movement was female, because it functioned according to different logics than any movement Italy or the world had previously known. It functioned according to logics of difference, horizontality, and dispersion; no central group or singular ideology could control it, and it was propelled by an energy, from places, that exceeded those of traditional forms of leftist organization and practice. To him this was intimately tied to feminist notions of politics—and to the figure of woman.

After his remarks the room was filled with silence, smirks, smiles, and nods of agreement. I personally shared the ambivalence. On the one hand I was intellectually intrigued and somewhat in agreement with his claim, but on the other I was subtly disturbed. Besides a visceral reaction at the very use of the term *woman* to describe a movement, it made me uncomfortable because, throughout the meeting that lasted well over two hours, only two or three women had actually spoken. And when they did speak, they took much less time and spoke with much less authority than the many male activists that filled the rest of the meeting's time. Yet in spite of this rather blatant tension inherent in Federico's statement—the movement was a woman, but the women hardly spoke—something about Federico's words seemed significant. At the time I could not fully articulate why. I immediately thought of two earlier interviews that had already contributed to exploding all preconceptions I had held about what the Italian component of a global justice movement would be.

I recalled that, upon my arrival to Bologna, one of the first places I was directed to as I sought to make sense of the Italian GJSM was the Orlando Women's Center, located in the center of Bologna's historic Piazza Maggiore. I was told to speak with the center's director, Raffaela.

At the time, I only found it somewhat notable that a women's center was the first place I went. During the interview Raffaela recounted how, despite her earlier skepticism about the 'antiglobalization' or 'global justice movement'—both in Italy and in the world—she had come to believe that it was an incredibly important political development. Her change of mind took place after she was invited to attend the second WSF in Porte Alegre in January 2002. Since her return to Italy she had initiated and participated in a series of meetings with different components of the No Global movement in Bologna.

Throughout our conversation she was incredibly enthusiastic about the movement's prospects. (In fact, members of her staff told me that she must have been quite eager to talk about it, because she was usually too busy for interviews of this sort.) She stressed that there seemed to be something refreshingly new about this movement. It was something that, unlike leftist movements of the recent past—that especially in Italy had a rather troubled relationship to women's movements—pointed to immediate affinities between her work as a feminist and the myriad other actors who found themselves rethinking oppositional politics in the aftermath of the 'fall of Communism.'

She pointed out that both the themes and format of Porte Alegre and the larger No Global movement fit strongly with what she had been dedicated to for several years with her work at Orlando. In terms of *form,* she saw Porte Alegre as an 'open university' that embodied the sorts of relational, partial, horizontal, and knowledge-based political practices that had been lacking in previous leftist movements. Furthermore, the themes themselves—that she identified as 1) *sopravivencia, convivencia e felicíta* (survival, living together, and happiness); 2) economic alternatives; 3) the city; and 4) public space and democratic participation—not only reflected many of her political priorities but also stood in stark contrast to traditional leftist politics oriented at the state and organized through political parties or labor unions (Interview, June 2002). So even for Raffaela, although she did not put it in the terms Federico did, there was something significant about the relationship between a women-based politics and the emergent politics of the alternative globalization movement (AGM).

Shortly after my meeting with Raffaela, but still before attending the BSF, I was encouraged to speak with Giulia, a young woman studying political science at the University of Bologna. Interestingly, while I was told she was very active in the movement, Giulia had only recently begun to consider herself a political actor. Actually her activism began with the preparations for and attendance at the Genoa protests. Like many other young people, it was in the period leading up to Genoa and with the help of the political imaginaries coming from movements all over the world (especially since Seattle) that Giulia felt (for the first time) the desire and possibility to participate in meaningful political action. For her, as for Raffaela, there was something about the openness of the movement, its ideological and formal flexibility, and especially the breadth and the proximity to everyday issues of its thematic concerns that inspired her to get involved. Traditional political organizations had never appealed to her, but the movement that led up to and emerged from Genoa seemed, to her, to provide a space for real and qualitative participation in the goings-on of the city and in the world. (Giulia was one of several representatives of the Italian No Global movement to go to Palestine during that same year.)

Notably, in her interview—and this is the part I was thinking about in particular as I reflected on Federico's words—Giulia had also brought up the issue of women in relation to this movement. However, whereas for Raffaela the 'movement of movements' seemed to—at least schematically—coincide and match up with her feminism, for Giulia, experiences of marginalization, a sense of belittlement, and the hegemony of certain groups and practices over others in many movement spaces and at many events led her to identify a problem for the women in the movement. She argued that the movement seriously needed a woman-based politics—what she referred to as a "politics of relation" as the only way to be consistent with this movement's true goals and potential (Interview, June 2002).

While I am still trying to make sense of the myriad moments, discussions, and observations I had while in Italy and at various movement events—including social forums at Porte Alegre, Florence, and Paris—some things become quite evident from even the three moments I depicted above.

1. As I began to mention at the outset, there is a very strong identification of this movement as elaborating *a new type of politics:* one that specifically escapes and opposes traditional organizational

forms, and even challenges the nature of what counts as 'political'; a politics that instead focuses on sites and issues such as the city, happiness, relations, and participation and follows logics of openness, dispersion, inclusiveness, and specificity.

2. There is hardly any reference to a global scale or to affecting global policy. Unlike commonsense conceptions (and even my own initial assumptions) about what a *global* justice movement against neoliberal globalization is and ought to be, the moments I sketched above point to the fact that on the ground and to the people that comprise it, one is hard pressed to think about 'the global' in any simple way.

3. There is an interesting, even paradoxical relationship—both productive and problematic—between women, feminism, and the Italian global justice movement. For on the one hand there is an undeniable degree of overlap between feminist concerns, forms of organizing, and definitions of the political and those of the emergent AGM—even in the very practices of attempting to think through, name, and develop them. At the same time, however, we can see that the use of the concept of 'woman,' or the theoretical perspective of feminism can at times obscure and even hinder our ability to critically address the nature of women's *actual* participation and presence.

Toward a Place-based Political Approach

I do not think it was only because I was already involved in the 'Women and the Politics of Place' project or because of my own political desires and feminist dispositions—although I am certain they have something to do with it—that these three elements stood out to me. Rather, I believe—and this is the argument or notion that I would like to explore in the rest of this chapter—that the three characteristics I pointed to above (new form of politics, not emphasizing the global, and women-related) are themselves intricately, and even inextricably, related—to each other as well as to a larger political approach that can itself be understood as a corrective to the dominant ways of understanding and pursuing sociopolitical change.

That is, I believe that the AGM(s)—or at least significant parts of it—are potent examples of actual efforts to develop and use a set of political practices and strategies that, following the arguments in this book and elsewhere,[1] can be considered 'place-based.' I consider them place-based because they reorient and reinvent political practices to focus on the local, the present, the cultural, and other places 'closest-in.'[2] By doing so, they challenge older political models and generally go against commonsense definitions of globality. These practices are themselves closely related to, and in effect coconstituted by, the work of women's movements, their critiques, and their presence in local and international politics over the last three decades.

I use the term *coconstituted,* because ultimately these women's movements are themselves products of the influence and inspiration of various movements, events, and political experiences from around the world, some of which are not necessarily considered women-based or predominantly feminist.[3] In fact one of the questions that I would like us to keep in mind is precisely about the relationship between this feminist, or women-based, political theory and approach and the actual centrality of women to it. For, as we shall see, some moments, actions, and events that I would consider exemplary of these place-based politics do not—at least in any obvious way—have women at their center. At the same time, and as the moments I describe indicate, there is a difference between a theoretical and actual inclusion of women, as well as between theoretical and palpable practices of social change.[4]

Place-based Globalism

Coming to an understanding of this relationship, as well as of the notion of a place-based politics, has critical implications for how we make sense of the radical and transformative potentials of contemporary movements, as well as for what we understand *real* global, social, and political change to be. This is particularly important because, as of yet, the political challenges that these movements pose at all scales, and especially at that which we call the 'the global,' have been poorly understood—by people both internal and external to the movement. This has on the one hand contributed to misunderstandings of their current politics and, on the other, encouraged reductive visions of their political possibilities.

While I have already pointed to some of the characteristics above, it might be helpful to go more schematically through the notion of a politics of place—what, with respect to the AGM, I want to argue is actually a 'place-based globalism.' I do not want to suggest that all participants in the GJSM are taking part in this political approach, only that many do—some more consciously than others—and that, because of our own limited political lenses and biases, we often miss them.

The place-based political project becomes evident through a set of emergent practices and political forms—practices that are often experimental and that vary from place to place. Broadly speaking, we can say that these movements explicitly defy any simple economistic or political-institutional approaches to global social change. They do so by inventing new political forms and objectives that are based on a fundamental critique of representative democracy and include a greater attention to many aspects—such as culture, subjectivity, and process—that might be considered micropolitical and that can quite literally only be addressed in place. Direct action, networking, the use of carnival-like spectacle, democratizing all spaces and processes, and maintaining heterogeneity are some of the most common and indicative practices. Overall this means that participants in these movements work *locally* and in the *present* to point to and demonstrate the political relevance of many sites or terms that are usually either excluded from, or undervalued, in most definitions of 'the political.'

Place as Micropolitics

One of the most important elements of the place-based strategy that was quite evident in the examples I spoke of above is the very clear emphasis on the form and process of politics. In general, what this means is that while these movement actors work against particular policies and institutions, they place great importance on *the how*, or means of politics, rather than on their ends—at least when ends are defined in traditional political terms. Recall that Raffaela, Giulia, and Federico all spoke about the newness of this movement in terms of its openness and its decentered and antihierarchical nature. Movement actors work to build horizontal, flexible, and often temporary forms of political organization that in and of themselves enact—in the present and in place—the kind of social relations and political cultures they are struggling to nurture.

Taken directly from past women's movements, they pursue a 'pre-figurative politics,' "modes of organization that consciously resemble the world you want to create" (Grubacic, 2003). Rather than constantly deflecting their political aspirations to some distant future, as often required of traditional leftist movements, these activists believe they can only be effective if they live and work *today* consistently with their political visions for *tomorrow*. This shift in focus also forces people to recognize and pay close attention to the day-to-day and micropolitical ways in which oppressive relations of power are experienced. This is itself a response to what experiences like those of Giulia and myself with the Italian movement indicate—the fact that many of these oppressive practices are present even within political organizations and movements that consider themselves progressive and radical.

Although the experiences I spoke of at the outset might be considered 'negative' examples of the need for these prefigurative or micropolitical emphases, when one considers many other movement spaces, these focuses and commitments become very clear. For example, Intergalactika, an autonomous space at the periphery of the World Social Forum 2003, exemplified this centrality of process and form. It housed events and workshops committed to sharing experiences, debating ideas, and developing a political praxis based on the principles of horizontality, self-organization, antiauthoritarianism, participatory democracy, and direct action. In contrast to the rest of the Forum that was united against neoliberalism and war, this space was united, above all else, in its commitment to radically democratic *practices*.[5] Moreover, this commitment was far from abstract or ideological. The space itself embodied it: Participants were always seated in a circle so that experts never lectured to a mass. Attention was paid to the internal democracy of the meetings, so that if men were dominating discussions and few women were speaking, this was brought to the attention of the group and addressed. Although there was no explicit denotation of these spaces as focusing on women, the practices were feminist to their core.

Place as Difference

In addition, spaces like Intergalactika also pointed to another of the movement's characteristics: the importance placed on *difference* and *heterogeneity*. Apart from certain sessions committed to organizing specific direct-action events, the workshops were spent discussing specific experiences from which were teased general lessons and concepts that might be useful for other particular realities. There was never an attempt to come up with 'a' single model or 'a' campaign. Rather, speaking from particular and real experiences, the group collectively created a basis for thinking alternatives, always plural. Unlike traditional logics of leftist movements, maintaining the multiplicity and heterogeneity of the movement was not considered simply pragmatic or procedural—a tedious and necessary strategy to manage difference. Instead heterogeneity is seen as a necessary and constitutive element of worlds to be created. It is considered the basis for a new modality of being that is itself inherently opposed to authoritarianisms and universal logics of all sorts.

As such, implicit in these micropolitical and place-based practices, what I have elsewhere spoken of as 'cultural politics' (Osterweil, 2004b) is also a focus on social relations and subjectivity. For as the Notes From Nowhere Collective (2003) points out, "the fences of capitalism are also inside us. Interior borders run through our atomized minds and hearts, telling us we should look out only for ourselves, that we are alone." This means that these place-based actors believe that an effective politics must work *to create other ways of being,* not as a secondary or bonus goal but as part and parcel of the politics of the AGM.

Place as Network

This does not mean, as many have claimed, that these 'new' movements limit their purview and political desires to the local and small scale. It simply means a different modality of arriving at larger political issues and scales. Place-based movements see working from place—where place is understood not as closed or fixed but grounded and porous; not as outside of the global but as constitutive of it—as the only adequate way of dealing with the complex injustices and political paralysis experienced as a result of capitalist globalization.

As an organizer from Napoli states

> It is not anymore the 20th century, with "the political" on one side, and "the social" on the other; the labor unions on yet another. Our objective, even if it is unconscious, is to reactivate the processes of participation, to *re-appropriate in our own hands our own resources of our own communities, contexts, territories: From the little, without the big. Related to "the big," related to general themes, to grand values, grand issues, universal struggles, but, within the dynamic of the small, of the quotidian*—to construct forms of political participation that also make society. . . . Because ours is in fact the problem of building a global movement, not a global movement, that is, a movement that is well rooted in the concrete. (Interview, Porte Alegre. January, 2003; emphasis mine)

As is already clear, this has significant consequences for the ways these movements conceive of and work globally. For example, individuals certainly referred to their global ties with the Zapatistas and other actors from the 'global' movement, but those ties were not thought of as traditional forms of transnational coalition or solidarity groups. Instead, their relations were defined by the "great task of mutually creating and using symbols and practices with the Zapatistas to make struggles and battles in the territory" where they were (Interview, Bologna, 2002). Rather than opposing particular policies in global campaigns, the nature of these relations was based very explicitly on a *network* form that allowed for interconnection and mutual exchange, while the various individual nodes or groups of nodes each retained their specificity and individual profundity.

In this structure the various nodes (places) of the network are able to share new forms of organizing, new narratives, and new notions of the objectives of social movements, while at the same time being grounded in the 'real' and everyday concerns of people in particular places. This greatly contrasts with the sort of obvious and official connections required by older forms of internationalism and coalitions in which a centralized platform or program, often even an organizing structure, directed the relations and objectives of diverse participants without much attention to the coalition's relevance or usefulness to the particular place. Again, while not specifically focused on women in this particular example, one can clearly see both the influence of and potential for women's movements—especially considering the tremendous diversity in cultural and socioeconomic contexts that often make transnational solidarities and coalitions very complicated and difficult to sustain.

Place as Rethinking Globality

It is critical to understand that the use of networks is not about matching the changing nature of finance capital and other global flows, as some tend to argue (e.g., Castells, 1996). Unlike such dominant conceptions of networks, these movements' conceptions emphasize the fact that networks are comprised of myriad locally situated realities that cumulatively—both in intentional and less intentional cooperation—build a global politics. That is to say, based on both a strategic and ethico-political vision, activists deliberately choose to employ dispersed and small-scale strategies, viable only in a network form, in order to achieve global change. As such, they do not deny the importance of or ignore the global level, but pursue what they consider to be a more holistic globality.

For as Raffaela, Giulia, and myriad others have pointed out, older modes of international politics were missing something in their distance from the messier specificities and complexities of lived and particular places. Although they may internationalize themselves rhetorically and through the repetition of global themes and slogans that are important in multiple places, these international campaigns simply did not resonate on the ground, because they failed to touch down for long enough in any given place.

Unlike conventional definitions of globality—that I think are still the commonplace among many parts of the movement—these place-based globalists see 'true' or qualitative globality as comprised of many nodes, places, interconnections, and relations that at no point are totally consolidated into a singular global entity. Instead, in their diffuseness and local rootedness, they touch and involve increasingly more parts of the globe. For example, people often consider a movement to be global simply because it has chapters or groups throughout the world. But, as women's politics have exemplified, if they are not rooted in the priorities and real lives of the people in these various places their presence is almost simply nominal. As such, for something to be truly global, the quality and intensity of its presence needs to be taken into consideration. Globality as a total or universal project is never complete. Because it is impossible to see 'the global' as a totality if we acknowledge that we are always gazing from a particular place, body, or moment, one can refer to 'the global' as solely departing from concrete places/spaces that are themselves particular—and partial—takes on the global. For women in the movement this is particularly important, because, as we have seen, the moment one does not locate political practice in the messy specificities of a given space or action, its effects are often inconsistent with its theoretical goals.

As should be evident then, place-based globalism is not simply a tactical or technical perspective for effectively reaching the global scale; it also constitutes an ethico-political vision, a basis for revisioning political practice at a global scale without succumbing to a totalizing or universalizing approach that ignores and negates difference and specificity.

Concluding Thoughts

I do not want to come to any real conclusions, especially because I believe we are very much at a beginning. As I see it, these movements and their politics have the potential to be the beginning of a phase of transformative political invention and creativity. I could even argue that the place-based globalism whose traits and traces I have pointed to above has the potential to be *a truly feminist intervention* in the terrain of global politics; even more feminist perhaps than women's movements of the recent past, precisely because of its capacity to include so many different people and so many of those different people's most important issues.

At the same time, I must temper my optimism and hope with a cautionary criticality. For, as my interviews and experience with the Italian *movimenti* point to, there is a very fine line between the movements' potentially transformative feminism and a politics that masks new forms of exclusions under the rhetoric of feminism. This difference is something so material I have worn it on my body. For, whereas I vividly remember moments with the movement in which I got goose bumps because I truly felt like—even for just a few moments—we were already living in another world, in which the very ways people related to one another had been transformed. My same body has far too many memories of being saddened and angered by the fact that at times I could experience more sexism and exclusion in an activist space than in many other facets of my daily life. For me the key is to work to make both the potentials and inconsistencies in the political practices of these various actors visible, to push our movement to make its practices coherent with the politics of place many of us are already speaking about and doing.

Notes

*This piece was made possible in part through research funding from the National Science Foundation.

1. See specifically *Development* 41.2, and 45.1; Harcourt, et al., (2001) and Gibson-Graham (2004b).

2. Notions of places 'closest-in' have been developed mostly by feminist theorists such as Judith Butler and Elizabeth Grosz (see Harcourt, et al., 2001).

3. For example, the Feminist Encuentros that took place all over Latin America during the 1980s and 1990s both influenced and were influenced by various other movements. Notably the history of these Encuentros, as with the Zapatista-organized Encuentros For Humanity (1996, 1997), is not often referred to in the 'official' history of things like the World Social Forum, which are clearly at least partially outcomes of these experiences. For more information about the Feminist Encuentros, see Alvarez, et al., 2004.

4. For more on this question see J. K. Gibson-Graham, 2004b.

5. For more on this see Osterweil, 2004a.

Part Four

Displacements:
Women on the Move

12

Zapatista Women:
Place-based Struggles and the
Search for Autonomy

Marisa Belausteguigoitia

Introduction

During the last ten years Mexico has been exposed to the demands of indigenous people, which are related to their status as citizens and their juridical and cultural autonomy inside the nation. The nation as a whole and the world in general have been bombarded with communiqués and various performances referring to the unfair and marginal conditions in which Indians live in Mexico. Discussions about race and gender in relation to equality and citizenship have multiplied geometrically.

An increasing migration to the northern border—the United States—and the southern border, which is unstable because of rebellions and uprisings of Indian minorities such as the Zapatistas, has been the scenario of this decade, dominated by the erasure of local demands in global negotiations.

Feminist researchers in Mexico have focused on the particularities of women's participation in these processes of rebellion and migration and generally in every space, which involves female strategies for autonomy inside and outside their communities. Traditionally women, especially Indian women, had to negotiate intensely the specificity of their forms of liberation. Regularly their demands for change, be they in relation to access to equal payment, better working conditions, equal access to education, land ownership, or violence-free spaces, have been

190

relegated to the fulfillment of other forms of liberation, such as those represented by class or racial struggles for equality and the granting of equal opportunities for poor regions. My personal research focuses on the analysis of Mexico's southern and northern borders and the ways in which women negotiate the 'visibility' of their own voices and demands parallel to the solidarity and communality with these 'bigger' forms of liberation.

In this chapter, I look at the strategies for cultural and political autonomy developed by the Zapatistas, particularly by Zapatistas' indigenous women in the southern border region of Mexico.[1] I focus on the role of indigenous women in the strategies designed by the Zapatistas in order to construct their autonomy from a gender perspective.

The Zapatistas' rebellion erupted on Janaury 1, 1994, the very day that the North American Free Trade Agreement (NAFTA) began to operate. The Zapatistas' uprising was rapidly known not only because of the fairness of the movement demands, but also because of the development of creative communication strategies. Since then, the world has been bombarded—through the Internet, in staged events, and in numerous texts—by the Zapatistas' rhetoric and strategic ways of resisting and fighting for political and cultural autonomy, along with the development of coalitions for the construction of a democratic nation.[2]

A crucial document was included in the "Declaration of War" that was sent by the Zapatistas on January 1, 1994: the "Revolutionary Women Laws."[3] My critical position of the state and of the very Zapatistas' movement derives from the implications of "Revolutionary Women Laws," created originally by two Zapatista commanders—Susana and Ramona, as they are called inside the Zapatista Army. It represents the demands made by Indian women, in their own words and within their own frame of modernity and tradition, to the state and to Indian tradition. A document without precedent, the "Revolutionary Women Laws" began to change the way in which academics, activists, and intellectuals interpreted Indian women. It represented the first step of the Indian female struggle for autonomy and rights without mediation.

The intervention of women inside the Zapatista movement provoked the analysis of many feminists who were mediating and 'speaking for' the other. The Zapatistas' rebellion and the participation of women inside it has been one of the most important events for everyone interested in the development of a real democracy, but especially for feminist researchers who are strongly involved with the agency of Indian women with their speaking out in their own voices and with their cultural and political directions.

The "Revolutionary Women Laws" was released to the mass media along with the Zapatistas' declaration of war in early January 1994. The laws are considered laws because the Zapatistas want them to operate as rigorously as any other official and legitimate form of rights control. They are revolutionary because they both come from a revolutionary movement and demand an equal and better treatment of women, not only by the state but also by their own male revolutionaries and communities.

The laws synthesize the demands of indigenous women belonging to the different ethnic groups integrated under the *Ejército Zapatista de Liberación Nacional,* or the Zapatista Army of National Liberation. They refer to the right to participation in the revolutionary struggle, regardless of race, creed, color, or political affiliation; the right to work and receive a fair salary; the right of each woman to decide the number of children she wishes to have; the right to participate in the affairs of the community and the right to hold authority positions; the right to health and education; the right to choose a partner and not to be forced into marriage; the right not to be beaten or physically mistreated. They also call for severe punishment for rape.

The role of Zapatista women inside the movement has been extremely important for the movement itself and for a national and international civil society. Indigenous women have been immersed in a tradition that silences them and constrains them to the roles of mother and caregiver. Zapatista women have created a leadership that is parallel to the struggle for autonomy and justice within the modern world and has fought against laws, practices, and values of their own tradition that discriminate and marginalize them.[4] They have emphasized the particularity and locality of the female question and demands in front of the 'globality' and the national tendency to erase local tensions and specificities.

In this chapter, I analyze this long and complex process of autonomy developed by Indian women through three different scenarios. The first one looks at the construction of national identity through the analysis of a national and central mythical figure, *La Malinche.* Through revisiting the myth of *La Malinche,* I intend to unpack the hegemonic notion of national identity, which marks Indian women as betrayers.[5]

The remaining two scenarios represent two moments in the indigenous women's expression of the struggle for autonomy and citizenship. In the second scenario I look at the massacre that took place in Acteal (in the county of Chenalho in the Chiapas highlands) on December 22, 1997, during which forty-five women and children were massacred. In the third scenario I analyze Comandante Esther's discourses in congress and in the inauguration of *Los Caracoles* (The Snails) during the World Trade Organization (WTO) meeting held in Cancun on September 9, 2003. (The third scenario is described in three parts.) Both the Acteal massacre and the inauguration of *Los Caracoles* represent different moments of the ripping and suturing of indigenous women's bodies and tongues in their exercise of autonomy and citizenship. Both are related with the Zapatistas' rebellion that erupted in the state of Chiapas, Mexico, in January 1994. *Los Caracoles* represent the most recent territorial and cultural manifestation of autonomy by the Zapatistas.

Through the framing of myth, body, and discourse, I want to show the particular ways in which the Zapatistas have constructed their notion of autonomy, based on a specific appropriation of 'place-based strategies.' Place-based strategies point to the importance of local politics and cultures, but may obscure its own margins. There are also dangers of place-based strategies when they involve women. Actions toward autonomy are sometimes held with the total deprivation of women agency and at other times with strategic counterpoints; but rarely are they held with the complete power of representation in the hands and tongues of indigenous women. It is this exceptionality that I want to analyze.

The notion of autonomy, critical of practices that conform to *one* national identity, is linked to the appropriation of a specific notion of 'place.' Malinche, Acteal, and *Los Caracoles* work slowly within three strategic 'places' that transform dominant notions of tradition, national belonging, and identity into more flexible entities that involve minorities and women, local specificities, and demands. Therefore the nation's resources for hegemonic identity linked to the erasure of place-based strategies, along with the ethnic erasure of their own female agency, are strongly revisited.

Several questions emerge from these placebound strategies: In what ways does the notion of 'place'—as the preservation of tradition, local practices, and traditional knowledge—change when it is appropriated by indigenous women? What are the limits of these appropriations when they involve Indian women? And, as Wendy Harcourt and Arturo Escobar (2002) ask, how do women, locally and globally, communicate their place-based politics in ways that are transforming their communities' lives and, therefore, global interactions?

Transforming Images of Women

Little by little the Zapatista communities have changed the imagery of 'purity and contamination' related to the favors or maladies of modernity and tradition; and have accepted and reproduced practices, such as birth control, equal education, and participation in community decision-making processes, that were once considered 'poisonous' to Indian traditions. In the uprising, the Zapatistas favored female presence and representation. Modern practices, such as birth control, have been strongly opposed by traditional knowledge, but since the beginning of the rebellion, Zapatista women have voiced demands related specifically to gender oppression by the state and their own community, as stated in the famous "Revolutionary Women Laws."

Since the outbreak of the Zapatista rebellion in January 1994, the presence and representation of indigenous women has gone through various transformations. Indigenous women face a particular form of violence in these hybrid versions of modernity and tradition. Other questions frame the difficulty of obtaining autonomy for Indian women: How might the image of indigenous women change from one of women representing betrayal to one of women as citizens with agency, voice, and autonomous bodies? What kind of 'places' allow for these changes?

The First Scenario: Malinche/
The Indigenous Woman as Mother and Betrayer of the Nation[6]

The myth of Malinche contributes to the idea that indigenous women's actions for autonomy or independence are repaid by betrayal. Specifically, Octavio Paz (1994), a Nobel Prize winner for literature, describes the birth of the Mexican nation as the birth of a country of betrayed people.[7] In Paz's interpretation of the myth, Malinche is the one who, through her sexual nature—being 'open'—tends to betray.[8]

Historically representations of indigenous women have been used to organize divine and evil narratives for nationalist imageries. Discourses about both the good and bad indigenous women provide the images needed to construct the nation's vices and virtues, in the flesh by the virtuous virgins and the perverse indigenous women.

Malinche was an indigenous woman who was given as a present to Hernando Cortez, the Spanish conqueror, after his victory in the battle against the indigenous people of Cintla. Malinche's mother remarried after her husband died, and she conceived a second child. Fearing the splitting of the family inheritance, Malinche's stepfather convinced his wife to get rid of her. For Malinche, the ultimate betrayal was the one she suffered at the hands of her own family, her mother, who sold her as a slave.[9]

Malinche was Cortez's translator. Spanish chroniclers claim that she was knowledgeable, beautiful, and extremely well suited to translate the unknown world for the conquerors. This act of translating for the enemy was considered the ultimate betrayal against the nation and Malinche's own people, a kind of opening, a tearing apart of the nation's confidence in their women. Malinche is accused of selling her own people, which raises several questions: Who sold whom? Can a slave betray the master? Where was the nation she betrayed?

The myth of Malinche has been reiteratively used to convey women's, particularly indigenous women's, 'inherent' capacity for betrayal. Together, gender and race are seen as creating the vice and action of betrayal. There is no possibility whatsoever to elucidate Malinche's agency and personal voice in this myth; we know her only through those who used her for translation and those who sold her.

In this precise, historic, and mythic scenario, the act of slitting and raping refers to both the damage done by the body and tongue of an indigenous woman to a nonexistent nation, and the act of raping the body of a slave woman and 'kidnapping' her words for translation.[10]

Malinche as such, a translator and Cortez's lover, stood at the borders of communication: the divide between Europe and America, between Spanish and indigenous languages and between genders, female and male.

Notwithstanding the capture of her body and voice, feminist intellectuals have reconstructed a possibility of autonomous expression in

Malinche, albeit a fragile one that leans more toward a reinvention of her voice.

The Second Scenario: Massacre in Acteal/The Openings, the Splits

On December 22, 1997, forty-five indigenous people—thirty-two women and children and thirteen men—were split apart in a village called Acteal.[11] Women were raped; their bodies were slit open and mutilated. Their breasts were sliced off, and pregnant women were cut in half.

Witnesses report hearing the cry, "Let's kill the seed" when the bodies were attacked. What kind of interpretation transforms the call, 'Women and Children First'—a call emanating from the patriarchy, the power structure that protects its homeland by defending the bodies of women and children—to a call that depicts women and children as dangerous: the cry of 'Let's kill the seed'?

Raping and ripping were the acts of the ones who located the 'seed of contamination' and betrayal in female indigenous bodies. There are several interpretations of the reasons behind these acts of mutilation and assassination. One of them refers to the sympathy shown by members of the attacked community, a group called '*Las Abejas*' (the Bees), toward the Zapatistas. Solidarity was considered a form of betrayal expressed toward both the state and forms of resistance that were more ethnic and essentialist than the form the Zapatistas represent. At Acteal, the act of cutting and literally opening up indigenous female bodies asserts visibly the women's betrayal of the patriarchy.

Traditional practices define indigenous women in fixed forms, such as having an arranged marriage, having 'as many children as God gives them,' or, most commonly, going to the city to work as a maid. Indigenous women represent a 'remedy' against modernity; they are symbols of tradition in communities that are defined as ethnically pure.[12] The condition of being Mexican rarely offers these women a place from which they can exercise their rights. As women and as indigenous people they are sold into marriage, and therefore cannot decide whom to marry, and they cannot inherit land. These are only three of the most traditional forms of discrimination against these women.[13] Zapatista women, the insurgents, and women who enrolled in the military found other forms of femininity, citizenship, and tradition. They practiced birth control, married whomever they chose, and claimed inheritance and ownership of land. In spite of these 'modern' or nontraditional practices, these women still spoke their traditional languages and praised and practiced sewing and other forms of traditional women's work. However, such a mix of tradition and modernity created expectation of autonomy among indigenous women and concern among indigenous men.

The Zapatistas underwent an intense process of education against sexism, as several of Subcomandante Marcos's communiqués exhibit.[14] Even if these educational moments were incomplete, they nonetheless created real possibilities for female agency. As microscopic as they may have been, they represented another way of being traditional and female from a woman's perspective, a mix of modernity and tradition.[15]

Indigenous women are reconstructing their identities through the incorporation of modern practices and values linked to the notion of place-based strategies, which favor local traditions but with the inclusion of the sanctions and demands of change expressed by Indian women.

The Third Scenario:
Los Caracoles/Places for Hybridity and Autonomy

In August 2003, the Zapatistas announced a new cycle in their struggle. They announced the renaming of the autonomous zones from *Los Aguascalientes* to *Los Caracoles.* The Zapatistas decided to launch a new call during the recognition of the more than five hundred years of oppression through the dedication of *Los Caracoles.* They named this celebration 20/10 Fire and Words to indicate the twenty years of existence of the Zapatistas and the ten years since the start of the rebellion.[16]

Los Caracoles was the 'gift' of this national celebration and one of the effects of the learning process, the particular pedagogy developed by the Zapatistas during the rebellion. These places call for a transformation of the relationship between civil society and Indians, a relationship framed with the recognition of autonomy and voice emanating from Indians, not from the mediators, academics, or politicians who study or 'speak for them.'

Five autonomous regions constitute *Los Caracoles,* which is governed by a *Junta del Buen Gobierno: Corazón Céntrico de los Zapatistas frente al Mundo* (JBG; Committee of Good Governance: *Core Hear* of the Zapatistas in front of the World). This committee fosters dialogue between

Zapatistas and non-Zapatistas, autonomous regions and governmental counties, and between ethnic groups that practice different religions.[17]

Los Caracoles allowed the Zapatistas to redo what they know best: offering words, narratives, and symbols as weapons for their struggle. In spite of its literal meaning, 'The Snails,' *Los Caracoles* allows for multiple interpretations. According to the Zapatistas, snails represent the slow advance toward a new project for the nation, forming concentric circles as snails' movement would. The project involves education, jurisprudence, and culture and allows for a growing autonomy. Snails are the registers of memory of the state's betrayals. And according to Mayan culture, snails stand for both the heart and the guardians of heaven; they are the guardians of the people's hearts.

After the last visible climax of the Zapatista rebellion, known as 'The March of the Color of the Earth,' and the presence of Comandante Esther defending the *Acuerdos de San Andrés* (San Andrés Accords)[18] in Congress in March 2002, the government launched different, widely announced projects involving health, nutrition, and education programs directed specifically toward disenfranchised indigenous communities in Chiapas.[19] The Zapatistas responded with silence and refusal. They have established several autonomous regions where they govern and live according to their own cultural framework, renamed *Los Caracoles*.[20] These places existed already as zones of resistance prior to this renaming. These communities refuse all financial support, all educational or health programs—anything to do with development—from the government. The living conditions in these regions are extremely difficult; there are hundreds of displaced communities, and harvesting and any kind of work is difficult or impossible because of military intervention and forced migration. Under these conditions, the decision to remain Zapatista and be autonomous in these regions is a very tough one.

The relationship with civil society has also had its difficult moments. As stated by Subcomandante Marcos,[21] the renaming of the zones, the place of encounter between civil society and the Zapatistas also represents the need for civil society to change its attitudes toward indigenous people. In one of the communiqués, Subcomandante Marcos illustrates the misconception of solidarity toward Indians. He tells how, in one of the big deliveries of humanitarian aid made up of objects, clothes, and devices that urban people donated, he found an unmatched, pink, imported, high-heeled slipper. He states

> ... I preserve a sample, of how our people benefited through this war. It belongs to the 'humanitarian' aid collected for the indigenous people of these regions: a pink high heeled slipper, imported ... with no other half. I carried it with me in my back pack to remind myself, in between interviews, photographs, photo-reports, what we are for civil society after that 1 January: a Cinderella... How can we tell these good people, who sincerely sent a pink high heeled slipper, size 9, imported, without a pair... that we do not want to be the shame of Mexico? We do not want to be the part of the country that has to be made-up in order not to deface the rest. No, we do not want to live like that anymore. (*La Jornada,* August 10, 2003)

The Third Scenario:
The Voice of Esther/From Betrayers to Citizens

Comandante Esther´s Speech Before Congress: In August 2001, recently elected president Vicente Fox invited the Zapatistas to defend the San Andrés Accords before Congress. The rebels took the opportunity to travel from Chiapas to the capital of the nation. Subcomandante Marcos, as the Zapatistas' spokesman and internationally known figure, was expected to be the one to defend the Accords. Instead, however, the Zapatistas declared that Comandante Esther, an indigenous woman, would speak for the approval of the San Andrés Accords.

Comandante Esther's speech in Congress represents the fact that Indian women speak for themselves. Within indigenous cultures women generally hold the place of subordination. The "Revolutionary Women Laws" precisely show, in women's own words, the practices these women want to change or eliminate.

Comandante Esther demanded the recognition of their negotiations for their cultural and juridical autonomy. She related cultural and national prudence in such a way that the rights for indigenous women were considered of national interest. Through her speech, she repositioned the imaginary and real place of Indian women inside the nation and tradition. In Esther's words, "In the law (the Accords) it is clearly stated that . . . the dignity and integrity of women ought to be respected. . . . We do not want to be a separate nation. We want to be included inside the Mexican law" (*La Marcha del Color de la Tierra* 2001: 219).

In the second half of her speech Esther addressed the conditions of indigenous women. She spoke about their daily living, describing their survival strategies, cultural practices, and wrong practices that women want to be changed (*La Marcha del Color de la Tierra* 2001: 391–2).

Esther demanded access to national laws by making a clear distinction between what she considers bad habits and what she considers practices that preserve her culture.

The Third Scenario:
Esther's Message from Los Caracoles to the WTO

The WTO convention was held in Cancun in September 2003. During this convention Comandante Esther contacted civil society from one of *Los Caracoles's* zones and sent a message to the WTO convention. The message was addressed to the 'indigenous and peasant sisters.'

Act I: Gender and the Visibility of Women. In her message, Esther referred to the many ways in which national and transnational trade will make indigenous people and peasants disappear. To the categories of indigenous and peasant, she added the category of 'woman,' making visible this particular form of oppression and existence, which was formerly subsumed under the categories of race or class.

After referring to the market dynamics that exclude indigenous people from the competition for low prices, she refers to other problems. She pointed directly to men, rich and poor, indigenous and white, revolutionary and conservative. For indigenous women there are the issues of NAFTA, racism, and the way women are treated by men. In Esther's words, "We have to develop more courage to fight against humiliation and exploitation. We also want to say to men that they should respect our rights as women. . . . We are going to oblige men to respect us" (*La Jornada,* August 10, 2003).

Act II: Visibility of Patriarchy. The content and place of Esther's announcement represent a huge distance from the splits and rips of former scenarios. Here Esther's voice is contravening cultural norms of behavior and is demanding—not asking for—changes beyond free agreements and the state's forms of neglect and violence. "Because we are women, the rich want to humiliate us, but also the men who are not rich, I mean the ones who are poor, such as our husbands, our brothers, our fathers, our sons, our brothers in struggle, and the ones who work with us" (*La Jornada,* August 10, 2003).

Husbands, sons, fathers, rebels, conservatives, rich, and poor men agree on the place they grant indigenous women. Esther is conscious of this and no longer takes it silently. According to her statement, the notion of patriarchy functions alongside the structure of racism and class discrimination.

Act III: Visibility of Ripping, Raping, and Opening of Female Bodies at the Other Pole of the Nation. The Zapatistas have made several references to different problems related to the northern border (migration, violence, resistance to globalized markets) and multiple contacts between the Zapatistas, Chicanos, and migrant workers. During the 20/10 Fire and Word observance, several migrant organizations of *braceros* (wetbacks) held dialogues with Zapatistas and their advocates. The National Assembly of *Braceros* participated in these events, and narrated the common fights of Zapatistas and 'wetbacks.'

Zapatista advocates and *braceros* sat in a dialogue in which both groups referred to the promises made by the government, the land they worked that is not theirs, the new movement that was being constructed by them—mainly old people—and the ways in which they needed the understanding and collaboration of a wide range of associations, communities, and individuals.

Commandante Esther was no exception in these extensions of the concept of place-based struggles to the northern border of the nation. She ended her message with a reference to working women in the cities, specifically the ones who work in *maquiladoras* (sweatshops). She referred to the exploitation of urban workers, focusing on one case in particular: the assassination, raping, and mutilation of more than three hundred young women and children in Ciudad Juárez, Coahuila, on the northern border of Mexico. Esther spoke as a representative of *Los Caracoles,* and extended her voice to embrace the other side of the nation, the north, and the opposite pole that encompasses female exploitation and abuse. She stated that the assassination, mutilation, and raping were done because the victims are women, all poor and all young. She referred to the values of these bodies: "If the disappearing, raped, ripped, and kidnapped ones were male and rich, you would see how soon the government and the police would find the perpetrators."

The girls and young women who work in the sweatshop industry have been found ripped and raped, mutilated and opened. Many of them were left in the desert, half naked, with their nipples torn off, cigarette burns and deep cuts on their bodies, and in some cases . . . with only one shoe: a slipper.[22] Another way to consider poor women as the 'Cinderellas' of development is as the leftovers of a modernity that cannot protect, educate, and repair their slit, split young women.

Conclusion

The Zapatistas' struggle involves granting autonomy to indigenous communities inside the nation; it involves allowing these people the possibility of being indigenous and Mexican at the same time, to be ruled and governed under a mixed juridical and political system that represents modernity but allows for specific forms of traditional knowledge and governance that underscores the indigenous identity. This form of autonomy refers to the first level of visibility: the cultural, juridical, and political one.

Today the place of women inside the Zapatista struggle and their particular demands are sustained, sometimes even against the opposition of sectors of their own community. As a rule, the men of their communities allude to their acts of betrayal and to their defense as a 'fake' form of discrimination; that is, gender versus the real discrimination: racism.

The accusations of betrayal are constant and pervasive. The foundation of this betrayal defines indigenous women as particularly 'suited' to 'open' themselves to outsiders or forms of discrimination that are not considered central and, as such, to rip communal unity.

The tenuous voices of Indian women inside *Los Caracoles* show that place-based strategies, local forms of resistance, need to be strongly interrupted by women. Place-based forms of resistance are mainly constructed upon the silence of the most marginalized sections of the local region.

Indian women inside the Zapatista movement have spoken; the construction of autonomy defined within official documents has taken them into account, but in reality there has been little change. Place-based strategies are still regulated by patriarchal frameworks that involve silencing the "Revolutionary Women Laws."

The voices of female Zapatistas are tenuous and do not emerge when survival is the first priority. There is not much evidence, on the other side of the transformation, of civil society's 'behavior' toward the indigenous communities. Indian women's bodies have been terrain for dispute and punishment, as demonstrated by the massacre in Acteal. The voices of Indian women, such as Esther's, show the readiness of these women to represent themselves. Malinche may also speak for herself and eloquently underline what she wants with all the power of her words.

If Los Caracoles, representing both autonomous regions and place-based strategies, keeps silencing the specific demands uttered by its Indian women, the central feature of the movement—emancipation, cultural, and juridical autonomy as a call for plurality and diversity inside the Mexican nation—will be either a utopia or a lie. Snails walk slowly; they do not miss their direction.

Notes

1. For an accurate account of the origins and causes of the Zapatista rebellion, see Collier (1994).

2. A great diversity of texts has been written that allude to the creativity and singularity of this movement. See Ben Clarke and Clifton Ross, eds., *Voices of Fire: Communiqués and Interviews* (1994), José Rabasa (1997), and Josefina Saldana (2003).

3. See Clarke and Ross (1994).

4. For more on women and Zapatistas, see Lynn Stephen (1997), Marisa Belausteguigoitia (2002), Rosa Rojas (1994), and Giuomar Rovira (1997).

5. The notions of 'rip' and 'rape' both represent the 'openings,' or wounds, suffered by traditionally expelled subjects such as the Indians and particularly Indian women, when entering modernity. I am alluding to the notions of *rajada* (ripped) and *violada* (raped) constructed by Octavio Paz in his seminal text, *The Labyrinth of Solitude*.

6. There is canon that not only challenges the myth of Malinche by constructing her as the mother and betrayer of the Mexican nation but also presents a newly constituted myth that reinforces the sexist and racist interpretation of

the original tale. See Margo Glantz (1999), Cherrie Moraga (1983), Norma Alarcón (1989), Marta Lamas (2001), and Fernanda Nuñez (1992).

7. Along with his discussion of the notion of the 'bad woman,' Malinche, Paz identifies her counterpart, the 'good' woman figure, the Virgin of Guadalupe, who redeems the sins of the 'bad' one. In Mexico, such pairing of myths is not unique; several of the narratives describing the founding of Mexico are based on female counterparts of sin and virtue.

8. Octavio Paz portrays the female sexual openness, *rajada,* as both a sexual organ that is 'open'—as opposed to the masculine organ, which is 'closed'—and as a slit. This 'split' suggests that women tend to 'open' themselves more easily toward the outside world. As translator and as Cortez's lover, Malinche had to 'open' her body and her voice for translation. A former slave, she did not have the possibility to decide what to do with her body or her skills as a translator.

9. There are of course many other interpretations of Malinche that contest and critique Paz's interpretation, such as those by Chicanas and Mexican writers, which give Malinche a voice and attempt to revert this imaginary of betrayal mentioned above.

10. It is interesting to note that Malinche married Cortez. She gained status as a married woman—a 'signora'—and also inherited, although she had to fight for this right.

11. This community was displaced from a village called Los Naranjos because of the occupation of the military in regions that were Zapatista or contained Zapatista sympathizers.

12. To explore further images of indigenous women as 'remedial' supplements of modernity, see Chatterjee (1989) and Alarcón, et al. (1999).

13. The "Revolutionary Women Laws"—which included laws stating that women could not be sold into marriage, were allowed to participate in the decisions of the community, and had the right to education—left out women's right to inherit and possess land. In spite of this omission, indigenous women fully subscribed to the document.

14. See Clarke and Ross (1994).

15. Nobody could say that the indigenous women's exercise of autonomy and the consequent accusation of betrayal led to the massacre in Acteal, but it definitely played a role in the perversion, hate, and the actions of ripping and raping.

16. The celebration and campaign, 20/10 lasted for more than three months on the Web and in specific locations in Chiapas, Mexico City, France, Greece, and Spain—places where the Zapatista presence is visible. A wide array of events was arranged: conferences, dialogues, demonstrations, film festivals, and parties.

17. The latest dispute in which they had to mediate occurred in San Juan Chamula. See *La Jornada,* June 12, 2004.

18. The San Andrés Accords are the result of the dialogue between the Zapatistas and the government, which began on February 21, 1994 with the

discussion of 'Rights and Indigenous Culture.' See CONAI (1996) and Navarro and Herrera (1998).

19. The most aggressive one, the Plan Puebla-Panama, corresponds to the project of development involving tourism, in which a tourist corridor extending from the central state of Puebla, across the southern state of Chiapas, and into Panama will be created.

20. The former name for *Los Caracoles* was *Los Aguascalientes*. They were created as a space for encounter, dialogue, and celebration of civil and international society. The five *'Caracoles'* or autonomous regions include Oventik, La Realidad, La Garrucha, Roberto Barrios, and Morelia in Chiapas. There are other autonomous places—contact spaces—for indigenous people and civil society outside Chiapas, such as *Ojo de Agua* (Water Eye) at the National Autonomous University of Mexico in Mexico City.

21. After the failure to gain approval of the San Andrés Accords, Subcomandante Marcos no longer functioned as the mediator between the Zapatistas and civil society. He is only occasionally called for mediation.

22. A number of bodies have been found wearing clothes from other bodies and, strangely, with only one shoe or mismatched shoes.

13

Out of the Shadows:
Listening to Place-based Narratives
of Palestinian Women

RANDA FARAH

Introduction:
The Problem with 'Western' Images

I find it difficult to write a chapter on Palestinian-Arab women, both Muslims and Christians, for a primarily 'Western' audience without a brief observation on the existing stereotypes and biases, especially in today's political climate. Despite the fact that the 'West' is not a monolithic entity and that there are critical voices within it, these remain marginalized.

The recent military and political aggression in the Middle East led by the United States has only reinforced Orientalist[1] notions concerning the peoples of the region, especially Islam. One example of persistent Orientalist approaches is Raphael Patai's book, *The Arab Mind*. Published in 1976 and long discredited as unworthy scholarship, the book is littered with characterizations that describe Arabs as violent and as having an "all-encompassing preoccupation with sex" (Whitaker, 2004: 2). Nonetheless, the book reappeared recently as a guide for US policy makers and the military. According to Seymour Hersh (2004), who investigated the torture of Iraqis in the Abu Ghraib prison, the book was being used by the neoconservatives to understand 'Arab culture' and 'psychology.' *The Arab Mind* taught readers that to deal with Iraqis one must use force and manipulate their 'biggest weakness,' i.e., shame and humiliation surrounding sex (Hersch, 2004: 8). Although the book and

206

the war are condemned by many people within and outside the United States, the book's basic assumptions about Arabs and Muslims are not confined to the White House. Orientalism insidiously seeps into the public domain through mainstream media, including the reliance on 'Middle East' experts who apparently can analyze the 'Arab Mind' and 'Muslim culture.'

Orientalism also appears in the academic writings on women, who are generally depicted as passive victims and their bodies as markers that distinguish between Western 'civilization' and Eastern 'barbarism.'[2] This is especially reflected in writings on veiling and female circumcision.[3] In this body of literature Islam is assumed to be inextricably linked to patriarchy and to a culture of 'honor and shame.' Even in feminist works one encounters an unchanging 'Islamic' and 'traditional' experience of womanhood, while politics and history recede into the background (Shami, 1996: 18). As Shami observed, fixing Islam as a cultural configuration displaces and obscures other regional references of identity, including secular meanings such as 'Arab' with which Islam has intersected variously over time (ibid: 19).

Within Palestine

Stereotypical images of Arab and Muslim women are systematically reproduced in news reporting on the Palestinian-Israeli conflict. In a recent Israeli incursion in the West Bank and Gaza, the 'Western' audience does not generally see the cruel face of the Israeli occupation. Rather, channels such as CNN project images of Palestinian women screaming in demonstrations with masked, armed men vowing revenge, and stone-throwing children brainwashed by 'fundamentalists.' Meters away, women are collecting the remnants of clothing or perhaps an undamaged pot from a heap of rubble that once stood as home. Absent in the media is how women emerge from the debris to repair, console, and gather in neighborhoods to help one another and their communities survive death, home demolitions, and curfews.

The impact of the Israeli occupation on the Palestinian population is devastating at all levels of daily life. Land confiscation, the killing of civilians, collective punishment such as curfews, house demolitions, the uprooting of trees, and arbitrary arrests have a pervasive impact. Impoverished women have been especially vulnerable; the loss of land means robbing them of the only source of livelihood. Many of them have lost husbands or sons to Israeli gunfire or prisons, resulting in untold grief and increased poverty. Israeli checkpoints have hindered many women from access to basic health care; stories of pregnant women denied access to hospitals, sometimes leading to death, are not uncommon (Giacaman and Husseini, 2002; Wick, 2002).

Israelis blame Palestinian women for not 'keeping their children off the streets,' an accusation picked up by Sweden's Queen Silvia and echoed in a United Nations meeting in 2000. The underlying assumption is that Palestinian women are bereft of motherly instincts and complicit in 'terrorism.' Grieving mothers who lost their children to Israeli gunfire wrote a response to remind the Queen that it is the Palestinians who are under occupation, not the other way around. The obfuscation is obvious: the Israeli soldiers who shot the children were not required to account for their crimes; rather, the mothers whose children were killed were forced to defend their motherhood (Mabuchi, 2003).[4]

The Israeli attack on the Palestinian family, since the dispersal of Palestinians following the war in 1948, has had a dual and contradictory impact on women. On the one hand, the national calamity has reinforced a conservative trend that views women's identity in terms of a single purpose of motherhood. The male elite in nationalist and Islamist organizations share this perception that anchors women's identity in the domestic sphere. On the other hand, defending family and motherhood as a Palestinian strategy for national survival has granted women a focus for political activism against the occupation within Palestine and in countering exile and integrationist schemes in Arab host countries.

For months now, Palestinian women, often with Israeli women from the peace movement, have been resisting the construction of the separation wall in the West Bank, also known as the 'wall of apartheid.' According to Tanya Reinhart on Sunday, April 25, 2004, about thirty Israeli women answered the call by Palestinian women to protest the expropriation of land belonging to the Palestinian village, Biddu. As Reinhart reported, the wall would "enable territorial contiguity 'clean of Palestinians' from this corridor to the Jewish settlement of Givat Zeev, deep inside the occupied West Bank" (Reinhart, 2004). Audiences of mainstream Western media are rarely informed of Palestinian women's struggles, but also almost never of international or Israeli-Jewish solidarity movements.

Not unlike other movements that have emerged in the context of anticolonial struggles, the relationship between nationalism and feminism converges and diverges over time. Palestinian women's agendas only partially—though inextricably—overlap with the aims of a national movement seeking to rid itself of occupation. Many Palestinian women's organizations adopted the nationalist agenda, especially in the seventies, and delayed initiating social transformation dealing with gender discrimination, fearing it might create schisms and weaken the national front. Yet, there were historic turns, such as during the first Intifada[5]—when the Islamists called for the veiling of women and their return to their 'traditional' roles at home—an occasion when women felt their achievements were being threatened. Rather than standing in solidarity with the women's movement, the secular nationalist organizations abstained from actively supporting women against the conservative trend.

The conservative social agendas of organizations such as Hamas, compounded by the Palestinian Authority's policy that has not actively promoted women's participation and rights as integral to the building of state and society, signaled to women that they must reevaluate their strategies. In the call for protecting the nation and its culture, women must be wary not to abandon their priorities.

In Exile: The Lives and Narratives of Women

While the lives, experiences, and resistance strategies of Palestinian women in the occupied territories have been reshaped by the Israeli occupation and the policies of the Palestinian Authority, the experience and response of refugee women in exile have been shaped by the specific historical and political dynamics in the country of exile. The primary objective in this chapter is to bring out of the shadows the heterogeneous and often silenced voices of subaltern segments of society, including refugee women. One such method that has been used especially by women is the oral narrative or life-histories.[6] Palestinian women, especially refugees, are marginalized in the political process as well as in hegemonic discourses. Their neglect in the academic literature stems from the assumption that the only political and economic domains worth studying in Middle Eastern societies are the formal ones

(Paidar, 1995: 2). Women's activities and contributions in nonformal and formal sectors are undervalued or ignored. Life-histories are thus important instruments through which their lives, contributions, experiences, and voices may be delineated and brought into the public sphere.

Narratives of refugees expose the ways in which women negotiate, resist, and oppose displacement and power structures; they show how women reproduce a sense of place while out of place in numerous ways. These include basic strategies such as the refusal to relocate outside camps, how they reproduce a sense of place in their homes and neighborhood, and how they foster social networks that reestablish Palestinian belonging. The narratives also reveal how they transmit stories of Palestine while maintaining the peasant dialect; and how they insist on preparing Palestinian food, producing Palestinian embroidery, and so on. Refugee women in the camps participate in reinscribing these practices as a symbol of the original *balad,* a polysemic word that refers to original village but also home and homeland. Many refugee women I interviewed recalled the first years following their expulsion, when the camps were not so crowded, and how they planted gardens or tended poultry in front of their refugee shelters. Women attempted to bring the village of origin into the camp in order to carry on with the tasks, using the skills that had given them a sense of place in their original villages.

The narratives of refugee women show that their roles are not limited to the domestic arena. They reveal how larger political, economic, and cultural processes impinged upon women's lives and, in turn, upon how women navigated and resisted oppression while moving between ambiguous public and private domains. In addition to countering a Zionist discourse that denies a Palestinian national past, women's narratives challenge Palestinian hegemonic discourses wherein they are often viewed as simply the protectors of a 'tradition' that is imagined in terms of a female-centered 'home' and 'culture' (Sayigh, 2002: 317).

A first point to keep in mind is that recreating Palestinian fragments of 'home' has been essential for the maintenance of a sense of peoplehood and collective belonging in the context of fragmentation and dispersal. Thus, reproducing home in exile is not secondary to the political struggle. In nationalist discourse, 'home' is viewed as a double-edged sword: as a monolithic and isolated domain, either the place where women should be or as a space they should resist, as it confines them and constrains their liberation. In the narratives of refugee women, however, the dichotomy is neither this rigid, nor is the meaning of home essentialized or unchanging. Rather, women often appropriate this space to negotiate for their rights or as a focal point to gather Palestinian fragments and reestablish their social, political, and economic lives in exile.

Secondly, the boundaries between the personal and political, the private and public domains are fluid, and women move between these in various ways, often challenging normative gender roles. As such, women's life-histories have a political and critical dimension that reveal *different* and, in certain contexts, *oppositional* experiences to hegemonic discourses and normative values.[7]

Third, the approach to women's narratives is crucial; the aim is not to seek women's stories of the past simply to preserve culture,[8] although this is not an entirely unworthy cause; rather, it is to reposition them as active actors in the reshaping of Palestinian identity and political life. Moreover, life-histories are not meant to heroize or romanticize the refugee experience, but to destabilize the larger discourses that silence the voices of 'ordinary' women.

The power of Fatema's, Amneh's or Suad's life-histories that follow lie precisely in their ability to disrupt hegemonic and essentializing narratives (Farah, 2002: 26) and the hierarchical arrangements in which 'home' and 'culture' are perceived as secondary and separate from the male domain of 'politics' and 'history.' The narratives of these women of rural origin show that patriarchy is inextricably linked to other power structures, in this case produced by colonization and expulsion. Silencing women's narratives makes it difficult to discern how constructs such as patriarchy, Islam, or 'honor and shame' manifest themselves in women's social worlds and whether they are appropriate or not as analytical concepts. The narratives expose the variety of experiences that cannot be reduced to a monolithic paradigm such as patriarchy, through which Palestinian, Arab, and/or Muslim women's experiences can be filtered.

The women whose short excerpts I use below live in the same refugee camp in Jordan,[9] and they represent three generations defined by historical events, not by age. Fatema fled the war in 1948, Amneh fled from the West Bank to Jordan following the 1967 war, and Suad was born in exile. These women represent different phases and experiences of uprooting and exile, and their narratives show how they managed to reassert their identities while coping with political, social, and economic oppression. Following these excerpts I have added excerpts from my own life-history as an example of another Palestinian trajectory of exile and to highlight my belief that Palestinian feminism cannot be extricated from the Palestinian political and historical context.

Fatema: Challenging Gender Roles

Fatema is from Dayr Aban,[10] a village located twenty-one kilometers southwest of Jerusalem. The village was destroyed during the 1948 war. When I interviewed Fatema in the mid nineties she was in her early seventies, a small-built but strong and proud woman. She defined her political identity in terms of her village of origin and her most fundamental personal characteristic as a 'hard worker.' The interview took place in al-Baq'a refugee camp, which was established in 1968 following the influx of Palestinians fleeing the 1967 war and includes refugees of the 1948 war. The camp, located north of Amman, the capital of Jordan, has a population of approximately one hundred twenty thousand people living in an area of 1.4 square kilometers. The life-history was recorded while sitting on the roof of Fatema's neighbor's house, which was also the home of a few pigeons and a goat. The 'goat on the roof' incited a conversation on women's tasks in the village of origin and their role in domestic economies.

Fatema's life-history portrays a woman of remarkable endurance with a keen interest in politics and historical processes. Her narrative reveals junctures where she reverses gender roles, and points to the overlapping boundaries between the public and the private and women's roles in both domains. Her economic activities are more important to the household than those of her husband. She is interested in political events such as the 1936–39 Palestinian peasant rebellion.

In the village of origin, having their autonomous spheres, such as tending the household garden, did not isolate women from larger political events. The catastrophe or the *Nakba* of 1948 resulted in a radical transformation in their mode of livelihood and status. From farmers working on collectively held land, a process of proletarianization occurred following the war. However, in host countries, women's contribution to the household economy was concealed in its fragmented and seasonal nature. Nonetheless, like unsung heroines, refugee women quietly grinded the days of exile, creating networks and relationships that sustained both livelihood and Palestinian belonging.

In the quote below, Fatema challenges gender roles by anchoring her personal identity on her skills as a worker, generally conceived as a male domain. She 'challenges' men to carry a stone, thus deflating their physical power, and dismisses their role as providers. Work mediates her discourse on Palestine between home and exile; it is the common denominator that grants continuity and order in her disrupted life. Her representation of her life, like that of other refugees, is intricately inter-woven with the larger, collective national calamity.

> In the beginning, there was Islamic brotherhood among people in the Homeland, that is, if the girl went early to work in the fields, people did not gossip about her. As you know, all people's work was sowing, weeding, and peasant work—women fetched wood and went every-where. If the woman met a stranger (meaning a man), people did not gossip about her as they do now, never! . . . I am a peasant, peasant of the land, the land is ours, my daughter. . . . I was 18 when we fled . . . When we left the village I had two daughters then. One of them was seven months. I had her prematurely when I jumped off the camel. Of course strength is dignity without men! I swear, once I chal-lenged three men to carry a heavy stone for half a lira . . . they chal-lenged me and said, 'You can't carry it.' I said, 'I can and I will . . . just put it over my head!' . . . I swear, I won and took the half lira from them . . . . In al-Karameh (Jordan host country) we used to knead adobe blocks . . . when dry I used to carry them on my head and climb a ladder to give them to the builder . . . I think I used to make eight-een hundred bricks in three days.

Amneh: Beyond the 'Preservation' of Culture

As they fled the bombs hurled at their villages, some of the refugees sought shelter in caves and open fields. During this period, women sus-tained families by preparing food from whatever they could improvise, picking vegetables or plants they could find, and building makeshift shelters from rags and other materials. In the excerpt that follows, Amneh is central to the survival of the family. She is originally from a village called al-Shweikah, in the district of Tulkarem. During the 1948 war, half of the village fell under what became Israel, thereupon she and her family moved to a refugee camp called al-Fare'a in the West Bank. The battle for survival is seldom told in official narratives; yet the actual survival of many Palestinians during that period depended on women's ability to 'make something' out of 'nothing,' day in and day out, as many of the refugee women explained to me while narrating the trauma of uprooting.

Amneh's narrative shows that her status within the family does not lack authority, and she is critical of the leadership of the national movement. Amneh passes on a Palestinian sense of belonging to the younger generation by telling them about her original village. Although the older men also played a role in reminiscing, the women's role was much more effective in that they spent long periods of time with children and grandchildren. In this 'telling' of Palestine, there is always a contrast made between the camp and the village of origin, where life is depicted as more dignified if not always more abundant. Amneh narrates

> In 1967 we left, walking from Ghawr al-Jiftlik to al-Shree'a (the Jordan River or Valley). We stayed at the edge of the River, slept there that night . . . We didn't have bread, we had kids, but we had nothing, but luckily I had brought with me a few eggs, a few potatoes, and a kerosene (stove). I lit the kerosene and boiled the eggs and potatoes and fed the children. Then my husband told us we had to cross the Shree'a over the Mi'bar (the crossing) . . . We kept on walking until we came to Abu Nu'aym where we rested for a while . . . We were around a hundred families . . . so we started gathering dried straw to make beds for the children. We had no covers over us and no mattresses under us . . . Then I told my husband, 'Did we flee with the children from Palestine so that they die here? Go get us some sacks . . . so we can make us a small shack, the children will die from the sun!' . . . And we made something like a shelter . . . My husband went back . . . I tell them (her children) about my village, and their father tells them about his, how we lived, how we farmed, and even when we had rough times, our life was much better than now . . .

Suad: Gender Oppression and Resistance in Exile

The major themes that emerged in the narratives of the first generation of refugees focused on their lives in the village of origin. The narratives of younger generations of women—those born in camps and/or exile—center around their experiences as refugees and how they managed to survive political and socioeconomic marginalization. Suad was in her early thirties when I interviewed her. Suad was divorced and secured a livelihood by learning how to sew, and called upon kin and neighbors to ensure she did not lose her children to her husband's family. When I interviewed her, her husband had returned after divorcing his second wife, and according to Suad he had learned his lesson and was acting properly toward her and the children.

For Suad, the place she calls home in the refugee camp is the result of a historical collective event. However, home was also threatened by gender discrimination and a husband who abandoned her. In her narrative, she explains how she reclaimed home and challenged her husband by relying on a wider network of women and family members. The episode of the almond seed that grew into a tree in the home in Palestine is a political statement to reclaim Palestine and symbolizes continuity and connection between her and a homeland she had not seen before.

> Five years! (Her husband had left her for five years) Aida knows; she used to come in and find me crying, why? Because I did not have two piasters to buy bread for my children, and that day Aida (her neighbor) cried with me. She went back and broke the bread she had into two equal parts. She did the same with the tomatoes . . . . There was nothing to eat . . . So I began to sew, during feasts, I knitted with wool, . . . sewing clothes to bring in a couple of piasters here and there to feed the children . . . After the Eid (a religious feast for Muslims) he (her husband) brought the divorce paper as proof to show Suad he had divorced his second wife, which she had demanded and began to beg me to go back with him . . .
>
> When the September war broke out . . . I remember . . . the Jordanian police came and took the men away, including my father . . . In Ajloun there are huge caves, shelters, a hundred and fifty people huddled in them. They bombarded the shelter we were in . . . We (Palestinian resistance) were different then, not like today (the post-Oslo period), these days, we lost everything . . . I have never seen my homeland Palestine, not once. I yearn to see it; I want to go there so much and see my land. My mother tells me the seed of an almond tree had fallen in our house (the 1948 house of her parents in Bayt Mahsir) during the war and had grown up and tumbled the house down, can you imagine right in the middle of the house . . . The day we built the house here I used to work from morning till evening . . . picking tomatoes so that we can afford building the house . . . All this house you see, the five rooms including the salon, I am the one who did it . . . I also worked in electric wiring, I tiled the floor with Chinese tiles in the bathroom. I can fix sewage pipes; if a tap does not work I fix it by myself. The five years alone I worked on everything . . .

Randa: Exile and the Academy

My interest in the Palestinian exile emanates from the fact that I am a woman of Palestinian origin. Like all Palestinians, I am in exile, defined as political disenfranchisement and the denial by Israel of a Right to Return to my Homeland as an individual and a member of a national community. Thus I am a refugee in the generic sense.

I was born in Haifa as a second-class 'non-Jew,' a classification meant to efface our existence and national identity. In the street, we were often called 'dirty Arabs' and exposed to similar derogatory terms. I lived with my family under Israeli 'Emergency Laws'; we were not allowed to repossess our property, reunite with family members who fled to neighboring countries, buy land, form political parties, or even specialize in certain academic fields. We were confined in our movement and ever-shrinking spaces, literally and metaphorically.

Jews and Arabs lived separately and unequally; the landscape did not differ greatly from other colonial maps and geographies, such as Algeria under French rule or apartheid South Africa. Nonetheless, despite the isolation and repression that governed our lives, we continued to struggle against land expropriation and for our political rights. Memories of childhood are filled with a home where many people debated politics; where a large extended family provided us with a sense of security in a new Israeli society in which we were invisible or simply a nuisance that needed to be silenced or removed.

There were spaces in Palestine that turned Israeli in 1948 that I knew 'we' simply could not go to, because we would be interrogated or humiliated if we did. Such places included Jewish 'kibbutzim'—hailed in the West as socialist outposts—and areas on which Israeli Jewish settlements were sprouting. Once a year my mother would take me to the Hadar, a commercial area in Haifa, to buy me shoes. I remember our fear of speaking Arabic lest we be spotted.

In 1965 I, together with my family, crossed into the West Bank, which had been annexed by Jordan following the 1948 war. However, two years later in 1967, Israel occupied the West Bank and Gaza. The memory of those days is bittersweet, especially my school years in Jerusalem, which was a flourishing Palestinian urban center. The public bus my sister and I took to school was often stopped at Israeli checkpoints.

Schoolbags were searched, as were the vegetable baskets of village women going to the urban markets. Every Palestinian had become a target of surveillance and control by the military authorities.

The years went by, and we ended up in Lebanon. Beirut remains central in my political and social awareness; it was there that I read Nawal al-Sadawi's book on Arab women as well as books on anticolonial struggles. It was also the time at which I began to realize that many of the men I demonstrated with in the streets and male students at the university paid only lip service to gender equality, even when they had a progressive political stand on Palestine. In their relationship with women, many abused the power they had in society as men. Every now and then I remember conversations with men who told me that women's liberation was not the 'priority,' that we had to focus on the main objective! I began to question and wonder why.

More recent memories of Beirut evoke the sound of Israeli F-16s, cluster bombs, and shining swift metal ominously sparkling in space, which violently disrupted my trajectory of exile. In June 1982, Ariel Sharon led his mighty Goliathan army into Lebanon. My son was six months at the time, and I recall seeking safety in corners and staircases as I tightly held on to him. Today I shudder when I remember the fate of Sabra and Shatila camps where the massacre of Palestinian refugees took place the following September. I try hard to suppress the memory of the war in Lebanon; it brings back the smell of death, devastation, suffering, and the sound of grieving mothers wailing, their pain reverberating in the Lebanese sky. Exile after exile, death that follows another reminds me of Mahmoud Darwish's poem: "Where should we go after the last frontiers, where should the birds fly after the last sky?"

I was lucky to escape death and injury, and was able to flee with my son and finally managed to immigrate to Canada. Yet the experiences of war—of being denied my homeland—inform my daily life in ways that only those who are witness to the sorrow of exile can comprehend. Thus, understanding my struggle as a woman was always intertwined with the larger Palestinian calamity and the experiences of uprooting. Personal and daily choices, such as marriage, fields of study, films to see, and friends to make, are as much colored by this larger history as by the exigencies of livelihood and place of exile.

When I conducted my research on Palestinian refugees, I had my Canadian citizenship. Compared to the refugees living in camps, I was privileged and had certain kinds of power, including those of movement and publicly representing what they told me privately. I was both an insider and an outsider, and my position changed depending on the context. Like fields of force, I was sometimes pulled to become an 'insider,' especially with women; other times, the outsider prevailed. The fact that I was of Palestinian origin, however, provided a fundamental common denominator.

Understanding, studying, and giving voice to the experiences of refugees and their resilience in Palestine and elsewhere was one of the ways in which I sought to speak out against forced displacement. Perhaps it is also a way to reconcile my chaotic trajectory, which at times seems like dislocated and disconnected fragments scattered across numerous political, cultural, and geographical boundaries and landscapes.

Conclusion

The power differentials between the refugee women I interviewed and myself were important, yet they actively sought to be heard through me. The women I met had reinscribed the camp as a Palestinian place to assert their political identities and grant continuity to their social lives, while I sought to bring into light their experiences as part of our collective, albeit heterogeneous, Palestinian lives as women. Thus neither the refugee women from the camp nor I told these stories without purpose. We knew that these would go into print, and we actively sought to engage a 'Western' audience.

The life-histories challenge hypotheses underpinning an Orientalist approach that views Arab and Muslim women as passive victims of an Islamic cultural tradition assumed to be inherently oppressive. These narratives also counter beliefs embedded in Middle Eastern scholarly literature that focus on the formal political and economic domains; or confine women's roles to those of the 'preservers' of culture and reproducers of men who fight the political and military battles.

Within the occupied territory, women reassemble their lives following each house demolition, protest land expropriation, and refuse to surrender their right to live as Palestinians. As for women in exile, they gather pieces of shattered and scattered lives, contributing to the remaking of home and place, their survival, and the reproduction as 'Palestinian,' defending them against policies that aim at their dissolution as a nation.

Patai's book, *The Arab Mind* and the Swedish Queen's view of Palestinian mothers share deeply embedded Orientalist assumptions about the Arab world and Muslims in general. Therefore, it is important to seek different ways of writing with and about Arab women, in order to question the assumptions upon which mainstream discourses are based and to bring forth women's experiences as political statements that destablize hegemonic narratives on issues such as displacement, identity, place, politics, and history.

Notes

1. By 'Orientalism,' Said mainly refers to the academic traditions with doctrines about the Orient as they evolved in late-eighteenth-century Europe; a style of thought based upon an ontological distinction made between the 'Orient' and the 'Occident'; and the "corporate institution for dealing with the Orient—dealing with it by teaching, settling it, ruling over it: in short Orientalism as a western style for dominating, restructuring, and having authority over the Orient" (Said, 1979: 1–3).

2. For a comprehensive critique of Orientalist approaches, see Said (1979, 1994, 1997), Ahmed (1992), and Asad (2003).

3. In early 2004, I supervised the MA thesis of Sarah Blekaitis (2004) at the University of Western Ontario on Western literature and female circumcision. She noted that there are consistent Orientalist representations that recur in the works of Fran Hosken, Mary Daly, and Alice Walker.

4. See Harel (2004) and UNRWA (United Nations Relief and Works Agency for Palestine Refugees in the Near East; 2004a and 2004b) reporting on the killing of Palestinian children by Israeli soldiers.

5. For a good discussion on women's roles during the first Intifada, see Hiltermann (1991).

6. The literature on the significance of oral history for women's studies is vast and crosses disciplinary boundaries. See Armitage, et al. (2002); Leydesdorff, et al. (1996); Passerini (1987); and Johnson, et al. (1982).

7. For more information about the political dimension of oral histories and narratives, see Farah (2004) listed in the references.

8. In the context of the Zionist-Israeli objective to wipe out the Palestinian past, a number of research projects have emerged with the aim of preserving the Palestinian cultural heritage and reconstructing the social histories of the eradicated

villages and urban centers. For more information about Palestinian oral history, see a special issue of *Al-Jana* (2002) titled "File on Palestinian oral history," published in Beirut by the Arab Resource Center for Popular Arts.

9. Based on author's field research in camps for the Ph.D. dissertation.

10. For information about destroyed villages, see Khalidi (1992).

14

Still Challenging 'Place': Sex, Money, and Agency in Women's Migrations

LAURA Mª AGUSTÍN

A uthor's note: I first wrote "Challenging 'Place'" in 2001 as part of the project, Women and the Politics of Place. I wanted to be talking with the others in the group, but I was afraid that my subject didn't fit in. So I wrote against place, challenging the tendency to sanctify it and associate it with women, and this piece has been translated and reprinted a number of times. Looking at it several years later, I find that most of the ideas are truer than ever and that I could comfortably continue to challenge 'place.' But I now have some different things to say; thus the title, "Still Challenging 'Place'". For those who read the first version, this one begins the same way, but develops differently. Have patience.

The story starts with the picture of the migrant's loss of home. People talking about migrants tend to sentimentalize home with warm images of close families, simple household objects, rituals, songs, and foods. Many religious and national holidays across cultures nostalgically reify concepts of home and family, usually through images of a folkoric past. In this context, migration is constructed as a last-ditch or desperate move and migrants as *deprived* of their 'natural' place, the one they are meant to 'belong to.' Yet for millions of people all over the world, the birth and childhood place is not a feasible or desirable one in which to undertake more adult, ambitious, or unconventional projects, and moving to another place is therefore a positive solution.

How does this decision to move take place? Earthquakes, armed conflict, disease, or lack of food impel some people in situations that

221

seem to involve little element of choice or any time to 'process' options. These people are sometimes called refugees or asylum seekers. Other migrations are characterized by and reduced to their economic element, and of these, men's decisions to migrate are understood to be the product of a normal masculine ambition to get ahead through work. But something else happens when women attempt to do the same.

What I Am Doing Here

For a long time I worked in *educación popular* in various countries of Latin America and the Caribbean and with Latino migrants in North America and Europe, in programs dedicated to literacy, AIDS prevention, and health promotion; preparation for migration and *concientización* (an exact translation does not exist in English, but combines something about consciousness-raising with something about 'empowerment'). My concern about the vast difference between what first world social agents (governmental, NGO workers, activists) say about women migrants and what women migrants say about themselves led me to study and bear witness to these questions. I deliberately located myself on the border of both groups—the migrants and the social agents—in Europe, where the only jobs generally available to migrant women are in the domestic, 'caring,' and sex industries. My work examines both the social agents and the migrants, so I spend time in brothels, bars, houses, offices, 'outreach' vehicles, and 'the street' in its many versions.

Knowledge about what migrant women say comes from my own research over many years on both sides of the Atlantic, as well as others' research throughout the European Union, with migrants from all over the world (Agustín, 2001; 2005b). The focus of my own research shifts the gaze from 'those poor migrant women' to the powerful Europeans who want to 'help' and be 'in solidarity' with them, problematizing the biopolitical projects and programs considered worthy and necessary in the West. I did more than a year's participant observation among social agents working on 'prostitution' issues in Spain (as part of a Ph.D. program) and also met many projects when I did evaluations for the International Labour Organization and the European Commission.

Finally, for three years I have been moderating a romance-language e-mail list in which individual and organized groups of sex workers and support personnel participate—religious, NGO, researchers, and activists. This list provides daily knowledge of the voices of the subjects of sex industry and migration discourses.

I do not reproduce the usual separation between migrant women who sell domestic or caring services and those who sell sex. No such separation actually exists, but is rather imposed from outside in an imaginary that finds domestic workers to be 'good' or 'safe' women, while those selling sex are either 'bad' or 'victims.' Domestic and caring work share many characteristics and dangers with some kinds of sex work; numerous migrants take on both kinds of jobs when trying to acquire as much money as possible in a short amount of time, and abuse and labor-related problems are rife among them all. Most importantly, this division creates an opportunity for isolating people who sell sex that is then used by researchers and others who try to speak on their behalf (Agustín, 2004).

This point is very important to my work, which centers on migration rather than the sale of sex, and I believe it is important to engage with academic theorists on points like these. Commercial sex is mostly discussed within feminism in terms of the morality and freedom of individual actions, while other academic fields skirt the issue, even migration studies (Agustín, 2005a). This discursive isolation affects NGO programs and services, as personnel working with women use—often for reasons of funding—feminist theories as the framework for their work. The predominance and extension of the theory of 'violence against women' has an enormous impact on the direct services offered to clients of such NGOs, while engagement with economic and legal issues—among others—is largely absent.

One of the ways in which my work seems to go against the grain of the 'women and place' project lies in my apparent resistance to the demand that I 'disaggregate' migrant women and tie their experiences to particular places. In reality I am not resisting. Women migrants doing low-prestige jobs around the world have much more in common than not, and precisely what I am trying to do is pull back so that this becomes visible. The larger issue is related to the absence of civil and labor rights that determine how migrants live, unless the state has issued them various kinds of bureaucratic permissions that tie one to a place (nation, city, or workplace); for example, work contract, work permit, or correct visa. In the absence of these, the particular national context and its laws are less important to a migrant than finding whatever illegal niches and opportunities seem best at the moment. Obviously, in places where society appears to be panicking that migrants will 'invade,' the migrants themselves may live in more ghettolike conditions than they might otherwise; but there is no evidence that the current European panic, for instance, actually impedes migrants from getting in and moving around if they set their minds to it. Unfavorable legislation and social climate in the European Union, for example, promote migrants' mobility in general, and the mobility of many who sell sex specifically, as they try to avoid becoming known to police and authorities and look for more secure and comfortable places. But this by no means applies only to Europe; the same happens in Southeast Asia, West Africa, or anywhere else.

In Europe, migrant associations that engage in politics are overwhelmingly run by men. Even the most apparently 'progressive' groups, such as the *sans-papiers* in Paris, do not support the situation of migrant women who sell sex, who are currently being hounded and demonized in most parts of Europe. In many countries, undocumented migrants are not granted the right to join associations or protests, so organizing is next to impossible. This leads to rampant ventriloquism on the part of those who seek to 'represent' migrant women's needs—and brings me again to the feminist conflict about sex and victimization.

Un-gendering Migration

It is striking that in the year 2005 women should so overwhelmingly be seen as pushed, obligated, coerced, or forced when they leave home to get ahead through work. But so entrenched is the idea of women as forming an essential *part* of home, if not actually *being* it themselves, that they are routinely denied the agency to undertake a migration. So begins a pathetic image of innocent women torn from their homes, coerced into migrating, if not actually shanghaied or sold into slavery: the 'trafficking' discourse. This is the imagery that nowadays follows those who migrate to places where the only paid occupations available to them are in domestic service, caring labor, or sex work.

The trafficking discourse relies on the assumption that it is better for (non-Western) women to stay at home rather than leave and get into trouble. In this context, 'trouble' is seen as doing irreparable harm to women (who are grouped helplessly with children), while men are routinely expected to encounter and overcome it.

In the sentimentalizing that occurs around 'uprooted migrants,' the myriad possibilities for being miserable at home are forgotten. Many women are fleeing from small-town prejudices, dead-end jobs, dangerous streets, overbearing fathers, and boring boyfriends. Home can be a suffocating place, as evidenced by the enormous variety of entertainment sites located outside of it. In many cultures only men are allowed to partake of these pleasures, occupy these spaces; women who travel to the West find themselves able to participate in many. Moreover, the possibility that some poor women might *like* the idea of being desirable to first world men (who may be seen as 'white,' 'rich,' or 'exotic') or that they might *like* being a dancer or artist, even if with a sexual element, is practically never considered. Valerie Walkerdine has criticized British middle-class abhorrence of little girls' talent contests popular among the working class.

> Girls form ambitions and desires around aspects of femininity, which are presented to them. In fact. . . the lure of 'fame,' particularly of singing and dancing, offers working-class girls the possibility of a talent from which they have not automatically been excluded by virtue of their supposed lack of intelligence or culture. (1997: 50)

The same can be said of third world women with limited prospects. Whether or not people are misled about the meaning of an offer to work, their own desires must be taken into account when considering their later experiences. A trip abroad, away from the limited prospects of home, may represent the attempt to fulfill important personal desires, those considered essential to 'self-realization' and the acquirement of personal 'identity' in the West. And if one of our goals is to find a vision of globalization in which poorer people are not constructed solely as victims, we need to recognize that strategies for fulfilling desires that seem less gratifying to some people may be successfully utilized by others. As one member of Babaylan, a migrant domestic workers' group in Switzerland, said

> We look at migration as neither a degradation nor improvement . . . in women's position, but a restructuring of gender relations. This restructuring need not necessarily be expressed through a satisfactory professional life. It may take place through the assertion of autonomy in social life, through relations with family of origin, or through participating in networks and formal associations. The differential between earnings in the country of origin and the country of immigration may in itself create such an autonomy, even if the job in the receiving country is one of a live-in maid or prostitute (Hefti, 1997).

Nor do the bad beginnings or sad, frightening, or even tragic moments of people's migrations need to forever mark them or define their whole life experience. Relative powerlessness at one stage of migration need not be permanent; poor people also enjoy multiple identities that change over life-courses composed of different stages, needs, and projects. Granting agency to migrating individuals does not mean denying the vast structural changes that push and pull them. On the other hand, granting them autonomy does not mean making them over-responsible for situations largely not of their own making. Global, national, and local conditions intervene in individuals' decisions, along with doses of good and bad luck (Agustín, 2003).

Many situations come up during a migration, in which migrants have to choose between doing things the 'right,' or legal, way or doing them so they might turn out the way they want. This brings to mind the conversation I had with a Colombian woman through the bars of a Bangkok detention center where she was being held after spending a year in prison. Her anguish did not derive so much from her having been in prison as from her own feelings of guilt because she had semi-knowingly broken the law, allowing a fake visa to be prepared for her in order to get into Japan. Her family had helped her with this, and her resultant conflicts over love and blame were tormenting her. While this woman had been a victim, she had also made choices and felt responsible, and I would not want to take this ethical capacity away from her.

By insisting on the instrumentality of migrating under less-than-ideal conditions, one does not deny the existence of the worst experiences nor the necessity to fight against them. The abuses of agents who sell ways to enter the first world extend to migrants who work as domestic servants and in sweatshops, *maquiladoras,* mines, agriculture, and sex or other industries, whether they are women, men, or transgender people. But these most tragic stories are fortunately not the reality for most migrants, according to their own testimonies (Agustín, 2005b).

Dealing with Displacement

Research among migrant women doing sexual or domestic work reveals little essential difference in their migration projects and demonstrates that migrations that may have begun as a kind of *dis*placement (a feeling of being pushed out, of having no reasonable choices) are not doomed to be permanently sad stories.[1] Even the poorest, and even the partially 'trafficked' or 'deceived,' look for and find spaces in which to be themselves, run away, change jobs, or learn to utilize friends, clients, employers, and petty criminals. In other words, they do the same as other migrants and, in all but the worst cases, tend to find their way eventually into situations *more* to their liking, if still imperfect, whether that means finding a good family to clean for or a decent brothel owner or the right contacts to work freelance. Consider the story of one Moroccan woman in Spain.

> I arrived in Almería through a friend's mediation. I began to work as a domestic, I was badly paid and mistreated. Sundays I came to the edge of the sea and cried. One Sunday a Moroccan man saw me crying, I explained my situation to him, he took me to his house. I was a virgin, he promised he was going to marry me . . . he got me a residence card. . . he found me work in a restaurant and let me stay in his studio. He told me I had to pay rent. I began to sleep with some clients from the restaurant . . . Now, I would like to go to France, I want to get married. . . My sister who lives in Bézier says she's going to find me a Frenchman, to get a residence card. (Lahbabi and Rodríguez, 2000: 18)

This testimony shows how migrant women, far from being passive victims, exploit their opportunities in any way possible. At the beginning, the woman is sad at being far from home and 'out of place'; the big trip has been made across the sea, and she returns to the sea for solace.

A countryman, perhaps because of his association with home, promises more consolation. But by the end, the woman's tone has changed and she's setting her sights on yet another country where she is prepared to live, if she can find a husband. 'Place' has become an endless space to move through.

Nowadays people everywhere are constantly exposed to media images depicting world travel as essential to education and pleasure and fomenting desire through the glamorous representation of places (for example, see Mai, 2001). But since the majority of the world's poor and desperate do *not* migrate, many of those who do must be people interested in exploring and capable of taking the risks involved in uprooting (even if they also feel frightened or forced to do it).

'Place' for migrants is often set up in terms of a dichotomy: *home* (which one loved and was forced to leave) pitted against *one's new country* (which is not yet home, but from which one does not want to be deported). This classic focus is problematized by the work of many migration scholars. Consider the titles of two texts written about the Dominican diaspora: *Between Two Islands* (Grasmuck and Pessar, 1991) and *One Country in Two* (Guarnizo, 1992). In this case, a large number of Dominicans are said to live in both Santo Domingo and New York City, or live between them, on the 'bridge' they have built during the past twenty years.

> Family arrangements in which one or both parents live in the United States with none or some of their children, while their other children live on the island, are frequent. Although having more than one household in two different countries might be a source of emotional stress and economic hardship, it also arms family members with special skills to deal with uncertainty and adversity. They become more sophisticated than non-migrant people in dealing with a rapidly globalizing world. (Guarnizo, 1992: 77)

The complicated relationships migrants have to home, which may or may not be a place they actually wish to visit or live in again, are too often excluded from discussions about them. People who sell sex also have private lives, go to films, bars, discotheques, restaurants, concerts, festivals, church parties, and parks. Their wish to leave work behind and be ordinary is no different from other people's wish; in the context of urban spaces they become *flâneurs* and consumers like anyone else.

Underdog Cosmopolitanism

The term *cosmopolitan* is often applied to 'sophisticated' travelers, 'globetrotters' who are seen as carefree and urbane. According to this view, "most ordinary labor migrants are not cosmopolitans either. For them going away may be, ideally, home plus higher income; often the involvement with another culture is not a fringe benefit but a necessary cost, to be kept as low as possible" (Hannerz, 1990: 243).

Here Hannerz fixes migrant identity in an early stage of reluctant leave-taking, self-protection, and wariness toward the new; fails to reflect differences found among people of different ages, classes, and cultures; and forecloses the possibility that migrants don't remain 'migrants' forever, as they change and are accepted into new societies.

More seriously, here the lives of migrants appear to be a series of (dull) instrumental decisions in which travel and sophistication play no part. But the concept of the cosmopolitan does not necessarily exclude poor travelers. Jamaica Kincaid (1990) and Bharati Mukherjee (1988) both wrote novels in which a woman from a country on the 'periphery' migrates to the 'center,' initially to work as an *au pair*. The protagonists, Lucy and Jasmine, are portrayed as cosmopolitan, their discoveries about the metropole and their ability to reflect on cultures as astute as anyone's. They are migrants who begin with very little, but who increase their cultural capital enormously as they travel. The cosmopolite eventually comes to have a special relationship vis-à-vis 'place,' considering the world his oyster, not his home.

In traditional center-periphery theory, people who live outside the West are conceived as, literally, peripheral to the main story of modernity. James Clifford's travel theory (1997), which emphasizes flexibility and mobility rather than identity and fixed location, and encompasses such popular notions as New York City being 'part of the Caribbean' and Los Angeles and Miami being 'capitals' of Latin America, *might* have a place for ordinary working migrants, including those cleaning houses and selling sex. Similarly, Arjun Appadurai's concept of the ethnoscape, a "landscape of persons who constitute the shifting world in which we live; tourists, immigrants, refugees, exiles, guest-workers and other moving groups and individuals," seems open to including everyone (1996: 33).

The wider issue is the disqualification of the experiences of post-modern working people who see mobility and adaptability as key to their futures. Whether these are maids, strawberry pickers or sex workers, they are often allotted marginal spaces in actual geography and in discourses of mobility. Why is it possible to view the illegal jobs of British women on the Costa del Sol as entrepreneurial (O'Reilly, 2000) while the illegal work of Rumanian or Moroccan women in the same location is seen as 'forced'?

It is common for migrant sex workers to have lived in multiple places. For a variety of legislative and social reasons, not least of which are the repressive policies of police and immigration everywhere, many migrant sex workers keep moving from city to city and even from country to country. This itinerant lifestyle creates a particular relationship to place that impedes doing the things migrants are 'supposed' to do: establish themselves and become good (subaltern) citizens. Moving a lot, migrants have met people from many countries and can speak a little of several languages, and some have inevitably learned to be flexible and tolerant of people's differences. Whether they speak lovingly of their home country or not, they are on their way to overcoming the kind of attachment to it that leads to nationalist fervor and to joining those who may be the hope of the world, people who judge others on their actions and thoughts, not on how they look or where they are from.

Sexing 'Place'

Sex is sold in places. Though many commentators talk as though 'the street' were the only place involved, in fact street prostitution is on the wane in many places and nonexistent in others. In the 'free markets' of advanced capitalism, products and services that didn't used to exist proliferate before our very eyes. Places to go have burgeoned and purchasable experiences continuously multiply, so the proliferation of sexually oriented shows and services on offer is hardly surprising. In some of these sites you can see women from Equatorial Guinea working alongside women from Brazil and Russia, and women from Nigeria alongside others from Peru and Bulgaria. What's called the 'milieu' are 'workplaces' for those selling sexual services in them, people who wear erotic uniforms and spend many hours in the bar, socializing, talking, and drinking with each other and the clientele as well as with cooks, waiters, cashiers, and bouncers. In the case of flats, some people live in them while others arrive to work shifts. The experience of spending most of their time in such ambiences, if people adapt to them at all, is another way to produce cosmopolitan subjects.

All of this is not particular to people who have migrated. The places associated with commercial sex are treated in hegemonic discourses as disgusting, perverted, or marginal, but the idea that they are few and irrelevant to the social mainstream is ridiculous, given that all kinds of sexual businesses together generate multimillions in profits. The people involved include not only those who directly sell sex but also consumers, business owners, investors, and nonsexual employees. Sites and forms embrace bars, restaurants, cabarets, clubs, brothels, dance halls, phone lines, saunas, massage and beauty parlors, escort services, films and videos, spectacles, puberty rituals, sex shops, stag and hen events, fashion shows, shipboard parties, Internet sites, and sometimes art exhibitions and theater plays, many of which promote nonsexual products and services as well. Clearly a great deal that societies consider to be 'cultural' and normatively 'social' is included in the range of activities that take in both commerce and sex. Yet societies' twin reactions to commercial sex—moral revulsion and resigned tolerance—have permitted its uncontrolled development in informal economies, which simply means that the places of sexual commerce are not counted. People who sell are stigmatized, activities bought are taboo, and places are either treated as invisible or zoned into marginal areas. But none of this inhibits the growth and proliferation of businesses or their use for many mainstream purposes.

This is a key issue. Pole dancing, lap dancing, and belly dancing exist on an erotic continuum that in many cases provides little more than an evocative background for activities that are not sexual in themselves. In most cultures, men who hold wealth and power routinely use sexual spaces to do business, entertain clients, demonstrate their wealth, amass more cultural capital, and reproduce their masculinity. John Urry (1990) divides touristic gazing possibilities into 'collective,' in which the presence of other people adds to the experience, and 'romantic,' in which privacy is important. Both kinds of experiences are available in the sex industry, whose sites are used by clients to drink, eat, take drugs, get together with friends, do business, impress partners, watch films, travel, be with a variety of sexual partners, and pay for a gamut of services. The sexual moment need not occupy a central place within the whole experience; for many, drinking and socializing in the presence of symbolic, decorative women or men may be more important (Allison, 1994; Leonini, 1999; Frank, 2002).

Meanings of Place

Many sites in sexual milieu are multiethnic, multicultural, and they are even borderlands: places of mixing, confusion, and ambiguity where the defining 'lines' between one thing and another are blurred. With so many foreign migrants employed in the sex industry, languages spoken include pidgins, creoles, signing, and lingua francas whether we look in Tokyo, Bangkok, Lagos, or Sydney. Performance and experimentation are routine in spaces where sexual identities are malleable: anyone can buy or sell anything, unhampered by his or her everyday character. Many clubs would appear to be carnival sites—the world upside down— and the sex worker like the *pícaro,* the half-outsider who substitutes trickery for dignified work, living the role of "cosmopolitan and stranger . . . exploiting and making permanent the liminal state of being betwixt and between all fixed points in a status sequence" (Turner, 1974: 232).

Cosmopolitan space seems to work against the grain of the 'women and place' project and involve exactly that which does *not* fix people in places. I am aware that many will continue to lament migrants' loss of home and see involvement in commercial sex as singularly tragic. But imagine what would be said if men were the large group using commercial sex as a strategy to migrate to good wages: it would be seen as a creative, entrepreneurial move, and not characterized as a tragedy. So one must give credit where credit is due, recognize the resourcefulness of most migrant women, and allow them the possibility of overcoming feelings of victimhood and experiencing pleasure and satisfaction within difficult situations and in strange places.

Note

1. Studies that follow migrants over time show that there are gradual changes in levels of feeling alienated, strange, excluded, and accepted or integrated into receiving societies.

15

Politics of Place in Multilevel Games: Are Arab Women Acting or Reacting?

LAMIS A. M. AL-SHEJNI

One of the main concerns of the Women and the Politics of Place (WPP) project is how should women act to bring about change at the different levels of place, i.e., in their local reality or at the international level, such as at the UN fora or the World Social Forum. The WPP approach suggests that women's politics of place can best be seen as the sum of different local movements that come together on an international scale with common aims that enable them to act together cohesively and coherently. Unfortunately, such a vision is far from being realized. There are many issues that involve the organization of a local women's movement—if it exists in the first place—and its contribution to a global one. This chapter takes up the Arab Region as one location and explores how subaltern women are engaging in different political games.

The Arab Region faces huge external economic and political pressure, as well as growing internal turmoil. The central questions of the chapter are: How is the Arab women's movement reacting to these external and internal pressures? How are they shaping their politics of place through their struggle for gender equality and women's empowerment? And how are they contributing to the global women's movement?

The chapter draws on my work in the region. My aim is not to study the Arab women's movement per se, but to use it as an example to analyze women's politics in the different levels of place (local, regional, and international) in order to understand how place and the institutions that represent it empower or restrain women as civil agents of change. I use multilevel game theory, applied in the field of international political economy and international relations, as a valuable instrument to study this form of civil activism. It is originally a theory of international bargaining developed as a two-level game to analyze state actors' behavior in local and international spheres (Evans, et al., 1993), which some expand into local, regional, international, and even social levels (Lake and Morgan, 1997) and with which the actors may be playing more than one game at the same time. In this approach 'places' are not treated as separate and independent constituencies.

Essentially, multilevel game theory argues that domestic politics influence international policies and international politics influence domestic decision making. Within this state actors, who primarily seek their survival and then the fulfillment of their goals, may find space to bargain, influencing either the actors' domestic constraints or international policies by playing a 'double-edge diplomacy.' Women activists can be seen as political and social agents that act on both domestic and international levels simultaneously, pursuing changes on one level to affect the other. The difference from the usual application of game theory to international relations is, here, bargaining will not occur between two states or more, but between civil organizations and governmental and intergovernmental institutions.

Background

The Arab Region has faced centuries of prejudice (Said, 1995).[1] As this chapter is written in English, and as many readers are not familiar with the unfair politicization of Arab peoples in American and European literature, history, and now mass media, let me explain my approach. To begin with, I use the term *Arab Region* rather than Middle East, because the majority of the people in the region view themselves as Arab and their country as part of an Arab Region.

Nevertheless, I must acknowledge that the Arab identity is still divisive, even domestically. Arabism was born in the late nineteenth century as a nationalistic movement to resist foreign imperialism and, more romantically, to create a great state that encompasses all Arab nations (*al-watan al-'arabi;* the League of Arab States). At its roots, nationalism is a secular movement that embraced all the different communities and ethnicities in the Arab Peninsula and North Africa. The common denominator is considered the Arab language and the common history that goes back to the Semites' migration from south of the Arab Peninsula to the North African coasts. And it is in this sense that many feminists in the region conceive Arabism. However, we cannot ignore that local states' institutions tend to give an Islamic flavor to contemporary Arabism—just as the international community is belligerently doing so since September 11, 2001—which pushes some non-Muslim communities in the region to resist Arabism. Therefore it becomes a point of division after being born as a point of encounter and unity.

To better understand the identity politics in the Arab Region, we must be aware that this part of the world has been experiencing the same political pattern for more than fifty years (Brown, 1984). Since the end of colonization, the 'interference' of the superpowers has been continuous: starting from naming the region 'the Middle East' in 1912 (Adelson, 1995) to drawing the map of the Nation-states (causing the displacement and dispersion of many populations) after World War II, to the incessant interference in domestic politics, economy, and, today, even in the teaching and practice of religion. Women have often been targeted and positioned as the symbol of the Arab cultural identity in the political dialect between 'inside' and 'outside.' Since colonial times, women's image and status have been used to ridicule the colonized and claim the superiority of the colonizers' culture, even if at home colonizers were conservative and opposed women's independence (Ahmed, 1992). The colonized, however, would react with patriotism, defending local culture. This dialectic set the shape of the politics that organized women face today. In most cases these women act no differently from the colonized patriots of the past.

The end of the Cold War, the collapse of the Soviet Union, and the growing power of the United States changed the local politics, including gender politics. The discourse on women's issues went backward as the world became more conservative; debates that were not aired in the eighties, such as the debate on women's clothing (locally), women's reproductive rights (internationally), and the five-year review of the Fourth World

Conference on Women's Platform for Action in 2000, came back on the agenda. All of these gains risked being lost in the nineties. Conservatism is flourishing in the Arab Region. With the end of the Cold War and the renewed influence of the United States and the European Union in the Arab Region, there has been a surge of neocolonialism characterized by economic and political influence escalating to military war with the recolonization of Iraq, the assassination of many Palestinian political figures, and the military attacks on Syria and Lebanon. The new order that the United States wishes to impose upon the region is leading to a radicalization of the Arab identity and a return to religious discourse among the masses. And within this women are once again being asked to hold up the traditional female image and gender role in society, which is a direct contradiction of the process of modernization that the Arab countries are undertaking. Thus gender and social tensions are extremely high.

Religious forces view social 'modernization' as a government weakness, accusing it of allying with colonial powers. Governments are pushing for social change in the direction of gender equality, especially in the face of international pressure. Arab governments are calling for the advancement of 'the other half of society,' as they move toward greater democratization. And although this may be viewed as 'lip service' in response to international pressures, there are some tangible achievements. New paths for advocacy are opening up. However, these initiatives are from the 'top'; from public and private international institutions and local governments, the question becomes: are women themselves acting as agents of political change?

Women and the Politics of Place in the Arab Region

According to many feminists in the region there is a women's social movement, *'al-harakah al-nissa'eiah,'* that is not so much regional as national. It is important to underline here that in all the Arab countries, with the exception of the Palestinian situation (Moghadam, 1997: 39–40),[2] there has been an absence of any real social movement during the past fifty years because of governmental and military oppression. Arab governments perceive any form of social organization as a potential threat, and there are strong laws regulating civil organization. In fact, the only social movements we can speak of are those of a political-religious background, such as the Muslim Brotherhood. If there is an Arab women's movement it is certainly not a popular one. Rather it is a collection of different types of women activists organized in different spaces, not all of which are recognized by local legislations. That is why I prefer to use the term *organized women,* for they take many organizational forms: Some are independent individuals. Others work through women's organizations, which can be grassroots, professional civil society organizations (CVOs),[3] voluntary organizations, religious associations, or governmental or semigovernmental organizations. Others work with organizations that address human rights, environment, or development in general. These usually have women/gender departments that are no less active than the women-centered organizations. The organized women's work can be categorized as follows, with considerable overlap: 1) services, 2) rights-oriented, 3) development, and 4) research.

The political background of organized Arab women differs, but they are all compelled by the need for gender equity and equality, although certainly they have different views of what that need means in concrete terms and how it should be achieved. Some of these women are declared feminists, while others would resist such a label vigorously, and still others are extremely religious. Among them, some see no contradiction between religion and women's rights or even feminism.[4] They do have a unified voice on issues such as the independence of Palestine, globalization as the cause of increased poverty, and hegemony of what they call the 'West.' Thus they can unify in the face of international threats, because historically the different populations in the individual Arab states tend to unify against the foreign aggressor. On the other hand, they are more fragmented around local issues: local governments, state-economy relations, individual freedoms, and the relationship between state and religion. But most importantly, the space for activism is a space for self-expression for these women, as much of their womanhood cannot be expressed in 'public spaces.'

It is important to keep in mind that many of these organized women and the professional CVOs in particular tend to be from elite groups (sometimes even elitist), or middle-class women who generally have a patron-client relationship with their beneficiaries (Moghadam, 1997: 25).

The organized women on the grassroots level are vast in the periphery, and respond to women's basic needs, but the organizations that dialogue with the central political authority and receive local and international funds are generally the urban organizations with some level of professionalism.

What follows is an analysis of these organized women's groups at the local level (referring here to the national level), regional level (referring to the Arab Region), and international levels (relations with spheres of the international community).

The Local Level

The 'network' of organized women at the national level is quite loose. There is no national agenda and no centralized network through which the women operate. National women's committees are created by governments to address 'the woman question—*massa'alt al mara'ah.*' They are set up in accordance with governmental lines that have considerable national influence, and often they represent the government at world conferences. The civil organizations, on the other hand, create their own programs—often in competition for funds and notoriety issues—but in some cases they do campaign together when there is an important subject that requires their unity, such as the honor killings in Jordan, the NGOs' law in Egypt, and the Family Status Law in many Arab states.

Without an efficient, democratic, governmental system, organized women influence policies through workshops, seminars, and information diffusion programs. This strategy aims to open different dialogues between governmental officers, pro-governmental personalities, religious figures, civil activists and intellectuals, and foreign experts. Within this domain the women's governmental and semigovernmental organizations have a positive function: bridging between the civil sphere and the state institutions. Also international supporters of organized women's activities help to give greater legitimacy to the local organized women's work and encourage the government to listen to the needs of women in society.

At the same time, there is suspicion of foreign funders and their hidden agenda to destabilize national security or change local traditions to conform to the widespread popular consumerist culture, which better suits the international market; for example, the launch of one European government's research program on women's sexual rights in Yemen. It was totally inappropriate given that Yemen is a tribal conservative society and women's sexuality is a subject that cannot be addressed publicly from a 'rightist' perspective or by 'foreigners' without creating tensions. The researchers involved in the project were threatened, and the project was abandoned. Women's rights are always caught among governmental suspicions, traditional forces (religious or otherwise), and the international (American/European) agendas of intergovernmental organizations, international CVOs, and donors' programs. Likewise, UN conferences and international funding for women's rights are not always catalysts for change at home and can be considered by governmental and religious authorities, and even local women, as transplants of 'foreign' ideas that undermine local traditions.

There is no way to ignore the religious domination in governmental or civil campaign attempts to bring about social change. All the religious communities tend to be conservative in the region, not just Islamic as it is usually pictured. The patriarchal hegemony is present in the deferent communities regardless of faith. However, it is important to point out that *Shari'ah* is the main pillar that holds solid the patriarchal and legislative power concerning gender roles. But Shari'ah is not the law of the Qur'an—as it is commonly referred; it is a set of laws that was developed throughout the history of Islam by male scholars who used, as a base, their interpretation of the Qur'an and the oral and written history on the Prophet's sayings and his life experience. These interpretations can also favor a women-centered approach, and organized Arab women work hard to gain the support of religious figures through their knowledge of the Shari'ah. Many feminists would like to open the door for women's interpretations, *ijtihad,* but often shy away because of incredible pressure from state and religious arenas. Yet there are a few women who have taken this path, such as Faridah Bennani, the Moroccan professor, lawyer, and writer. Others instead think it is better to completely abandon the religious method and base their struggle on a 'rightist' approach, but unfortunately Arab governments and traditional institutions do not completely approve of the codes of universal human rights.[5]

Some governmental policies imposed by international forces, such as family planning, would have been impossible to implement without the agreement of religious institutions declaring that contraceptives do not conflict with Shari'ah. In relation to the struggle to end female genital mutilation, without state and religious institutional support, women activists would not have had the success they have enjoyed to date.

The local discourse of social change and women's rights in particular is dominated by religious debates. As the Arab Region gave birth to the three main world religions, its people are understandably very attached to the concept of living everyday life in religious terms. Yet religion per se is not static, it is the patriarchal system that has the power over the domain of religion. And in order to change such a system, many organized women are realizing that they need to gain power in the religious domain. More and more women are seeking theological knowledge to dialogue with religious authorities in their same language, using their same tools.

The Regional Level

The places for regional level women's politics are the Arab Women Summits, the UN regional meetings, and the meetings organized by civil regional and subregional networks. However, there is no real regional agenda. There are moments within the preparation for an international conference, such as the UN Beijing Conference, in which some organization will organize (often with outside funding) a preparatory Arab meeting. It is unclear how participants are chosen for these meetings and what are the criteria with which the 'Arab Agenda' is prepared.[6]

The constraints that apply on the local level are also true on the regional level. However, what is positive about regional meetings is that they promote regional networking and build solidarity among Arab women. It should be noted that often the main driving force of a regional meeting is a UN agency's need to pull together an Arab Region statement for a UN conference or treaty, and that particular agency is the one funding the meeting and drafting the final statement or document.

The recently created Arab Women's Organisation (previously known as the Arab Women Summit) is dominating regional Arab women's discourse, but it excludes the majority of the organized women. The civil actors that are engaged have usually gained government approval and tend to be conservative. The Arab Women Forum on 'Women and Law,' organized by the Arab Region Organization (ARO) and held in Bahrain, came up with several recommendations, one of which was to unify the Family Law in the Arab states. Although this may be considered a positive outcome, it is unrealistic. The differences between the laws in Tunisia and Saudi Arabia, for example, are large, even if both populations are predominantly Muslim.

There are also other places where regional and subregional work is organized. Many regional CVOs and networks organize common advocacy strategies. An example is AISHA network, which coordinates among different organized women in the region. Another example is the Collectif '95 of the Arab Maghreb, which prepared a common agenda on reforming the Family Law in the Maghreb subregion.[7] And they are lobbying locally and internationally for consideration of their propositions.

Identity is the main language of regional settings, which takes as a basis the politics of contemporary Arabism rather than secular Arabism; therefore Islam and Shari'ah are often considered the common dominator, which again differs in interpretation and application from one state to another. Another symbol of Arabism politics that influences women's politics at this level is the colonization of Palestine and Iraq. Any meeting outcome at the regional level always contains calls to the international community and the Arab governments to end the injustices that Palestinian and Iraqi women are facing.

The International Level

The international level is the sphere of the international community, which in theory includes the globe, but in practice is the expression of the dominant powers, currently the United States and European Union. In this sphere, as in much of the rest of the organized Arab civil society, organized Arab women have hardly had any voice when it comes to 'global' issues. Their contribution to international policy tends to be very weak. International agendas are dominated by American and European women. We also need to recall that the Arab women who reach the international conventions are those with enough technical skills. Therefore they are well educated, upper middle-class women. They tend to show the local or regional progress that has been made (legal reforms, data on education level or employment, or successful projects), depending on the groups they represent, and then explain the obstacles and the goals that need to be reached—without upsetting local governments or traditions. In these conferences, the objective is usually to produce some kind of report or agreement, and therefore many compromises take place. The role of the organized Arab women on this level is to bring in local/regional 'Arab' issues. For example, relative to the UN Convention on the Elimination of All Forms of Discrimination against Women (CEDAW), although organized women had negotiated extensively with their governments, it was signed by less than half of the Arab states, and even those expressed their reservations because some articles conflicted with local traditions.

Another example is the 2000 World Conference against Racism held in Durban, South Africa, where the final document of the conference was totally different from the document that the NGOs produced. Here Arab women's organizations focused on the Palestinian crisis. Although highlighting Palestinian women, they sacrificed gender issues to give priority to regional and nationalist agendas; the outside hegemony threatening the Arab Region is viewed as more critical than the local struggle for women's rights.

It is interesting to note that these women are also constrained by identity politics from the outside. American/European feminists always see their identity as 'Arab women.' When Arab women are invited to an international roundtable, usually Islam, Shari'ah, and the veil are the main subjects they are expected to speak about, even when the participant is Christian. No one asks them to speak about the world economy, global governance, UN reform, the environmental crisis, or gender issues in Latin America or Europe or anywhere else.

On the other hand, the Arab women tend to group together at these meetings rather than build solidarity groups with participants from other regions. The networking for solidarity and experience exchange is limited; this might be because not many women share the 'constraints' Arab women face. Arab women actors focus on who can support their work in terms of funds and visibility within authoritative institutions; getting to know which person can be sensitive to their cases in an informal way, creating for them a safe space that can support their struggle.

In the case of the antiglobalization movement, Arab civil activists are confronted with the question of who is to speak for Arab women? If each woman speaks for her country, we find that it is difficult to set the priorities because of the lack of an agreed-upon national agenda. And these women tend to speak to nationalistic claims, especially in these environments where identity politics is the main game.

Conclusions

Even if the Arab Region differs on economic and social levels, gender politics across the region faces the same constraints. The organized women, as state actors, are concerned about their survival first and then the fulfillment of their gender objectives. They face restrictive traditional powers and governmental repression domestically, preventing any serious clashes that would lead to endangering their mission. Other constraints are financial; they need funding and, thus lacking bargaining power, they must find a compromise with donors' agendas, which may lead them to address questions that are not a priority. The 'outside' prejudice expressed toward Arab women confines them within the domain of identity politics.

Arab women see defending their place from externalities and colonization as a priority issue that takes much of their energy and focus from critically addressing gender inequalities.[8]

Yet, despite constraints, Arab women have found ways to create spaces within which to bargain. Locally, they make use of international pressures, which sometimes they themselves help induce, to negotiate with governments for change. Similarly, they dialogue with religious figures to gain support for international conventions and local projects and to insure domestic consent, so that governments will approve of them.

Regionally, the situation seems stagnant; a discursive politics rather than effective policies. There are a number of regional documents and amendments produced at this level, but nothing has been implemented. There are only two outcomes produced by women's regional politics that can be considered positive: One is the regional documents of the UN meetings, which contribute to international discussions. The other is the networking among the organized women in safe spaces that allow them to speak freely, exchange lessons, and build solidarity networks. External forces are less influential on this level. This is mainly because of the strength of identity politics and the impenetrability of regional institutions such as Arab Women's Summit and the UN regional organisms.

Internationally, there is a participation problem and lack of access to decision making in inter-governmental institutions. There is a lack of adequate participation of the diverse, organized women at regional and international intergovernmental institutions. And the present structures do not give them any power in decision making. The organized women also seek safe spaces through interpersonal communications to help their work locally, and inform and, if possible, lobby with sympathetic institutional personalities to put pressure on local governments.

Restricted by both domestic constraints and foreign intervention, Arab women seem to react rather than act in these different political levels. Arab Region women need international support for localized funding and to put political pressure on governments. Some work needs to be done domestically to relax the traditional forces through strategic use of religious interpretations and by ensuring that women's politics reflects local concerns, rather than being imposed from the outside.

There are two main problems that are not adequately addressed. The first problem is the question of representation: these women are working for women's empowerment, but are they really representing the needs and desires of the majority of women in their place? The second problem is the gender blindness and lack of women's consciousness: there is a lot of talk about whether an Arab women's movement exists or not. Yet there is little discussion on the gender blindness of the majority of women in the region—let alone the men—or among organized women themselves. The female population is not politically organized to demand their rights and empowerment, which in some cases are already granted by their local constitution but not applied. Such a popular movement would have strong bargaining power. The lack of a popular women's movement in this part of the world has led to a top-to-bottom strategy, in which the 'knowledgeable' women and institutions aim to empower themselves based on their views and/or international agendas.[9]

There is a need for Arab women to inhabit comfortably the global space in which they are currently considered 'foreigners.' They need to contribute to the building of global agendas that are not directly connected with 'Arab' or even 'gender' issues. The big test for the region is whether modernization can be carried through the preservation and celebration of the religious heritage. Governments need to have more faith in civil organizations as the bearers of political and economic, historical momentum. The system needs to be democratized and civil societies engaged, rather than use top-to-bottom approaches or external impositions. Civil society capacity building also needs to reach the popular level to be successful in promoting social justice and sustainable change.

A Last Word

More than ten years of work as an activist and writer, with different organized women in almost all the Arab states, has led me to give what some readers might consider a somewhat general picture.[10] Returning to my opening concern, how does a global women's movement empower these local organized women? Even if Arab Region women can contribute to the spaces where a global women's movement operates, they may not be able to take up the issues raised at the global level with the local authorities. The only way they gain bargaining advantage is through intergovernmental relations in which they can play double-edge strategies. A global civil women's movement has no validity in the Arab governments' eyes; on the contrary it is regarded as a threat. Thus, how can such a movement offer greater bargaining power to localized women's movements? Is revolution the only real alternative?

Who is authorized to ask for change, in the name of the people, in a nondemocratic system: is it the so-called intellectual class? In this chapter I have been critical of the concerns and objectives of the organized women in the region, but I wonder how much we can foster a popular women's movement in the Arab world. How can the majority of women become more aware of their rights or political possibilities for change? In the democratic canon the majority should rule, and minorities must be granted full respect. Perhaps this remains the real challenge for organized women: how to listen and engage with the majority of the women in the region.

Using multilevel game theory, I have argued that we cannot answer these questions unless we examine the complexity of factors that operate at various levels. Each level has its own possibilities and constraints, and they influence each other. These scalar factors need to be understood as part of any politics of place framework.

Notes

1. See Chapter 13.
2. The Palestinian women's movement, although started by the educated and middle-class women, has reached the grassroots level and has gained popular support.

3. The CVOs in Arab states are set up with varying legal status because of the repressive legislations regarding civil activism.

4. Many religious women activists see no contradiction between Islam and feminism; obviously they are against patriarchal institutions that interpret Islamic philosophy. There is an emerging field called 'Islamic Feminism.'

5. Governments and religious figures deny the rights of homosexuals, for example.

6. This may not be true of the meetings organized and led by the United Nations, as they tend to base their work on independent, 'scientific' researchers.

7. Their approach of reform is based on both 'rightist' and religious beliefs, as most members do not see a contradiction between the two.

8. Positive examples should be taken from the Palestinian women who, although living in a continuous conflict situation, still address inequalities and women's rights to the point that they are some of the best-organized women in the region.

9. Some organized women rely on funding agencies' programs.

10. This picture excludes Libya, Djibouti, Mauritania, Somalia, and the Comoros. In Libya civil organizations are more focused on charity work, although this is changing with the new policies of liberalization. Although they are members of the League of Arab States, Djibouti, Mauritania, and Somalia are usually excluded from what can be considered the Arab women's dialogue. I presume this is because, in terms of gender politics and constraints, they have more in common with other African countries than with the Arab states. The Comoros joined the League in 1993 and is not really part of the regional politics.

Afterword
The Politics of Place, the Place of Politics: Some Forward-looking Reflections

SONIA E. ALVAREZ

This anthology is the carefully crafted product of a continuous political-intellectual process involving sustained conversations among a group of engaged scholars and activist-intellectuals committed to promoting alternatives to patriarchal neoliberal globalization. What most distinguishes this collection is that the authors' abiding commitment to a feminist politics of place stems from a shared conviction that such alternatives are already 'out there,' are already *taking place* around the world, in women's and men's lived experiences of place, in their place-based—though not placebound—struggles with/against globalization.

I was instantly drawn to the Women and the Politics of Place (WPP) project by the extraordinary women and men involved and by the diverse range of intriguing places and processes it explored; but I confess that when my friend and long-time collaborator, coeditor Arturo Escobar, first approached me about participating in an April 2002 workshop in Eugene, Oregon (a core event in the extended process that resulted in this book), I did not fully understand the concept of 'place' and I had some misgivings that the notion might prove to be somewhat 'romantic' or even potentially 'parochial.' Of course, early on during the Eugene meeting and in subsequent dialogues with participants in the project, I realized my doubts had been seriously mis*placed*. Lingering concerns were directly addressed and definitively laid to rest by the analytically compelling essays assembled in this anthology. I will return

248

to my sole remaining reservation, shared by a couple of the contributors, at the end of these remarks.

I am fully persuaded that one of the most unique contributions of this volume is to *restore the rightful place of place* to the ways we go about theorizing social, economic, political, cultural, and ecological change in this so-called 'global era.' In academic debates, especially during the 1990s, it seemed as though "everything was going away from place . . . place was dead, place was not the place to go," as Escobar aptly put it during our conversations in Eugene. The emphasis instead, as he noted, "was on diaspora, nomadism, migration, traveling, and so on." The theoretical and political significance of historical particularities, specific practices, and particular localities was purportedly subsumed, when not completely erased, by (ever more phantasmagorical) global forces. Place was increasingly devalued and judged irrelevant, and place-based movements were portrayed as "defensive, and even conservative," as Gerda Wekerle reminds us. Yet the notion of place, as coeditor Wendy Harcourt rightly insisted during the Oregon seminar, highlights the fact that "nothing is ever purely local or global." Places, after all, are "constituted at the crossroads of global forces," as J. K. Gibson-Graham suggest. And women activists are making 'complex connections' across multiple scales, suggesting that place is hardly self-contained—much less parochial—but rather, as Khawar Mumtaz and Lamis al-Shejni sustain, "operates at various levels in global times." A focus on place, then, provides a novel and especially discerning analytical lens through which to re-vision our political responses to modernity and global capitalism. In short, the wide range of riveting and revealing stories recounted in this book amply attest to the fact that the WPP framework offers an innovative critical language from which we can approach globalization in different and productive ways.

In doing so, this book unsettles, disturbs, and ultimately *displaces* what the editors refer to as the seamless *globalocentric* narratives that prevail in both mainstream and progressive theorizing about the world economy and the environment—this volume's second critical contribution. The chapters expose the fissures, the gaps, and sometimes the outright fault lines at which resistances, reimaginings, reembodiments, reembeddings, and relocalizations *take place*. As Wekerle, Gibson-Graham, and several other contributors maintain, dominant scripts about the global are typically presented as degendered and universally valid. In the new gender and development regime that grew out of the UN conference processes of the 1990s, for instance, "the demands of a global discourse smoothed away the differences of place," as Harcourt conclusively shows in her chapter. But this book's focus on the *practices of difference* expressed through the diverse embodiments, environments, and econo- mies in evidence in a wide range of places—from global cities like Toronto to out-of-the-way places such as rural Finland and Papua New Guinea—decidedly debunks neoliberalism's favored mantra, that 'there are no alternatives.'

The book renders "legible" (see Chapter 5) already existing alterna- tives to the purportedly flawless teleology of global neoliberal capitalism by foregrounding "ongoing and emergent sites of resistance that are often grounded in place" (see Chapter 6) and bringing to light many experi- ences "beyond classically 'heroic' struggles," like those of women in the Rural Federation of Zambrana-Chacuey in the Dominican Republic, "the kind of struggle embodied by women herbalists, midwives, farmers, and political leaders" that "still seems to escape many social movement schol- ars and advocates" (see Chapter 5). Perhaps no place in this collection is neoliberalism's 'singular thought' or *pensamiento único* more effectively and thoroughly demystified than in J. K. Gibson-Graham's discussion of diverse, noncapitalist community economies in which women hold a dis- tinctive place—one that helps unsettle and thereby contest the hegemony of capitalocentric conceptions of the global economy. A key goal of Gibson-Graham's action-research project, like that of the WPP project more generally, is to render "visible and intelligible the diverse and pro- liferating practices that the preoccupation with capitalism has obscured," to highlight the "power of place as a site of economic diversity and poten- tial, rather than a colonized node in a capitalist world." Struggles such as those of the black women of the Pacific in Libia Grueso and Leyla Royo's account attest to the value of this conceptualization.

The contributors to this volume are not content to simply critique dominant global capitalist logics—though some of their critiques are certainly powerful, trenchant ones. This anthology's third and perhaps most important contribution, instead, is precisely that it seeks to *replace dominant globalocentric narratives with rooted, embodied, embedded stories* and to *set in place* a flexible, interpretive framework that can be productively deployed by those seeking to theorize *and* to enact creative forms of feminist place-based globalism. The WPP framework offers up more conceptual innovations than I can possibly do justice to in these brief concluding words; I simply wish to highlight just a few among the many that merit further theoretical reflection and elaboration.

WPP's conception of women's bodies as fluid sites of "power and political contestation" (see Chapter 2), as "sites of resistance . . . simultaneously constituted by places and discourses," for instance, provides us with an especially promising, critical lens through which to "understand how women's agency from a fleshy postmaterialist position has a transformative, not just a destabilizing effect," as Yvonne Underhill-Sem eloquently puts it. This fleshy, embodied, placed-based perspective, as she further argues, offers feminist analysts the possibility of assuming a "theoretical position that allows bodies and places to be both grounded and materially pinchable, and also to be fluid and discursively constituted."

Fluidity and groundedness also come together in several authors' shared emphasis on relationality, on women's embeddedness in relational webs, networks, and meshworks. Sociopolitical networks and, particularly, meshworks are central to the WPP framework, and are critical to how place-based struggles often connect translocally and forge what we come to normally refer to as 'global' movements. As Mumtaz contends, there is a "network component to all politics of place, meaning that place is neither simply local nor its politics placebound, even if it continues to be fundamental in people's daily lives." Meshworks are especially crucial to the prefigurative politics envisioned by this project and are defined by the editors as "nonhierarchical and self-organizing networks that often grow in unplanned directions," involving "two parallel dynamics: strategies of localization and of interweaving." Fluid, weblike 'enmeshments' rooted in—but extending beyond, into, and across—place(s) are said especially to characterize newer movements, such as the anti- or alternative globalization movement(s) or AGMs, which tend to operate simultaneously on several scales. For Michal Osterweil, the AGMs are "comprised of myriad locally situated realities that cumulatively—both in intentional and less intentional cooperation—build a global politics" in which "activists deliberately choose to employ dispersed and small-scale strategies viable only in a network form in order to achieve global change."

Rooted social-cultural networks and relational webs are also key protagonists in several of the stories compiled in this volume. For Underhill-Sem, "'webs of power' are critical in continuing to define the ways in which women's bodies are constituted, in a myriad of different places." In Liisa Horelli's account of place-based politics in rural Finland, "networks of social cohesion" are intimately intertwined with the creation and sustenance of diverse economies. These networks are also central to the re-creation and maintenance of senses of place even in refugee experiences, as Randa Farah documents for the case of Palestinian women in refugee camps. Dianne Rocheleau further insists that people's lives and livelihoods are rooted in networks and landscapes of home, in relational webs that reconcile "networks and territories, men and women, experience and expertise, insider and outsider." And it is precisely those relational webs, in her view, that make possible the "continuing performance, affirmation and creation of positive alternative cultures expressed in values, landscapes, artifacts, rituals and daily practice that draw their legitimacy from a domain beyond the control (and even the gaze) of recognized, dominant power."

While calling attention to the "tangled, gendered social relations of power that join and separate all of us," Rocheleau also enjoins us to "complicate our notions of power," to "consider more entangled and embedded workings of power-alongside, power-under, power-in-spite-of, and power-between"—a keen insight of the WPP approach. It is in a similar vein that Underhill-Sem suggests that the operations of "dominant power" are not always what they appear to be, that, for instance, "Christianity has always had localized meanings in Papua New Guinea because meanings are constantly in tension over colonial, religious, and local agents of change." It is within these place-based meanings, she maintains, "that some women have been able to contest global influences."

The strategic importance of 'localizing' global meanings, of crafting place-based translations of global scripts, is another critical dimension of the WPP framework. In translating local women's needs into what some have called the 'language of Geneva' and relegating women's place-based politics to relative (and not always benign) neglect, Harcourt suggests that many advocates and "gender experts" in the so-called "global women's movement" became party to a "biopolitics of the management of gender" that produced new "productive," "maternal," and "sexualized" bodies specifically regulated for the needs of global capital in the twenty-first century. In the absence of adequate translations grounded in localized systems of meaning, the 'generic,' women-targeted antipoverty program or microcredit global recipes advocated by the World Bank or UN agencies almost invariably produce disciplined bodies, "mannequins of neoliberal economic development" (see Chapter 10), rather than empowered subjects. Even the progressive place-based experiments in forging noncapitalist economies discussed by Gibson-Graham "cannot be transported to any site in the world and expected to work without modification. In each site the particular and contingent conditions will present their own challenges, shaping the decisions made and the pathways followed." Perhaps a further lesson to be drawn from the stories collected here is that the need for continual translation is most pressing for precisely those activists and intellectuals whose work already stretches across scales. Forging new forms of place-based globalism that builds on such work, moreover, may well be a growing trend in feminist and other forms of social justice activism.

Yet, as was the case with many feminists, it would seem that—especially during the 1990s—many in the environmental, human rights, urban reform, and other progressive movements bought into Geneva/UN/global-speak and perhaps "overestimated the progressive change resulting from global civic engagement," as Smitu Kothari lamented in his interview. Many rights and social justice advocates may indeed have *misplaced* their energies in first getting thoroughly entangled with the UN conference process of the first half of the 1990s and then with monitoring the implementation of endless UN documents, platforms, and agreements through the various '+5' and now '+10' sequels. Still, it is certainly the case, as Harcourt and Fatma Alloo note, that many in global women's movements are currently in a 'third moment' of "disengagement or at least a significant problematization" in relation to development discourse and especially in relation to the United Nations, and that many are shifting their attention toward other "sites of power and knowledge production" like the AGMs and the World Social Forum (WSF).

Indeed, the people whom a Brazilian friend of mine who is one of the founders of the WSF process refers to as "the orphans of the United Nations"—NGO activists who invested heavily in the UN process but who became deeply disenchanted with it by the late 1990s—have been quite prominent in the Forum from the outset. It is encouraging that many highly heterogeneous streams of social justice organizing are increasingly flowing together in AGMs at the various scales and in the multifaceted, variegated, enmeshed, and always-grounded forms in which they have been articulated. Much of what we typically refer to as 'global activism' is not only rooted in place but is also inspired by and grows out of place-based practices. That is arguably the case with the WSF itself, for instance, which to my mind is (still) clearly marked by the practices of the Brazilian social movement field in which it originated. Similarly, it is no coincidence that a feminist politics is clearly discernible in the 'new' politics of AGMs, as Osterweil discusses in her chapter. Feminist theories and feminist activists coming from *many places*—prominently from Brazil/Latin America and India/South Asia, in the case of the global WSF meetings held between 2001 and 2005— have been an organized, if often largely un- or underacknowledged, presence in AGMs and the WSF and have struggled mightily to ensure precisely the "logics of difference, horizontality, and dispersion," long-time feminist trademarks now often celebrated as a 'novelty' of the globalist 'left.' To account for the pronounced presence of feminists in place-based expressions of globalism such as the WSF, moreover, we must also acknowledge that many feminist activists remained very much 'in place' during the 1990s, even as they forged global linkages, and have been moving in the direction of 'multiscalar' feminist organizing for some time now.

The analyses presented in this book clearly suggest that it is imperative that we continue to build global connections while also focusing our energies on understanding "the global 'in place,'" as Harcourt fittingly puts it. Yet doing so will require foregrounding the *politics* part of the WPP framework, a dimension largely undertheorized in the present collection. Very different political movements, coalitions, and configurations of actors and forms/regimes of politics, operating at different political 'scales' (local/municipal, state/provincial, national/federal, regional, interstate/international)—in short, sharply differing *practices* surrounding politics—deeply inform the various embodiments, ecologies, and economies analyzed in this volume in critical ways. Taking a closer look at the practices of 'globalized' NGOs and 'gender experts' in their relation to place-based women's struggles, for instance, would seem particularly crucial to enacting the WPP framework in ways that further social transformation rather than, however inadvertently, fostering new disciplinary/managerial regimes. After all, as Laura Agustín reminds us, a "rampant ventriloquism" sometimes characterizes the actions of "those who seek to 'represent' . . . women's needs." Examining such representational, deeply political practices 'closer-in' would no doubt further illuminate how we might move forward in *repoliticizing feminist politics* in ways that create new possibilities for "forging linkages across and among scales" (see Chapter 6).

The task of collectively reimagining a more fluid, more interconnected cross- and multiscalar feminist politics would seem to be an especially urgent one, because less-than-egalitarian, hierarchical, patriarchal, racist, and sometimes blatantly antidemocratic 'snags' still pervade even the 'newest of new' movements such as the AGMs and their most globally diffused and most ostensibly horizontal and 'meshworked' expressions, like the WSF process. The relationship between the global justice movement, women, and feminism in particular is at once "productive and problematic," as Osterweil reminds us. Indeed, as she rightly stresses, "there is a very fine line between the movements' potentially transformative feminism, and a politics that masks new forms of exclusions under the rhetoric of feminism." More effectively negotiating that line represents perhaps one of the most formidable challenges facing those wishing to build place-based feminist globalist practices.

I want to end by making a brief reference to the lingering reservation about 'place' that I alluded to at the outset of these brief reflections—a concern shared with Agustín and Marisa Belausteguigoitia regarding the need for feminists to be vigilant about the frequent need for women to "disturb place-based strategies." There are clear "dangers of 'place-based' strategies when they involve women," Belausteguigoitia insists. And as Agustín succinctly puts it, "home can be a suffocating place." This is certainly the case for many women, as well as for lesbians, gays, and transgendered people, and for those from ethnic or racial groups who are not dominant 'at home.' 'Moving in movements' and making connections with other people in other places can therefore be enabling, can create more space for women and other subaltern groups when they return to place. This is precisely the power of UN conferences, of Porto Alegre, and other such 'global' spaces, of the temporary strategic displacements that help women gain a different perspective on how the global shapes their particular places. A *feminist* WPP project, in sum, must be centrally concerned with making space for women in (and beyond) place.

Bibliography

Adelson, Roger. *London and the Invention of the Middle East*. New Haven, CT: Yale University Press, 1995.

Agustín, Laura. "Mujeres inmigrantes ocupadas en la industria del sexo." *Mujer, inmigración y trabajo*, Colectivo IOÉ, ed., 647–716. Madrid: IMSERSO, 2001.

———. "Forget Victimisation: Granting Agency to Migrants." *Development*, 46 no. 3 (2003): 30–6.

———. "A Migrant World of Services." *Social Politics*, 10, 3 (2004): 377–96.

———. "The Disappearing of a Migration Category: Migrants Who Sell Sex." *Journal of Ethnic and Migration Studies* (2005a; forthcoming).

———. "Migrants in the Mistress's House: Other Voices in the 'Trafficking' Debate." *Social Politics* 12, 1 (2005b).

Ahmed, Leila. *Women and Gender in Islam: Historical Roots of a Modern Debate*. New Haven, CT: Yale University Press, 1992.

Alarcón, Norma. "Traddutora, Traditora: A paradigmatic figure of Chicana feminism." *Cultural Critique* (Fall 1989), 57–87.

Alarcón, Norma, Caren Kaplan, and Minoo Moallem. *Between Women and Nation: Nationalisms, transnational feminisms and the state*. Durham, NC: Duke University Press, 1999.

Ali, Rabia. *The Dark Side of 'Honour'; Women Victims in Pakistan*. Lahore: Shirkat Gah, 2001.

Allison, Anne. *Nightwork: Sexuality, Pleasure and Corporate Masculinity in a Tokyo Hostess Club*. Chicago: University of Chicago Press, 1994.

Alloo, Fatma, Imruh Bakari, and Xavi Perez. "Cultural Diversity, Cultural Production and Identity." *Another World is Possible* (Michael Hardt and Antonio Negri, eds; World Social Forum). London: Zed Books, 2003.

Alvarez, Sonia, with Nalu Faria, and Miriam Nobre. "Another (Also Feminist) World is Possible." *Challenging Empires: World Social Forum* (Jai Sen,

Anita Anand, Arturo Escobar, and Peter Waterman, eds.), 199–206. New Delhi: Viveka Foundation, 2004.

Amin, Ash, Angus Cameron, and Ray Hudson. *Placing the Social Economy.* London and New York: Routledge, 2003.

Anzaldúa, Gloria, and Analouise Keatin, eds. *This Bridge We Call Home. Radical Visions for Transformation.* New York: Routledge, 2002.

APDC. "Women, Environment and Development." *Issues in Gender and Development.* Special Issue 4 (September 1992). Kuala Lumpur: Asia Pacific Development Centre.

Appadurai, Arjun. *Modernity at Large.* Minneapolis, MN: University of Minnesota Press, 1996.

———. "Deep democracy: urban governmentality and the horizon of politics." *Environment and Urbanization* 13, 2 (2001): 23–43.

Armitage, Susan H. with Patricia Hart, and Karen Weathermon, eds. *Women's Oral History.* Lincoln and London: University of Nebraska Press, 2002.

Asad, Talal. *Formations of the Secular: Christianity, Islam, Modernity.* Stanford, CA: Stanford University Press, 2003.

Barabási, Albert-László. *Linked. The New Science of Networks.* Perseus, 2002.

Barker, John. "Cheerful pragmatists: Anglican missionaries among the Maisin of Collingwood Bay, Northeastern Papua, 1898–1920." *The Journal of Pacific History* 22, no. 2 (1987): 66–81.

———. "Encounters with evil: Christianity and the response to sorcery among the Maisin of Papua New Guinea." *Oceania* 61 (1990): 139–155.

Belausteguigoitia, Marisa. "The Color of the Earth: Indigenous women 'before the law." *Development* 45, no. 1.

Beneria, Lourdes. *Gender, development and globalization: Economics as if people mattered.* New York: Routledge, 2003.

Betances, Emilio. *State and Society in the Dominican Republic.* Boulder, CO: Westview Press, 1995.

Blekaitis, Sarah. "Female Circumcision: Critiquing Western Feminist Literature." MA Thesis, submitted to the University of Western Ontario, Department of Anthropology, September 2004.

Booher, David E., and Judith E. Innes. "Network Power in Collaborative Planning." *Journal of Planning Education and Research* 21, no. 3 (2002): 221–236.

Brandt, Barbara. *Whole Life Economics: Revaluing Daily Life.* Philadelphia, PA: New Society Publishers, 1995.

Brenner, Neil, and Nik Theodore. "Cities and the geographies of 'Actually existing neoliberalism.'" *Antipode* 34 (2002): 349–379.

Brown, L. Carl. *International Politics and the Middle East.* Princeton, NJ: Princeton University Press, 1984.

Butler, Judith. *Gender trouble: Feminism and the subversion of identity.* London and New York: Routledge, 1990.

Callard, Felicity J. "The body in social theory." *Environment and Planning D: Society and Space* 16 (1998): 387–400.

Callon, Michel, ed. *The laws of the markets*. Oxford and Malden, MA: Blackwell Publishing, 1998.

Cameron, Jenny, and J. K Gibson-Graham. "Feminising the Economy: metaphors, strategies, politics." *Gender, Place and Culture* 10, no. 2 (2003): 145–157.

Castells, Manuel. *The Rise of the Network Society*. Oxford and Cambridge, MA: Blackwell Publishing, 1996.

Charkiewicz, Ewa. "Beyond Good and Evil: Notes on Global Feminist Advocacy." Paper given at the NCRW, New York, 2004.

Chatterjee, Partha. "The Nationalist Resolution of the Woman's Question." *Recasting Women* (Kum Kum Sangary, and Sudesh Vaid, eds.). New Delhi: Kali for Women, 1989.

Chatterton, Paul. "Making autonomous geographies: Argentina's popular uprising and the 'Movimento de Trabajadores Desocupados' (Unemployed Workers Movement)." *Geoforum* (forthcoming; 2005).

Clarke, Ben, and Clifton Ross, eds. *Voices of Fire: Communiqués and interviews from the Zapatista National Liberation Army*. Berkeley, CA: New Earth Publications, 1994.

Clifford, James. *Routes: Travel and Translation in the Late Twentieth Century*. Cambridge: Harvard University Press, 1997.

———. Indigenous articulations. *The Contemporary Pacific* 13 (2) 9 (2001): 468–490.

Colectivo Situaciones. "Causes and happenstance (dilemmas of Argentina's new social protagonism): research manuscript #4." *The Commoner*, Autumn/Winter 2004; www.thecommoner.org.

Collier, George A. *Basta: Land and the Zapatistas rebellion in Chiapas*. Oakland, CA: Food First, 1994.

Comisión Nacional de Intermediación (CONAI). *Primeros Acuerdos de San Andrés. Mesa 1: "Derechos y Cultura Indigena."* Mexico City: CONAI, 1996.

Community Economies Collective. "Imagining and enacting noncapitalist futures." *Socialist Review* 28, 3+4 (2001): 93–135.

Connolly, William E. *Why I am not a secularist*. Minneapolis, MN: University of Minnesota Press, 1999.

Cook, Paul, Patricia Boekholt, and F. Tödtling. *The Governance of Innovation in Europe. Regional Perspectives on Global Competitiveness*. London: Pinter, 2000.

Cooper, Barbara M. "Gender, movement and history: social and spatial transformations in 20th century Maradi, Niger." *Environment and Planning D: Society and Space* 15, 2 (1997): 195–221.

Correa, Sonia. *Population and Reproductive Rights: Feminists Perspectives from the South*. London: Zed Books, 1994.

Davies, R. "Improved representations of change processes: Improved theories of change." Paper presented at the EES 5th Biennal Conference, October 1012, 2002, in Sevilla, Spain.

Delphy, C. *Close to home: A materialist analysis of women's oppression* (D. Leonard, trans.). London: Hutchinson, 1984.

Diaz, Vincente M., and J. Kehaulani Kauanui. "Native Pacific cultural studies on the edge." *The Contemporary Pacific* 13, 2 (2001): 315–341.

Dinnen, Sinclair, and Allison Ley, eds. *Reflections on Violence in Melanesia.* Sydney: Hawkins Press and Asia Pacific Press, 2000.

Dirlik, Arif. "Women and the politics of place: a comment." *Development* 45, 1 (2002): 14–18.

Domingo, R. W. "Bulk of OFW inflows 'unproductive.'" ADB funded study (2004). www.inq7money.net.

Douglas, Bronwyn. "Prologue." *Oceania* 74, No. 1 and 2 (2003).

Elson, Diane. *Male bias in the development process.* Manchester, UK: University of Manchester Press, 1995.

Emery, M. "The persistence of subsistence in the United States: toward a political ecology of human-environment relations outside the market." Unpublished manuscript; Burlington, VT: University of Vermont, 2004.

Enloe, Cynthia. *The Curious Feminist: Searching for Women in a New Age of Empire.* Berkeley, CA.: University of California Press, 2004.

Escobar, Arturo, Dianne Rocheleau, and Smitu Kothari. "Environmental Social movements and the Politics of Place." *Development* (Special Issue on Place Politics and Justice: Women negotiating globalization) 45, 1 (2002): 28–36.

Escobar, Arturo, and Wendy Harcourt. "Women and the politics of scale." *Development* 45, 1 (2003): 7–14.

Escobar, Arturo. *Encountering Development: the Making and Unmaking of the Third World.* Princeton: Princeton University Press, 1995.

———. "An Ecology of Difference: Equality and Conflict in a Glocalized World." Prepared for UNESCO. Unpublished manuscript (1999).

———. "Culture Sits in Places. Reflections on Globalism and Subaltern Strategies of Globalization." *Political Geography* 20 (2001): 139–174.

———. "Displacement, Development and Modernity in the Colombian Pacific." *International Social Science Journal* 175 (2003): 157–167.

———. "Identity." *A Companion to the Anthropology of Politics* (D. Nugent, and J. Vincent, eds.), 248–266. Oxford: Blackwell, 2004.

Evans, Peter B., Harold K. Jacobson, and Robert D. Putnam, eds. *Double-Edged Diplomacy: International Bargaining and Domestic Politics.* Berkeley, CA: University of California Press, 1993.

Eyerman, Ron, and Andrew Jamison. *Social Movements. A Cognitive Approach.* Philadelphia, PA: Pennsylvania Press, 1991.

Fainstein, Susan. *The city builders: property development in New York and London 1980–2000* (Second Edition, Revised). Lawrence, KS: University of Kansas Press, 2001.

———. "Can we make the cities we want?" *The urban moment* (R. Beauregard and S. Body-Gendrot, eds.). Thousand Oaks, CA: Sage Publications, 1999.

Farah, Randa. "Popular Memory and Reconstructions of Palestinian Identity: al-Baq'a camp, Jordan." Ph.D. dissertation, Department of Anthropology, University of Toronto, 1999.

————. "The Significance of Oral Narratives and Life-Histories." *al-Jana: File on Palestinian Oral History* (Rosemary Sayigh, ed.). Beirut, Lebanon: Arab Resource Center for Popular Arts, 2002.

————. "'But Where Shall I Return? Where To?' 1948 Palestinian Refugees: Land and Return." *Mediterranean Journal of Human Rights, Special Edition* 8 no. 2 (2004): 157–185.

Field, Debbie. "Putting food first: women's role in creating a grassroots system outside the marketplace." *Women working the NAFTA food chain: women, food and globalization* (D. Barndt, ed.). Toronto: Second Story Press, 1999.

Fitzpatrick, Tony, with Caron Caldwell. "Towards a Theory of Ecosocial Welfare: Radical Reformism and Local Exchanges and Trading Systems (LETS)." *Environmental Politics* 10, no. 2 (2001): 43–67.

Folbre, Nancy. "A patriarchal mode of production." *Alternatives to economic orthodoxy: A reader in political economy* (R. Albelda, C. Gunn, and W. Waller, eds.), 323–38. Armonk, NY: M.E. Sharpe, 1987.

————. *The invisible heart: Economics and family values.* New York: The New Press, 2001.

Foucault, Michel. *The History of Sexuality, Volume 1.* Harmondsworth: Penguin, 1976.

————. *Discipline and Punish: the Birth of the Prison* (A Sheridan, trans.). London: Penguin, 1977.

————. "Afterword." *Michel Foucault: Beyond structuralism and hermeneutics* (H. L. Dreyfus and P. Rabinow, eds.). Chicago: University of Chicago Press, 1982.

Frank, Katherine. *G-Strings and Sympathy: Strip Club Regulars and Male Desire.* Durham: Duke University Press, 2002.

Franke, Richard W. "The Mararikulam experiment: women-owned cooperatives in Kerala, India—a people's alternative to corporate dominated globalization." *GEO: Grassroots Economic Organizing* 57 (May/June, 2003): 8–11.

Frankel, Stephen, and Gilbert Lewis, eds. *A Continuing Trial of Treatment: Medical Pluralism in Papua New Guinea.* Dordrecht: Kluwer Academic Press, 1989.

Friends of Dufferin Grove Park. "Food in the park." www.dufferinpark.ca/oven/food.html, updated October 2 (2004a).

————. "Zamboni kitchen." www.dufferinpark.ca/oven/zambonikitchen.html. updated October 2 (2004b).

Gegeo, David Welchman. "Cultural rupture and indigeneity: the challenge of (re)-visioning 'place' in the Pacific." *The Contemporary Pacific* 13, 2 (2001): 491–507.

Giacaman, Rita, and Abdullatif Husseini. *Life and Health during the Israeli Invasion of the West Bank. Institute of Community and Public Health.* Bir Zeit: University of Bir Zeit, 2002.

Gibson, Katherine. "Women, Identity and Activism in Asian and Pacific Community Economies." *Development* 45, no. 1 (2002): 74–79.

Gibson, Katherine, Lisa Law, and Deirdre McKay. "Beyond heroes and victims: Filipina contract migrants, economic activism and class transformations." *International Feminist Journal of Politics* 3, 3 (2001): 365–386.

Gibson-Graham, J. K. *The end of capitalism (as we knew it): A feminist critique of political economy.* Oxford, UK and Malden, MA: Blackwell Publishing, 1996.

———. "Beyond global vs. local: economic politics outside the binary frame." *Geographies of power: Placing scale* (A. Herod and M. Wright, eds.), 25–60. Oxford and Malden MA: Blackwell Publishing, 2002.

———. "Enabling ethical economies: cooperativism and class." *Critical Sociology* 29, 2 (2003a): 123–61.

———. "Politics of empire/politics of place." Unpublished paper, University of Massachusetts, Amherst and Australian National University (2003b).

———. "Surplus possibilities: postdevelopment and community economies." *Singapore Journal of Tropical Geography* (2004a; forthcoming).

———. "The violence of development: two political imaginaries." *Development* 47, 1 (2004b): 27–34.

Gibson-Graham, J. K., Stephen A. Resnick, and Richard D. Wolff, eds. *Class and its others.* Minneapolis, MN: University of Minnesota Press, 2000.

———. *Re/Presenting class: Essays in postmodern Marxism.* Durham, NC: Duke University Press, 2001.

Gilroy, Rose, and Christine Booth. "Building Infrastructure for Everyday Lives." *European Planning Studies* 7, no. 3 (1999): 307–324.

Glantz, Margo. *La Malinche, sus padres y sus hijos.* Mexico City: Taurus, 1999.

Godbout, Jacques T. in collaboration with Alain Caillé. *The world of the gift* (D. Winkler, trans.). Montreal and Kingston: McGill-Queen's University Press, 1998.

Goodman, David, and E. Melanie DuPuis. "Knowing food and growing food: beyond the production-consumption debate in the sociology of agriculture." *Sociologica Ruralis*, 41, 1 (2002): 5–22.

Gottlieb, Robert. *Environmentalism unbound: Exploring new pathways for change.* Cambridge, MA: MIT Press, 2001.

Graham, Julie. "Women and the politics of place: ruminations and responses. *Development* 45, 1 (2002): 18–22.

Grasmuck, Sherri, and Patricia Pessar. *Between Two Islands: Dominican International Migration.* Berkeley, CA: University of California Press, 1991.

Grubacic, Andrej. "Life After Social Forums: New Radicalism and the Question of Attitudes Towards the Social Forums." (2003) http://www.zmag.org/content/showarticle.cfm?SectionID=41&ItemID=3010.

Grueso, Libia. *"Participación política de las organizaciones de comunidades negras y específicamente de las mujeres negras en el escenario nacional."* Document prepared for the Cali workshop of Afro-Colombian organization, October 1997.

Grueso, Libia, Carlos Rosero, and Arturo Escobar. "The Process of Black Community Organizing in the Southern Pacific Coast of Colombia." *Cultures of Politics/Politics of Culture. Revisioning Latin America Social Movements,* 196–219. Boulder, CO: Westview Press, 1998.

Guarnizo, Luís Eduardo. *One Country in Two: Dominican-owned firms in New York and in the Dominican Republic*. Doctoral dissertation, Johns Hopkins University, 1992.

Gudeman, Stephen. *The anthropology of economy: Commodity, market, and culture*. London: Blackwell Publishing, 2000.

Habermas, Jürgen. *The Theory of Communicative Action, Vol. 1 Reason and the Rationalisation of society*. London: Heineman, 1984.

Hannerz, Ulf. "Cosmopolitans and Locals in World Culture." *Theory, Culture & Society* 7, no. 2/3 (1990): 237–251.

Haraway, Donna J. "The virtual speculum in the new world order." *Feminist Review* 55 (1997): 22–72.

———. *The Haraway Reader*. London and New York: Routledge, 2002.

Harcourt, Wendy, Arturo Escobar, and Michal Osterweil. "Women and the Politics of Place: An Introduction." Unpublished ms./working paper (2001). http://www.eurofem.net/info/Politics.html.

Harcourt, Wendy, and Arturo Escobar. "Lead Article: Women and the Politics of Place." *Development* 45, 1 (2002): 7–14.

Harcourt, Wendy. "Medical Discourse Related to the Female Body in Late 19th Century Melbourne." Unpublished Ph.D. thesis, Australian National University, Canberra (1986).

Harcourt, Wendy, ed. *Women@Internet: Creating Cultures in Cyberspace*. London: Zed Books, 1999.

Harcourt, Wendy. "Women and the Politics of Place. Rethinking Cultural Diversity, Equality and Difference in Response to Globalization." Prepared for UNESCO (unpublished manuscript), 1999.

———. "The Reproductive Health and Rights Agenda under attack." *Development,* vol. 46 no. 2 (2003): 1–5.

———. *The Road to the UN Millennium Development Goals: Some insights into the International Debate*. NCDO, 2004.

Harding, Sandra. *The Feminist Standpoint Theory Reader: Intellectual and Political Controversies*. New York and London: Routledge, 2003.

Harel, Amos. "IDF suspends commander implicated in death of girl, 13." *Haaretz.* October 12, 2004 http://www.haaretzdaily.com/hasen/spages/487788.html.

Hartsock, Nancy. "Foucault on power: a theory for women?" *Feminism/Postmodernism* (Linda Nicholson, ed.). New York and London: Routledge, 1990.

Harvey, David. *Spaces of hope*. Edinburgh: Edinburgh University Press, 2000.

Hassanein, Neva. "Practicing food democracy: a pragmatic politics of transformation." *Journal of Rural Studies* 19 (2003): 77–86.

Healey, Patricia. *Collaborative Planning: Shaping Places in Fragmented Societies*. London: Macmillan, 2003.

Hefti, Anny Misa. "Globalization and Migration." Presentation at conference, Responding to Globalization, September 19–21, 1997, Zurich.

Henderson, Hazel. *Paradigms in progress: Life beyond economics*. Indianapolis, IN: Knowledge Systems Inc., 1991.

————. *Building a win-win world. Life beyond global economic warfare.* San Francisco: Berret-Koehler, 1996.

Hendrickson, Mary K., and William D. Heffernan. "Opening spaces through relocalization: locating potential resistance in the weaknesses of the global food system." *Sociologica Ruralis* 42, 4 (2002): 347–369.

Hersch, Seymour M. "Annals of National Security, The Gray Zone, How a secret Pentagon program came to Abu Ghraib." *The New Yorker Fact,* May 24, 2004. http://www.newyorker.com/printable/?fact/040524fa_fact.

Hiltermann, Joost R. *Behind the Intifada. Labor and Women's Movement in the Occupied Territories.* Princeton, NJ: Princeton University Press, 1991.

Hindess, Barry, and Paul Hirst. *Precapitalist modes of production.* London: Routledge and Kegan Paul, 1975.

Horelli, Liisa. "Engendering evaluation of structural fund interventions." From "a minuet to progressive dance." *Evaluation* 3, no. 4 (1997): 435–450.

Horelli, Liisa, ed. "Proceedings of the EuroFEM International Conference on Local and Regional Sustainable Human Development from the Gender Perspective." Hämeenlinna: EuroFEM, 1998.

Horelli, Liisa. "Young people's participation, Lip service or serious business." *Youth, Citizenship and Empowerment* (Helena Helve and Claire Wallace, eds.), 57–71. UK: Ashgate Publishing Ltd, 2001.

————. "European women in defence of place – with a focus on women's resource centres in Finland." *Development* 45, no.1 (2002a): 137–143.

————. "A Methodology of participatory planning." *Handbook of Environmental Psychology* (R. Bechtel and A. Churchman, eds.), 607–628. New York: John Wiley, 2002b.

————. *Valittajista tekijöiksi, nuoret valtautumisen areenoilla Pohjois-Karjalassa* (From complainers to agents, young people on platforms for empowerment). Espoo: Helsinki University of Technology, Centre for Urban and Regional Studies, 2003.

————. "Environmental Child-friendliness, a challenge to research and practice." *Search of Child-Friendly Environments, Approaches and Lessons* (Liisa Horelli and Miretta Prezza, eds.), 11–35. Espoo: Helsinki University of Technology, Centre for Urban and Regional Studies, 2004.

Horelli, Liisa, Christine Booth, and Rose Gilroy. *The EuroFEM Toolkit for Mobilising Women into Local and Regional Development* (Revised edition). Helsinki: Helsinki University of Technology, 2000.

Horelli, Liisa, and Tiina Sotkasiira. *Karelli-hankkeen arviointi* (Evaluation of the Karelli-project of the Recife network of RECITE II). Joensuu: Karellikeskus, 2001.

Horelli, Liisa, and Kirsti Vepsä. "In Search of Supportive Structures for Everyday Life." *Women and the Environment. Human Behavior and Environment* (Irwin Altman and Arza Churchman, eds). Vol. 13: 201–226. New York: Plenum, 1994.

Horelli, Liisa, and Sirkku Wallin. "In search of gender-sensitive policy evaluation." Paper presented in the Fifth European Conference of Evaluation of the Structural Funds, June 26–27, 2003, Budapest, Hungary.

Ironmonger, D. "Counting outputs, capital inputs and caring labor: estimating gross household output." *Feminist Economics* 2, 3 (1996): 37–64.

Johnson, Richard, Gregor Mclennan, Bill Schwarz, and David Sutton, eds. *Making Histories. Studies in history—writings and politics* (The Centre for Contemporary Cultural Studies). Birmingham: Hutchinson & Co, 1982.

Jolly, Margaret, and Martha MacIntyre. *Family and Gender in the Pacific: Domestic Contradictions and the Colonial Impact.* Cambridge: Cambridge University Press, 1989.

Jolly, Margaret. "Woman-Nation-State in Vanuatu: Women as signs and subjects in the discourses of *Kastom,* Modernity and Christianity." *Narratives of the Nation in the South Pacific* (Ton Otto and Nicholas Thomas, eds.). Amsterdam: Harwood Academic Press, 1997.

———. "Introduction: Colonial and postcolonial plots in histories of maternities and modernities." *Maternities and Modernities: Colonial and postcolonial experiences in Asia and the Pacific* (Kalpana Ram and Margaret Jolly, eds.). Cambridge: Cambridge University Press, 1998.

Kaplan, Temma. *Crazy for democracy: women in grassroots movements.* New York: Routledge, 1997.

Kari, Karo, TorTora, Siyahkari, and Kala Kali. "There is no 'honour' in killing." National Seminar Report. Lahore: Shirkat Gah, 2002.

Katz, Cindi. "On the grounds of globalization: a topography for feminist political engagement." *Signs* 26 (2001): 1213–34.

Keane, Helen, and Marsha Rosengarten. "On the biology of sexed subjects." *Australian Feminist Studies* 17, 39 (2002): 261–277.

Khalidi, Walid, ed. *All That Remains: The Palestinian Villages Occupied and Depopulated by Israel in 1948.* Washington, DC: Institute for Palestine Studies, 1992.

Kickert, Walter J. M., Erik-Hans Klijn, and Joop F. M. Koppenjan, eds. *Managing Complex Networks: Strategies for the Public Sector.* London: Sage Publications, 1997.

Kincaid, Jamaica. *Lucy.* New York: Farrar, Straus & Giroux, 1990.

Kostiainen, Juha. "Learning and the 'Ba' in the Development Network of an Urban Region." *European Planning Studies* 10, no. 5 (2002): 613–631.

La Marcha del Color de La Tierra. *Comunicados, cartas y mensajes del Ejército Zapatista de Liberación Nacional.* Mexico City: Rizoma, 2001.

Lahbabi, Fatima, and Pilar Rodríguez. "Les immigrés marocains en Andalousie: Le cas des femmes marocaines prostituées a Almería." Unpublished doctoral research (2000). Université Toulouse-le-Murail and Universidad de Almería.

Lake, David A., and Patrick M. Morgan, eds. *Regional Order: Building Security in a New World.* University Park, PA: Pennsylvania State University Press, 1997.

Lamas, Marta. "Las Nietas de la Malinche. Una Lectura Feminista" de *El Laberinto de la Soledad,* en Memorias del Coloquio Internacional por el *Laberinto de la Soledad* a 50 años de su publicación. Mexico City: Fondo de Cultura Económica, 2001.

Latour, Bruno. *We Have Never Been Modern* (Catherine Porter, trans.). Cambridge, MA: Harvard University Press, 1993.

Lehto, Esko, and Jukka Oksa. "Maaseudun menestystarinta." *Rural Success Stories— Networks of Sotkamo's Development in International Comparison.* Kajaani: University of Oulu, 2004.

Leonini, Luisa, ed. *Sesso in acquisto: Una ricerca sui clienti della prostituzione.* Milan: Edizioni Unicopli, 1999.

Lernoux, Penny. *Cry of the People.* Garden City, NY: Doubleday & Company, Inc., 1980.

Leydesdorff, Selma, Luisa Passerini, and Paul Thompson, eds. "Gender and Memory." *The International Yearbook of Oral History.* New York: Oxford University Press, 1996.

Lind, Amy. "Gender, development and urban social change: Women's community action in global cities." *World Development* 25, 8 (1997): 1205–1223.

Longhurst, Robyn. *Bodies: Exploring Fluid Boundaries.* London and New York: Routledge, 2001.

Losonczy, Anne-Marie. "Del ombligo a la comunidad. Ritos de nacimiento en la cultura negra del litoral pacifico colombiano." *Revindi* 1 (1989): 49–54.

Luxton, Meg. "The U.N., women, and household labour: measuring and valuing unpaid work." *Women's Studies International Forum* 20, 3 (1997): 431–9.

Mabuchi, Kanako. "The Meaning of Motherhood during the First Intifada: 1987–1993." M.Phil Thesis in Modern Middle Eastern Studies, St. Anthony's College, University of Oxford, May 2003. http://users.ox.ac.uk/~metheses/Mabuchi.html

Mai, Nicola. "Italy is Beautiful." *Media and Migration: Constructions of Mobility and Difference* (R. King and N. Wood, eds.). London: Routledge, 2001.

Malaska, Pentti. "Globalization, Finland and the Finns." A Lecture in the Future Research Society, March 18, 2004, Helsinki.

Marston, Sallie A. "The social construction of scale." *Progress in Human Geography* 24, 2 (2000): 219–42.

Marston, Sallie A., and Neil Smith. "States, scales and households: limits to scale thinking? A response to Brenner." *Progress in Human Geography* 25, 4 (2001): 615–619.

Martínez Alier, Joan. *The Environmentalism of the Poor.* London: Edward Elgar, 2002.

Massey, Doreen. *Space, Place and Gender.* Minneapolis: University of Minnesota Press and Cambridge: Polity Press, 1994.

———. "A Global Sense of Place." *Studying Culture* (A. Gray and J. McGuigan, eds.). London: Edward Arnold, 1997.

Matthaei, Julie. "Healing ourselves, healing our economy: paid work, unpaid work, and the next stage of feminist economic transformation." *Review of Radical Political Economics: Special Issue on Feminist Political Economics* 33 (2001): 461–94.

McDowell, Linda. "Space, place and gender relations: Part II. Identity, difference, feminist geometries and geographies." *Progress in Human Geography* 17, 3 (1993): 305–18.

Mellyn, Kevin. "Worker remittances as a development tool: Opportunity for the Philippines." Consultant report to the Asian Development Bank (ADB). Manila: ADB, 2003.

Moffatt, Deborah, and Mary Lou Morgan. "Women organizers: building confidence and community through food." *Women working the NAFTA food chain: Women, food and globalization* (D. Barndt, ed.). Toronto: Second Story Press, 1999.

Moghadam, Valentine. "Women's NGOs and North Africa." *Organizing Women* (Dawn Chatty and Anika Rabo, eds.). Oxford, New York: Berg, 1997.

Moraga, Cherrie. *Loving in the War Years. Lo que nunca pasó por sus labios,* Boston: South End Press, 1983.

Morrison, Roy. *We build the road as we travel.* Philadelphia: New Society Publishers, 1991.

Mukherjee, Bharati. *Jasmine.* New York: Fawcett Crest, 1988.

Mumtaz, Khawar, and Farida Shaheed. *Women of Pakistan; Two Steps Forward One Step Back?* London: Zed Books; Lahore: Vanguard Books, 1987.

Mumtaz, Samiya. "Masters, not Friends." *Newsline* November 2002: 84–92.

Nancy, Jean-Luc. *The inoperative community.* Minneapolis, MN: University of Minnesota Press, 1991a.

———. "Of being-in-common." *Community at loose ends* (Miami Theory Collective, eds.), 1–12. Minneapolis: University of Minnesota Press, 1991b.

Naples, Nancy, ed. *Community activism and feminist politics.* NY: Routledge, 1998.

Navarro, Luis Hernández, and Ramón Vera Herrera, eds. *Acuerdos de San Andrés.* Mexico City: Era, 1998.

Notes from Nowhere, ed. *We Are Everywhere: the irresistible rise of global anti-capitalism.* London: Verso, 2003.

Nuñez, Fernanda. "Malinche." *Debate Feminista* año 3, vol. 5 marzo 1992.

O'Reilly, Karen. "Trading Intimacy for Liberty: British Women on the Costa del Sol." *Gender and Migration in Southern Europe. Women on the Move* (F. Anthias and G. Lazaridis, eds.), 227–249. New York: Berg, 2000.

Osterweil, Michal. "De-centering the Forum: Is Another Critique of the Forum Possible?" *Challenging Empires: World Social Forum* (Jai Sen, Anita Anand, Arturo Escobar, and Peter Waterman, eds.), 183–190. New Delhi: Viveka Fdtn, 2004a.

———. "A cultural-political approach to reinventing the political." *International Social Science Journal.* Vol. 182 (2004b): 495–506.

———. "Place-based globalists: rethinking the *global* in the alternative globalization movement." Unpublished paper, Department of Anthropology, University of North Carolina, Chapel Hill, NC (2004c).

Ousmane, Sembene. *God's Bits of Wood.* New York: Anchor Books Place, 1970.

Paidar, Parvin. *Women and the Political Process in Twentieth-Century Iran.* Cambridge: Cambridge University Press, 1995.

Passerini, Luisa. *Fascism in Popular Memory.* Cambridge: Cambridge University Press, 1987.

———. *Autobiography of a Generation, Italy 1968.* Middletown, CT: Wesleyan University Press, 1996.

Paz, Octavio. *El laberinto de la soledad. Postdata. Vuelta al laberinto de la soledad* (2nd ed.). Mexico City: Fondo de Cultura Económica, 1994.

Petchesky, Rosalind Pollack. *Global Prescriptions. Gender health and human rights.* London: Zed Books in association with UNRISD, 2002.

Pietilä, Hilkka. "The triangle of the human economy: household—cultivation—individual production. An attempt to make visible the human economy in toto." *Ecological Economics* 20, no. 2 (2004): 113–127.

Planning Commission GOP. Between Hope & Despair; Pakistan Participation Poverty Assessment. Balochistan Report; NWFP Report; Punjab Report; Sindh Report; AJK Report; FANA Report; FATA Report. Islamabad, 2003.

Pratt, Geraldine, and Brenda Yeoh. "Transnational (counter) topographies." *Gender, Place and Culture* 0, 2 (2003): 159–66.

Prescott-Allen, Robert. *The Wellbeing of Nations, A Country-by-Country Index of Quality of Life and the Environment.* Island Press, 2001. http//www.iucn.org.

Qadir Shah, Hassam. *Don't let them get away with murder (Booklet on criminal procedures); Basic questions answered.* Lahore: Shirkat Gah, 2002.

Rabasa, José. "Of Zapatismo: Reflections on the Folkloric and the impossible in a Subaltern Insurrection." *The Politics of Culture in the Shadow of Capital* (Lisa Lowe, ed.), 400–430. London: Duke University Press, 1997.

Rabinow, Paul, ed. *The Foucault Reader.* London: Penguin, 1984.

Rankin, Katharine N. "Governing development: neoliberalism, microcredit and rational economic woman." *Economy and Society* 30, 1 (2001): 18–37.

Reinhart, Tanya. "Biddu: The Struggle against the wall." *Nthposition.* May, 2004. http://www.nthposition.com/bidduthestruggleagainst.php.

Resnick, Stephen A., and Richard D. Wolff. *Knowledge and class: A Marxian critique of political economy.* Chicago: University of Chicago Press, 1987.

———. *Class theory and history: Capitalism and communism in the U.S.S.R.* New York: Routledge, 2002.

Rich, Adrienne. *Blood, Bread and Poetry: Selected Prose 1979–85.* London: W. W. Norton and Co., 1986.

Ricourt, Milagros. "From Mama Tingo to Globalization: The Dominican Women Peasant Movement." *Women's Studies Review* 9 (2000): 1–10.

Rocheleau, Dianne, and Laurie Ross. "Trees as Tools, Trees as Text: Struggles Over Resources in Zambrana-Chacuey, Dominican Republic." *Antipode* 27, 4 (1995): 407–428.

Rocheleau, Dianne E., Laurie Ross, Julio Morrobel, and Luis Malaret, with Ricardo Hernandez and Tara Kominiak. "Complex communities and emergent ecologies in the regional agroforest of Zambrana-Chacuey, Dominican Republic." *Ecumene* 8, 4 (2001): 465–492.

Rocheleau, Dianne, Barbara Thomas-Slayter, and Esther Wangari, eds. *Feminist Political Ecology.* New York: Routledge, 1996.

Rocheleau, Dianne. "Listening to the Landscapes of Mama Tingo." *A Companion to Feminist Geography* (Joni Seager and Lise Nelson, eds.). Oxford: Blackwell Publishing, 2004.

Rodney, Walter. *How Europe Underdeveloped Africa.* Dar-es-Salaam: London and Tanzanian Publishing House, 1972.

Rojas, J., with the team of facilitators of the Network of Black Women of the Pacific. "Plan general para el desarrollo de las organizaciones y redes de mujeres negras del Pacífico." Cali workshop of Afro-Colombian organization, October 2000.

Rojas, Rosa. *Chiapas ¿y las mujeres qué?* Mexico City: La Correa Feminista, 1994.

Ross, Laurie. "What Happens When a Grassroots Organization meets an International NGO?" Master's Thesis, program in International Development and Social Change, Clark University, Worcester, MA (1996).

Rovira, Guiomar. *Mujeres de Maíz.* Mexico City: ERA, 1997.

Rowbotham, Sheila, and Stephanie Linkogle, eds. *Women resist globalization: Mobilizing for livelihood and rights.* London: Zed Books, 2001.

Said, Edward W. *Orientalism.* New York: Vintage Books, 1979.

———. *Culture and Imperialism.* New York: Vintage Books, 1994.

———. *Orientalism.* London: Penguin Books, 1995.

———. *Covering Islam: How the Media and Experts Determine How We See the Rest of the World.* New York: Vinatage Books, 1997.

Saldana-Portillo, Maria Josefina. *The Revolutionary Imagination in the Americas and the Age of Development.* Durham: Duke University Press, 2003.

Santos, Boaventura de Sousa. "The WSF: toward a counter-hegemonic globalization." *World Social Forum: Challenging empires* (J. Sen, A. Anand, A. Escobar, and P. Waterman, eds.). New Delhi: The Viveka Foundation, 2004. http://www.choike.org/nuevo_eng/informes/1557.html.

Sassen, Saskia, "Whose city is it? Globalization and the formation of new claims." *Public Culture* 8 (1996): 205–203.

Sassen, Saskia. *Globalization and its Discontents.* New York: New Press, 1998.

Sayigh, Rosemary. "Gender, Sexuality, and Class in National Narrations: Palestinian Camp Women Tell Their Lives." *Women's Oral History* (Susan H. Armitage, ed., with Patricia Hart and Karen Weathermon), 317–337. Lincoln and London: University of Nebraska Press, 2002.

Scheyvens, Regina. "Church women's groups and the empowerment of women in the Solomon Islands." *Oceania* 74, 2 (2003).

Scott, James. *Seeing Like a State: How Certain Schemes to Improve the Human Condition Have Failed.* New Haven, CT: Yale University Press, 1999.

Shami, Seteney. "Transnationalism and Refugee Studies: Rethinking Forced Migration and Identity in the Middle East." *Journal of Refugee Studies* Vol. 9, No. 1 (1996): 3–26.

Smith, Neil. "Homeless/global; Scaling places." *Mapping the futures—local cultures, global change* (J. Bird, B. Curtis, T. Putnam, G. Robertson, and L. Tickner, eds.). London: Routledge, 1993.

———. "Social justice and the new American urbanism: The revanchist city." *The urbanization of injustice* (Andy Merrifield and Erik Swyngedouw, eds.). New York: New York University Press, 1997.

———. "New globalism, new urbanism: gentrification as global urban strategy." *Antipode* 34, 3 (2002): 427–450.

Starr, Amory. *Naming the enemy: Anti-corporate movements confront globalization.* London: Zed Books, 2000.

Starr, Amory, and Jason Adams. "Anti-globalization: The global fight for local autonomy." *New Political Science* 25, 1 (2003): 19–42.

Stephen, Lynn. "The Zapatista opening: the movement for indigenous autonomy and state discourses on indigenous rights in Mexico, 1970-1996." *Journal of Latin American Anthropology* 3, no. 1 (1997): 32.

Swyngedouw, Erik. "Neither global nor local: 'Glocalization' and the politics of scale." *Spaces of globalization: Reasserting the power of the local* (Kevin Cox, ed.). New York: Guilford, 1997.

The Research Group for the New Everyday Life. *The New Everyday Life—ways and means.* Copenhagen: Nord, 1991.

Thomas Isaac, T. M., Richard W. Franke, and Pyaralal Raghavan. *Democracy at work in an Indian industrial cooperative: The story of Kerala Dinesh Beedi.* Ithaca: ILR Press (imprint of Cornell University Press), 1998.

Tickell, Adam, and Jamie Peck. "The return of the Manchester men: Men's words and men's deeds in the remaking of the local state." *Transactions of the Institute of British Geographers* 21, 4 (1996): 595–616.

Tsing, Anna, Lowenhaupt. *In the Realm of the Diamond Queen.* Princeton, NJ: Princton University Press, 1993.

Turner, Victor. *Dramas, Fields and Metaphors.* Ithaca: Cornell University Press, 1974.

Underhill-Sem, Yvonne. "'Tragedies' in out-of-the-way places: oceanic interpretations of another scale." *Feminist Futures: Re-imagining Women, Culture and Development* (Kum-Kum Bhavani, John Foran, and Priya Kurian, eds.). London: Zed Press, 2003.

UNDPI. "Earth Summit Agenda 2 The United Nations Programme of Action from Rio." New York: United Nations, 1992.

UNRWA. "Israeli Gun Fire Hits 11-Year-Old Girl Sitting at Her Desk in an UNRWA School." *UNRWA Press Release.* No. HQ/G/33/2004 October 12, 2004(a). http://www.un.org/unrwa/news/releases/pr-2004/hqg33-04.pdf.

———. "Child Shot in UNRWA School Dies." *UNRWA Press Release* HQ/G/34/2004 October 13, 2004(b). http://www.un.org/unrwa/news/releases/pr-2004/hqg34-04.pdf.

Urry, John. *The Tourist Gaze: Leisure and Travel in Contemporary Societies.* London: Sage Publications, 1990.

Van Parijs, Philippe. *What's wrong with a free lunch.* Boston: Beacon Press, 2001.

Vaughan, Genevieve. *For-giving: A feminist criticism of exchange.* Austin, TX: Plain View Press, 1997.

Villalba, May-an. "Women migrant workers transforming local communities: the Iloilo women's group." *Development* 45, 1 (2001): 80–84.

Walkerdine, Valerie. *Daddy's Girl: Young Girls and Popular Culture.* Cambridge, MA: Harvard University Press, 1997.

Waring, Marilyn. *Counting for nothing: What men value and what women are worth.* Auckland and Wellington NZ: Allen and Unwin, in assoc. with Port Nicholson Press, 1988.

WEDO. *Official Report World Women's Congress for a Healthy Planet.* New York: WEDO World Women's Congress Secretariat, 1992.

Wekerle, Gerda R. "Women's rights to the city: gendered spaces of a pluralistic citizenship." *Democracy, citizenship and the global city* (Egin Isin, ed.). London: Routledge, 2000.

———. "Food justice movements: policy, planning and networks." *Journal of Planning Education and Research* 23, 4 (2004): 378–86.

Whatmore, Sarah. *Hybrid Geographies: culture natures spaces.* London and Thousand Oaks: Sage Publications, 2002.

Whitaker, Brian. "Its best use is as a doorstop." *Guardian Unlimited.* May 24, 2004. http://www.guardian.co.uk/elsewhere/journalist/story/0,7792,1223525,00.html.

WICEJ. *Seeking Accountability on Women's Human Rights: Women Debate the Millennium Development Goals.* New York (2004).

Wick, Laura. *Birth at the Checkpoint, the Home or the Hospital? Adapting to the Changing Reality in Palestine.* Institute of Community and Public Health, Birzeit University, June 15, 2002.

WIDE. "Special on Women and the Environment." *WIDE Bulletin,* 1. Ireland: Shanway Press, 1992.

Williams, Colin C. *A commodified world? Mapping the limits of capitalism.* London: Zed Press, 2004.

Wilson, Amrit. *US Foreign Policy and Revolution.* London: Pluto Press, 1989.

Window on the World. *Development* 45, 1 (2002): 143–147.

Window on the World. *Development* 46, 2 (2003): 112–116.

Window on the World. *Development* 48, 1 (2005): 132–136.

Zia, Shahla. "Some Experiences of the Women's Movement: Strategies for Success." *Shaping Women's Lives: Laws, Practices & Strategies in Pakistan* (Farida Shaheed, et al., eds.). Lahore: Shirkat Gah, 1998.

Index

About the Contributors

Laura Mª Agustín is Research Associate for a collaborative project of three British universities, 'Regulating the spaces of sex work,' and author of many publications based on 12 years research in Latin America and Europe on migrants who sell domestic, caring, and sexual services in Europe and the large social sector which proposes to help them.

Lamis A.M. al-Shenji, based in Rome, Italy, is the Founder and President of the Organization for Alternative Development and Global Justice (ODAG).

Fatma Alloo is a media expert working in Zanzibar, Tanzania in development. She is founder of ten African and international network including TAMWA the Tanzania Media Women's Association.

Leyla Andrea Arroyo is affiliated with Process of Black Communities (PCN).

Sonia Alvarez is Professor of Anthropology at the University of California-Santa Cruz and a well-known writer on Latin American Feminism.

Marisa Belausteguigoitia is Professor of Education and Director of the University Program of Gender Studies, Autonomous University of Mexico, in Mexico City.

Arturo Escobar is Professor of Anthropology at the University of North Carolina at Chapel Hill.

Randa Farah is currently Assistant Professor of Anthropology at the University of Western Ontario.

Katherine Gibson is Professor and Head of the Department of Human Geography in the Research School of Pacific and Asian Studies at the

Australian National University. She and Julie Graham have worked together on feminist re-thinkings of 'economy' since the late 1970s and publish under the joint name J.K. Gibson-Graham.

Julie Graham is Professor of Geography at the University of Massachusetts, Amherst.

Libia Grueso is a social worker and co-founder of the Process of Black Communities (PCN), and is one of the most prominent intellectual-activists in the Afro-Colombian civil rights movement.

Wendy Harcourt is Editor of Development, the SID quarterly journal of the Society for International Development and a well-known writer in gender and development. Currently she is Chair of Women in Development Europe (WIDE).

Liisa Horelli is Senior Research Fellow of the Finnish Academy, Helsinki University of Technology, Centre for Urban and Regional Studies.

Smitu Kothari is based in New Delhi, India as a researcher and activist working towards a non-party people's political movement for just, sustainable, and inclusive development.

Khawar Mumtaz is one of Pakistan's leading women's rights activists and co-coordinator of Shirkat Gah-Women's Resource Center, Pakistan

Michal Osterweil is a National Science Foundation Graduate Fellow at the University of North Carolina at Chapel Hill, Department of Anthropology, and is currently working on her Ph.D. on global movements.

Dianne Rocheleau is Associate Professor of Geography at Clarke University, Worcester, M.A.

Yvonne Underhill-Sem is Associate Professor of Geography, Center for Development Studies, University of Auckland, New Zealand and member of the Development Alternative with Women for A New Era (DAWN) Steering Committee.

Gerda Wekerle is Professor of Geography in Faculty of Environmental Studies, York University, Canada and writes extensively on gender and urban planning.